Sports Economics, Management and Policy

Volume 16

Series Editor
Dennis Coates, Baltimore, USA

The aim of this series is to provide academics, students, sports business executives, and policy makers with information and analysis on the cutting edge of sports economics, sport management, and public policy on sporting issues.

Volumes in this series can focus on individual sports, issues that cut across sports, issues unique to professional sports, or topics in amateur sports. Each volume will provide rigorous analysis with the purpose of advancing understanding of the sport and the sport business, improving decision making within the sport business and regarding policy toward sports, or both. Volumes may include any or all of the following: theoretical modelling and analysis, empirical investigations, or description and interpretation of institutions, policies, regulations, and law.

More information about this series at http://www.springer.com/series/8343

Bernd Frick
Editor

Breaking the Ice

The Economics of Hockey

Editor
Bernd Frick
Management Department
University of Paderborn
Paderborn, Germany

Department of Sport Economics and Sport
Management
Schloss Seeburg University
Seekirchen/Salzburg, Austria

ISSN 2191-298X   ISSN 2191-2998   (electronic)
Sports Economics, Management and Policy
ISBN 978-3-319-67921-1   ISBN 978-3-319-67922-8   (eBook)
https://doi.org/10.1007/978-3-319-67922-8

Library of Congress Control Number: 2017958352

© Springer International Publishing AG 2017
This work is subject to copyright. All rights are reserved by the Publisher, whether the whole or part of the material is concerned, specifically the rights of translation, reprinting, reuse of illustrations, recitation, broadcasting, reproduction on microfilms or in any other physical way, and transmission or information storage and retrieval, electronic adaptation, computer software, or by similar or dissimilar methodology now known or hereafter developed.
The use of general descriptive names, registered names, trademarks, service marks, etc. in this publication does not imply, even in the absence of a specific statement, that such names are exempt from the relevant protective laws and regulations and therefore free for general use.
The publisher, the authors and the editors are safe to assume that the advice and information in this book are believed to be true and accurate at the date of publication. Neither the publisher nor the authors or the editors give a warranty, express or implied, with respect to the material contained herein or for any errors or omissions that may have been made. The publisher remains neutral with regard to jurisdictional claims in published maps and institutional affiliations.

Printed on acid-free paper

This Springer imprint is published by Springer Nature
The registered company is Springer International Publishing AG
The registered company address is: Gewerbestrasse 11, 6330 Cham, Switzerland

Contents

Part I Labor Relations and Player Behavior

From Strikes to Lockouts: Consequences of the Shift in the Balance of Power from the Players' Union to the Owners in the National Hockey League 3
Joel Maxcy

Fighting as a Profit-Maximizing Strategy: The American Hockey League 17
Duane W. Rockerbie

Part II Salary Determination and Player Careers

Returns to Handedness in Professional Hockey 41
Dennis Coates

All-Star or Benchwarmer? Relative Age, Cohort Size and Career Success in the NHL 57
Alex Bryson, Rafael Gomez, and Tingting Zhang

Part III Diversity and Discrimination

If You Can Play, You Get the Pay!? A Survey on Salary Discrimination in the NHL 95
Petra Nieken and Michael Stegh

The Source of the Cultural or Language Diversity Effects in the National Hockey League 113
Kevin P. Mongeon and J. Michael Boyle

Team-Level Referee Discrimination in the National Hockey League 131
Kevin Mongeon and Neil Longley

Part IV Ticket Demand and Ticket Pricing

The Effect of 'Superstars' on Attendance: NHL-Players in the German and Czech Hockey League 151
Christian Deutscher and Sandra Schneemann

An Exploration of Dynamic Pricing in the National Hockey League 177
Rodney J. Paul and Andrew P. Weinbach

Index 199

Contributors

J. Michael Boyle Department of Operations & Information Systems, David Eccles School of Business, University of Utah, Salt Lake City, UT, USA

Alex Bryson Department of Social Science, University College London, London, UK

Dennis Coates Department of Economics, University of Maryland Baltimore County, Baltimore, MD, USA

Christian Deutscher Department of Sports Science, Bielefeld University, Bielefeld, Germany

Bernd Frick Management Department, University of Paderborn, Paderborn, Germany

Department of Sport Economics and Sport Management, Schloss Seeburg University, Seekirchen/Salzburg, Austria

Rafael Gomez Centre for Industrial Relations and Human Resources, University of Toronto, Toronto, ON, Canada

Joel Maxcy Center for Sport Management, Drexel University, Philadelphia, PA, USA

Kevin P. Mongeon Department of Sport Management, Brock University, St. Catharines, ON, Canada

Neil Longley Department of Sport Management, Isenberg School of Management, University of Massachusetts, Amherst, MA, USA

Petra Nieken Karlsruhe Institute of Technology, Institute of Management, Karlsruhe, Germany

Rodney J. Paul Falk College of Sport and Human Dynamics, Syracuse University, Syracuse, NY, USA

Duane W. Rockerbie Department of Economics, University of Lethbridge, Lethbridge, AL, Canada

Sandra Schneemann Department of Sports Science, Bielefeld University, Bielefeld, Germany

Michael Stegh Faculty of Economics and Management, University of Magdeburg, Magdeburg, Germany

Andrew P. Weinbach E. Craig Wall Sr. College of Business Administration, Coastal Carolina University, Conway, SC, USA

Tingting Zhang Centre for Industrial Relations and Human Resources, University of Toronto, Toronto, ON, Canada

Introduction

Why Hockey Economics?

The National Hockey League (henceforth NHL) is the smallest and the least studied among the major team sports leagues in the US. This is surprising insofar as the annual revenues in the NHL are significantly higher than in four of the five well researched top divisions in European Football (only the Premier League generates more money). Moreover, one of the now seminal papers in sports economics specifically addressed hockey quite early already (Jones 1969), suggesting that the interest in that league has been rather low for decades.

This volume tries to close that research gap. It includes nine papers addressing some of the most important questions related to the economics of professional team sports leagues: labor relations and player behavior, salary determination and player careers, diversity and discrimination and, finally, ticket demand and ticket pricing.

Bernd Frick

Part I
Labor Relations and Player Behavior

From Strikes to Lockouts: Consequences of the Shift in the Balance of Power from the Players' Union to the Owners in the National Hockey League

Joel Maxcy

Abstract The development of a players' union in the National Hockey League lagged behind the organization of unions in the other American major team-sport leagues by a decade. Moreover, the union leadership was ineffectual until Bob Goodenow succeeded Alan Eagleson as the head of the NHLPA in 1992. Under Goodenow the players used strikes and the threat of strikes to leverage mobility rights including unrestricted free agency and salary arbitration, all of which substantially and steadily increased salaries and the players' share of revenue for more than ten years. In 1995 ownership locked out the players, a radical move at the time as it was the first owner-initiated work stoppage to cancel scheduled games. The lockout enabled owners to roll back some of the mobility concessions gained by the union. Yet, the league was unable to implement a desired salary cap and player salaries continued to grow. Nine years later a second lockout resulted in the cancelation of the entire 2004–2005 season. The outcome this time was very favorable to owners including a hard salary cap and a limit on individual player salaries. In this chapter the NHL eras before and after the salary cap are compared. Competitive balance and payroll dispersion across teams are examined empirically through means tests. The analysis indicates that the players' share of revenue is much lower under the salary cap and that payroll dispersion across clubs has diminished. The results also show a significant improvement over three different dimensions of competitive balance. Finally, it is anticipated that owners will continue to leverage their bargaining position and gain more concessions.

J. Maxcy (✉)
Center for Sport Management, Drexel University, Philadelphia, PA, USA
e-mail: jmax@drexel.edu

© Springer International Publishing AG 2017
B. Frick (ed.), *Breaking the Ice*, Sports Economics, Management and Policy 16, https://doi.org/10.1007/978-3-319-67922-8_1

Introduction

The National Hockey League's (NHL) entire 2004–2005 schedule of games was canceled because of a bitter labor dispute between the club owners and the players' union. The players in the four major American team-sport leagues, which include Major League Baseball (MLB), the National Basketball Association (NBA), and the National Football League (NFL), all have organized as unionized work forces. Collective Bargaining Agreements (CBAs), the set of union-management negotiated policies regulating compensation, hours, and working conditions under American Labor Law (NLRB 1935) were in place for each league by 1970. Federal labor law governs negotiations, a process which may bring conflict leading to work stoppages. Strikes and lockouts are the stoppages initiated by the players' union and the owners, respectively. Such industrial actions are permissible by law. Work stoppages had cancelled games in each of the leagues on several occasions prior, including the 1994 MLB championship tournament (the World Series). Notwithstanding, a league's entire season's schedule had not before been voided.

The pivotal issue of contention was the owners' demand for a *salary cap*. NHL payrolls at that time, like MLB, but in contrast to the NBA and NFL, were not subject to any limits. The salary cap proposed by the owners, however, invoked strict bounds on both team payrolls and individual player salaries. This combination would make the NHL's salary rules the most restrictive of the American major leagues. For instance, the NBA had limited individual salaries since 1999, but its payroll restraint, in place since 1984, allows exceptions so as to be termed a *soft* payroll cap. The NFL meanwhile has employed a no-exception or *hard* payroll cap since 1994, but except for the contracts of first-year players (rookies), the policy does not directly limit individual players' salaries. Most importantly, the NHL owners' proposal greatly diminished the players' negotiation leverage and aimed to reduce their share of league revenue. The union was accordingly acrimonious to any mandated restriction on salaries and payrolls; the conflict over this issue motivated the work stoppage.[1]

The National Hockey League Players' Association (NHLPA) was the last of the four unions to organize, and through most of its history lagged behind the other sports unions in terms of power and influence (Cruise and Griffiths 1991). However, with the appointment of Bob Goodenow as the NHLPA's Executive Director in 1992, the organization changed course. Goodenow invoked a considerably more aggressive approach to bargaining than his predecessor, Alan Eagleson. Following the MLB union's (MLBPA) tactic of instigating work stoppages at the point in the season of peak profitability for owners, Goodenow swiftly called a strike on the eve of the 1992 playoffs. The owners acquiesced before any missed games. The outcome was a modified CBA which loosened the rules for free-agent eligibility and

---

[1] The NBA's *soft cap* refers to the policy that allows teams to exceed the predetermined payroll limit under several stipulated circumstances. Most common is when re-signing a player who is already on the club's current roster. The NFL *hard cap* allows no exceptions to the payroll limit, but can nevertheless be circumvented.

expanded opportunities for salary arbitration to settle contract disputes between ice hockey players and their teams (Dowbiggen 2007). The changes initiated a less restrictive, more fluid labor market, and represented a significant gain for players.

The NHL labor rules had quickly come to resemble MLB's, generally considered the most favorable to players in professional sports. Under Goodenow's leadership, from the 1992–1993 through 2003–2004 seasons, the average NHL player's salary rose from $276,000 to $1.8 million (Dater 2012). All advancement aside, a mild restraint of free agent and salary arbitration eligibility and the implementation of a strict salary cap for first-year players followed from a new CBA negotiated after an owners' lockout that cancelled about one-third of the scheduled 1994–1995 contests. The 1994–1995 lockout is of consequence, not as much for the rather modest rollback of union gains, but for changing the dynamics of labor relations in the NHL and American professional sports.

The 2003–2004 championship season was the last one before the expiration of the CBA, which began with the lockout settlement in 1995. Negotiations for a new agreement were attempted on several occasions over that season (Kahane 2006), but proved futile given the club owners' demand for payroll limits and Goodenow's unyielding resistance to a restricted labor market. Typical of sports labor disputes, leveling the playing field and improving competitive balance was stated as the primary goal. However, owners' objectives were also to reverse the flow of income and increase their share of the total generated revenues.

The owners, as they had done in 1994, timed the lockout so as to inflict the highest cost on players, just as preseason training camps were scheduled to open in September 2004 (Stoudohar 2005). There was little compromise from either side until early February when the union accepted as inevitable a payroll cap; however, the two sides differed substantially on the dollar value of the cap's upper bound. The NHLPA offered $49 million per team per year and the owners countered at $42.5 million, a $6.5 million gap. Summed across all 30 NHL teams, the difference between the two sides' positions totaled $195 million (Stoudohar 2005). Unable to compromise and with insufficient time to complete a schedule, NHL Commissioner Gary Bettman announced on February 16, 2005 that the season was cancelled (Kahane 2006).

Cracks in the union's solidarity were revealed the following summer as owners indicated the resolve to continue the lockout into a second season. Various players, under the pressure of losing a second year of hockey income, urged the union to concede, and accompanied by Goodenow's forced resignation, the NHLPA did just that (Dowbiggen 2007). The conditions of a new CBA, to extend through 2011–2012, were announced in July 2005. The union accepted a hard payroll cap at $39 million per team for the 2006–2007 season, with annual adjustments to fix the cap so that the players' share was a maximum of 54% of league revenue. Moreover, any individual player's salary was capped at 20% of his team's total payroll, amounting to an annual limit of $7.8 million in 2005–2006 (Stoudohar 2005). Kahane (2006) provides a detailed table of the resultant CBA. The approved payroll bound was not only 25% less than the union's bid in February, it was also 10% below the owner's tender. The deteriorating negotiating leverage of the union as the lockout persisted was clearly revealed.

The NHL's success with lockouts appears to have influenced at least the NBA and NFL owners to adopt similar strategies. Both leagues at once faced expiring CBAs in 2011 and locked out the players. The NBA had already used the method to their benefit in 1998. The NFL resorted to a lockout for the first time after 18 years of labor peace. The NFL owners actually accelerated the CBA expiration so as to take earlier advantage of the lockout opportunity. (The NFL followed up with a lockout of their referees in 2012.) In each case, the owners made considerable gains and reduced the players' share of revenue from about 60% to less than 50%.

The NHL likewise exercised its third lockout in 2012, cancelling 34 games for each team before terms of a new CBA were reached in December. The new CBA made no substantial changes in either salary or payroll cap policy. However the players' percentage share was reduced from 54% to 48% (Brehm and Allen 2013). Bob Goodenow's warning regarding a payroll cap during negotiation in 2004 appears to have come to pass. He surmised at the time that once a cap is imposed, the owner's enthusiasm to adjust the players' share down will not cease (Dowbiggen 2007).

The NHL's experience in the aftermath of the lockout brings about two areas for consideration. First, the imposition of the hard salary cap facilitates an empirical examination of the effect of the policy on talent distribution and competitive balance. The NHL's cap represents a significant change as the league moved to a highly restrained market from a talent distribution that was the outcome of a relatively free labor market. Salary cap effects on sports leagues have been heretofore difficult to distinguish empirically. The NBA's soft cap is not truly a payroll limit. The NFL invoked their salary cap system and at once loosened free agent rules; the changes modified what was already a highly restricted labor market. Second, the NHL's success from the lockout strategy was a resounding success from the owners' perspective and this did not go unnoticed by the other American leagues. The lockout strategy has become the standard choice of actions by owners in the other American sports when engaging in collective bargaining negotiations.

This chapter proceeds as follows. The next section reviews the literature regarding salary caps and their effect on talent distribution and compensation patterns in team-sport leagues. That section is followed by empirical tests measuring several dimensions of competitive balance in the NHL before and after the imposition of the salary cap, including an account of those results. The chapter concludes with a broader discussion of the outcomes, including the advancement of the lockout strategy.

Literature Review

Transformations in labor policies, both hypothetical and existent, have long motivated analyses by sports economists. Simon Rottenberg's (1956) seminal work established one primary tenet of sports economics; that the assignment of property rights to players' labor service does not alter the distribution of players (talent) across clubs in a team-sport league –the *invariance principle*. Rottenberg wrote specifically about the MLB reserve clause, which contractually authorized to owners the property rights to the players' labor service. Free agency conversely shifts those property rights to the player.

The invariance principle has been interpreted by some to broadly suggest that all changes in labor policies that reallocate the distribution of income between owners and players will not alter competitive balance in a sports league. Analysis of labor policy shifts, in particular the institution of free agency in American sports and the corresponding elimination of, or restrictions on transfer payments in European football, predominate the sports economics literature. Fort and Maxcy (2003) discuss the significant body of literature that considered the effects of league policy changes on competitive balance to that point. Fort (2006) follows with a comprehensive review of the literature on competitive balance in American team-sport leagues.

Rottenberg's work applied invariance only to MLB's reserve clause, but the presumption remains that it extends to other policies and events that manipulate sports labor markets. Even when a policy may theoretically improve balance, economists researching this area frequently suggest that it is overwhelmingly labor market control and profits that motivate the rule changes (e.g. Quirk 1997). The argument for improved balance is simply a smokescreen and incidental to the true objective.

Empirical tests are mixed and vary across both the policy change examined and the measure of competitive balance employed. Fort et al. (2016) provide a thorough and critical review of the economic research that addresses the effects of all types policy changes by team-sport sport leagues on competitive balance. A sample of those papers is discussed here. Papers by Spitzer and Hoffman (1980), Cymrot (1983), and Besanko and Simon (1985) each find empirical evidence from the early years of MLB free agency that support the invariance principle. There are several studies that reject invariance including Hylan et al. (1996), Marburger (2002), and Maxcy (2002). Nevertheless, Fort and Lee (2007) employ a time series analysis of the most common measure of balance—the ratio of the actual to ideal standard deviations of win percent (RSD)—and find no structural changes coincidental with drafts, free agency, salary caps, or most labor disputes in the NBA, NHL, or NFL.[2] Other researchers disagree on the theoretical generalization beyond a strict transfer of property rights. For example, Késenne (2000a) argues that invariance does not hold for alternate revenue sharing schemes.

Generally the evaluation of competitive balance in the NHL has been included with works that encompass all four American major leagues (e.g., Sanderson and Siegfried 2003, Schmidt and Berri 2003). Very little work has considered the NHL in isolation. Jones and Walsh (1987) find that rival league competition in the 1970s from the World Hockey Association (WHA) mirrored free agency outcomes and significantly increased players' salaries. Richardson (2000) evaluates the invariance principle with respect to free agency in the NHL and finds a gradual, though cyclical improvement in RSD. Yet, he cannot ascertain that changes in free agency are

---

[2] This followed Lee and Fort (2005) who found the same lack of structural change applied to MLB.

responsible. To this point there is no known research that has isolated salary cap effects in the NHL.

Mandated limits (salary caps) on club payrolls and/or individual player's compensation have become commonplace at all levels of American sport leagues. Major League Soccer (MLS), the Women's National Basketball Association (WNBA), and the Arena Football League are among those team-sport leagues that enforce a hard salary cap. Bounds on payroll have been implemented in three of the four major professional leagues, and in several lower-level leagues. Salary caps, at least by conventional wisdom, are at once considered the solution to (small market) teams' financial troubles and the panacea to competitive imbalance. Although some adherents to invariance may include cap policy with the group of rules that do not alter the distribution of talent, there is theoretical support for the effectiveness of salary caps in the moderation of competitive balance.

Quirk and Fort (1995) and Rascher (1997) consider payroll cap effects as modifications within broader theoretical models of sport leagues. Both papers weigh the circumstances under which a cap is expected to improve competitive balance. Késenne's (2000b) model shows that in addition to improving balance, salary caps will level (improve) the salary distribution within and across teams. Notwithstanding, there has been scant empirical examination as to the effect of these polices on sports labor markets.

Larson et al. (2006) employ Gini Coefficients to measure allocation outcomes and find some evidence that the NFL's salary cap is consistent with improved balance. However, they find that unrestricted free agent rights are also responsible, and both policies were instituted at once with the league's 1994 CBA. Lee (2010) found that with the 1994 CBA, the NFL's combination of labor policy changes, including the payroll cap, improved inter-seasonal balance. Booth (2005), using the familiar RSD method, finds that imposition of a salary cap in 1986 improved competitive balance in the Australian Rules Football League. However, as with NFL free agency, another policy was implemented concurrently. In this case a player draft was imposed the same year as the payroll cap. Again, it was not possible to distinguish the changes in competitive balance as consequences of one policy, the other, or a combination of the two.

Quirk (1997) maintained that a theoretically effective cap differs considerably from those caps that have been implemented in practice. He alludes to the NBA cap outcomes, which are shown to neither improve balance nor restrain payrolls, as the incongruence between the implemented soft cap policy and a true hard cap. Maxcy (2011) conversely evaluates MLB's luxury tax on team payrolls—a restraint similar to a soft cap—and finds the policy to be mildly effective at inhibiting the flow of the most productive players toward the highest revenue generating clubs. At any rate, the effect of salary and payroll restraints on sports labor market outcomes remains unclear. Perhaps, despite the current prevalence of these restraints, an opportune setting in which to study their effects, and the corresponding data necessary to support a proper empirical examination, has not before been present.

The NHL case provides a clear shift of policy and the cap is strict, enforced, and not entangled with other policy tools. The empirical examination assesses several dimensions of competitive balance and analyzes changes in the distribution of salaries across teams and players.

Empirical Analyses

Two simple propositions with respect to the effect of the NHL's payroll cap are tested:

Proposition 1: The dispersion of annual payroll values across teams will be less under a payroll cap system.

Proposition 2: Imposition of a payroll cap will level the distribution of talent across teams and improve competitive balance.

The effect of the salary cap is tested by comparing the periods before and after implementation of the salary restrictions following the lockout in 2005. The initial period of comparison is defined by the *Goodenow era*, encompassing eleven seasons starting in 1992–1993. Although the removal of mobility restrictions had gradually loosened NHL labor markets prior, this period marks the apex of free labor market conditions for NHL players. Basic testing of mean values is used to compare the before-cap (1992–1993 – 2003–2004) and after-cap (2005–2006 – 2013–2014) periods. Changes in salary dispersion across teams and measures of three alternate dimensions of competitive balance are examined. Data were collected from Rod Fort's (2014) sport business database and HockeyReference.com (2014).

The analysis of salary dispersion across teams checks Késenne's (2000b) theory and the first proposition, that a salary cap equalizes team payrolls. Though the correlation between team payroll and winning is far from perfect (e.g. Hall et al. 2002), a closer distribution of payrolls theoretically reflects a more even distribution of talent across a league. Table 1 presents the average club payroll and standard deviation for each year of the two periods for which data is available.[3] Correctly accounting for dispersion requires calculation of the coefficient of variation (COV = standard deviation ÷ mean). A comparison of the before and after means shows that the cap is clearly consistent with payroll dispersion. Average team payrolls increased substantially over the 20 year period from $8.25 million in 1992–1993 to more than $62 million for 2013–2014, and average payrolls in the post cap period are nearly double the pre cap years. Notwithstanding, the comparison of payroll dispersion, as measured by the COV, shows that payrolls were much more concentrated in the years following the imposition of the cap. The COV is more than double in the earlier era (0.355–0.149) and the t-test shows this to be a highly significant result (p-value = 0.000). The results leave little doubt that the payroll cap accomplished

---

[3] NHL payroll data is not available for the 1997–1998 season.

Table 1 NHL payroll dispersion: pre and post salary cap

Period of analysis	Season	Average payroll	Standard deviation	Coefficient of variation
	1992–1993	$8,275,648	$4,514,633	0.546
	1993–1994	$12,950,000	$3,702,327	0.286
	1994–1995	$15,967,500	$4,302,599	0.269
	1995–1996	$19,769,666	$4,944,225	0.250
	1998–1999	$28,552,225	$9,587,472	0.336
	1999–2000	$30,529,312	$11,640,445	0.381
	2000–2001	$33,375,943	$11,657,873	0.349
	2001–2002	$38,011,852	$14,162,670	0.373
	2002–2003	$41,939,715	$16,876,630	0.402
	2003–2004	$44,400,490	$15,898,399	0.358
	2005–2006	$34,657,712	$6,247,900	0.180
	2006–2007	$40,211,713	$4,699,260	0.117
	2007–2008	$44,388,537	$7,601,233	0.171
	2008–2009	$51,387,176	$8,104,458	0.158
	2009–2010	$51,750,270	$7,948,647	0.154
	2010–2011	$54,173,190	$11,046,770	0.204
	2011–2012	$56,657,728	$9,777,196	0.173
	2012–2013	$60,699,742	$6,311,335	0.104
	2013–2014	$62,200,365	$4,956,297	0.080
Full period	1992–2014	$38,415,725	$8,630,546	0.257
Pre cap	1992–2004	$27,377,235	$9,728,727	0.355
Post cap	2005–2014	$50,680,715	$7,410,344	0.149
Difference		$23,303,480[a]	$2,318,383	0.206[a]

[a]Significant at 0.01
[b]Significant at 0.05
[c]Significant at 0.1

the goal of smoothing club payrolls. However additional tests are needed to confirm that competitive balance also improved.

Fort (2006) summarizes other researchers and offers three dimensions of outcome uncertainty that can be used to measure competitive balance. These are game uncertainty, end of season uncertainty, and seasonal discontinuity. Numerous statistical measures have been employed to assess the various aspects of competitive balance. The three chosen here attempt to capture each of the three aforementioned dimensions. RSD, the most used measure of balance, explains the variation in talent distribution over the course of each full season. Arguably it captures end of season uncertainty as the more closely grouped the teams are, the less certain end-of-season outcomes are, for instance which teams will qualify for the playoffs. Table 2 shows the absolute standard deviations of win percent and the RSD results over the course of both the pre and post cap eras. RSD shows a much tighter and statistically significant distribution of talent in the post cap years (1.602 post cap compared to 1.832 pre cap, p-value = 0.035).

Table 2 NHL standard deviation of win percent: pre and post salary cap

Period of analysis	Season	SDWP	ISD	RSD
	1992–1993	0.145	0.055	2.660
	1993–1994	0.102	0.055	1.875
	1994–1995	0.111	0.072	1.541
	1995–1996	0.116	0.055	2.092
	1996–1997	0.078	0.055	1.411
	1997–1998	0.096	0.055	1.742
	1998–1999	0.097	0.055	1.752
	1999–2000	0.104	0.055	1.880
	2000–2001	0.108	0.055	1.950
	2001–2002	0.092	0.055	1.658
	2002–2003	0.093	0.055	1.693
	2003–2004	0.095	0.055	1.729
	2004–2005	NA	NA	NA
	2005–2006	0.109	0.055	1.979
	2006–2007	0.102	0.055	1.852
	2007–2008	0.066	0.055	1.193
	2008–2009	0.088	0.055	1.586
	2009–2010	0.085	0.055	1.543
	2010–2011	0.085	0.055	1.532
	2011–2012	0.080	0.055	1.449
	2012–2013	0.109	0.072	1.510
	2013–2014	0.097	0.055	1.768
Full period	1992–2014	0.098	0.057	1.733
Pre cap	1992–2004	0.103	0.057	1.832
Post cap	2005–2014	0.091	0.057	1.602
Difference		0.012[a]	−0.001[b]	0.230[b]

[a]Significant at 0.1
[b]Significant at 0.05
[c]Significant at 0.01

Game uncertainty is evaluated by examining goal differential across teams over the course of each season. HockeyReference.com (2014) reports total goals scored and allowed each season for all NHL teams. Goal differential (GD) is the calculated difference between the two and may take either a positive or negative value. Two work stoppage seasons (1994–1994 and 2012–2013) had only 48 games, thus GD was adjusted to a per-game average. The standard deviation of goal differential (SDGD), both absolute and adjusted across teams in the league, was calculated for each season and the computed values are shown in Table 3. Once again a clear improvement in competitive balance in the post cap era is apparent. The SDGD per game dropped from 0.61 to 0.48 (p-value = 0.002). In addition to tighter groupings of teams in the standings, the SDGD comparison indicates that scoring differential was on average much closer following implementation the cap.

Table 3 NHL standard deviation of goal differential: pre and post salary cap

Period of analysis	Year	SDGD	Games	SDGD/games
	1992–1993	78.35	82	0.933
	1993–1994	54.02	82	0.643
	1994–1995	31.58	48	0.658
	1995–1996	58.38	82	0.712
	1996–1997	38.32	82	0.467
	1997–1998	44.26	82	0.540
	1998–1999	42.98	82	0.524
	1999–2000	50.22	82	0.612
	2000–2001	48.79	82	0.595
	2001–2002	42.36	82	0.517
	2002–2003	43.59	82	0.532
	2003–2004	45.75	82	0.558
	2004–2005	NA	82	NA
	2005–2006	46.71	82	0.570
	2006–2007	46.10	82	0.562
	2007–2008	28.33	82	0.345
	2008–2009	36.99	82	0.451
	2009–2010	35.55	82	0.434
	2010–2011	37.13	82	0.453
	2011–2012	25.26	82	0.308
	2012–2013	24.09	48	0.502
	2013–2014	40.76	82	0.497
Full period	1992–2014	42.834	78.909	0.543
Pre cap	1992–2004	48.218	79.167	0.608
Post cap	2005–2014	35.657	78.222	0.458
Difference		12.561[a]	0.944	0.150[a]

[a]Significant at 0.01
[b]Significant at 0.05
[c]Significant at 0.1

The Spearman's Rank Correlation Coefficient (SRCC) is used to evaluate seasonal discontinuity. This method, which measures the correlation of each team's rank in the league standings over two consecutive seasons, is standard practice in the sports economics literature. For example, Daly and Moore (1981) and Maxcy (2002) have used this method to evaluate the seasonal discontinuity dimension of competitive balance in American team sport leagues. A league where a club can quickly move from last to first is thought to exhibit good balance, while little year-over-year change of the order of finish reflects poor balance; the SRCC captures this. SRCC coefficient values range from $R_s = -1$ to $R_s = +1$ with -1 representing a perfect reordering of league standings and thus the best possible balance. A value of $+1$ indicates exactly the same order of finish and thus higher coefficient values indicate worse balance.

Table 4 NHL Spearman's rank correlation coefficient: pre and post salary cap

Period of analysis	Year	SRCC = R_s
	1992–1993	0.385
	1993–1994	0.441
	1994–1995	0.578
	1995–1996	0.746
	1996–1997	0.403
	1997–1998	0.429
	1998–1999	0.541
	1999–2000	0.655
	2000–2001	0.817
	2001–2002	0.603
	2002–2003	0.579
	2003–2004	0.605
	2004–2005	NA
	2005–2006	0.481
	2006–2007	0.571
	2007–2008	0.480
	2008–2009	0.538
	2009–2010	0.464
	2010–2011	0.591
	2011–2012	0.520
	2012–2013	0.202
	2013–2014	0.523
Full period	1992–2014	0.531
Pre cap	1992–2004	0.565
Post cap	2005–2014	0.486
Difference		0.080[a]

[a]Significant at 0.1
[b]Significant at 0.01
[c]Significant at 0.05

Table 4 presents the SRCC calculations. Competitive balance is again shown to be significantly better in the post-cap era. The SRCC declines from an average of $R_s = 0.565$ over the period before the cap to $R_s = 0.486$ post cap (p-value = 0.077). The swing is not as dramatic as the within-season measures of balance. Nonetheless, the results confirm that imposition of a salary cap improved all three dimensions of competitive balance in the NHL, and the results are statistically significant in each case.

The empirical results evidently confirm both propositions. The imposition of firm, enforced limits on club payrolls both reduces payroll dispersion across teams and levels the distribution of talent, improving competitive balance. The results are counter to the view that labor market policy alternatives are irrelevant to the distribution of talent in team sport leagues. However, it should be cautioned that a strict interpretation of the invariance principle, which considers only a shift of property rights, is not necessarily breached by considering the effects of a payroll and salary cap.

The Lockout as a Strategy

Beginning with the 1994 NHL work stoppage, each and every work stoppage in American sports has been a lockout, with the cancellation of games being motivated by the owners and not the players. In all cases—three lockouts in the NHL, two for the NBA, and one for the NFL (plus the lockout of its referees)—the owners have rolled back prior concessions and gained a CBA considerably more favorable to their interests. Primarily in the three most recent lockouts, the players' share of revenue has fallen sharply, by about 10%, for each league that has locked out its players.

American labor law, by court interpretation, specifies that the terms of a CBA stay in effect after expiration until a new agreement is reached (Weiler and Roberts 2004). The spirit of the law authorizing lockouts is that it gives management a tool to balance a union's right to strike. The party satisfied with the current state of affairs must be pressed to change the status quo, and income-eliminating work stoppages are the most effective force. Logically the side with the most leverage to shift the terms in their favor will initiate a stoppage—and that has been entirely a one way street for 15-plus years.

Team owners were once hesitant to force a stoppage. MLB had locked out players from spring training facilities on several occasions, but never had a lockout resulted in canceled games. In fact, MLB owners had always yielded, ensuring that the perception of the responsibility for work stoppages lied with the union. All that changed in 1994 when the NHL, under Commissioner Gary Bettman, revealed that the public relations damage from a lockout and canceled games was minimal. Most importantly, any public relations costs to owners could be offset by a more beneficial CBA. As explained above, the first lockout only granted the NHL owners limited advances. In fact, they were thwarted on their primary demand, a salary cap. Nonetheless, the NBA, under the leadership of Bettman's former colleague David Stern, saw the potential, followed suit, and locked out the players in 1998.[4]

The NBA lockout, which also began as training camps were to open, resulted in the cancellation of roughly half of the 1998–1999 season's games. The outcome this time was a CBA far more favorable to owners' interests. The exceptions allowed under the league's soft salary cap permitted players a significant share of revenues, and NBA players earned by far the highest average salaries in American team sports. Michael Jordan's $30 million salary in 1997–1998 actually exceeded the league's team cap. The new NBA CBA imposed the first ever restraints on individual player's salaries. The NBA's positive experience undoubtedly motivated Bettman and the NHL owners to use the lockout strategy once more in 2004, and provided additional resolve to cancel an entire year in order to frame the CBA on their terms.

Modern day ownership is much better suited to weather the storm of a stoppage than their predecessors; owners are wealthier and more diversified, and with long-

---

[4] Bettman served as Stern's top assistant, Deputy Commissioner of the NBA, before taking the top NHL position in 1994.

term contracts for broadcast rights, luxury suites, and sponsorships, they are also less dependent on game-specific revenue. The NHL and NBA have locked out the union at the expiration of every CBA since their first try, and extracted, as Goodenow predicted, more from the players each time. The NFL, which boasted nearly 20 years of labor peace, jumped on board in 2011, actually accelerating the termination of their CBA, to lockout their players. Only MLB, once the primary sports labor battleground, has not followed suit, but the different dynamics holding labor peace there may also be changing.

So where does it go from here? What's to stop owners from locking out until all the gains for players made by unions and antitrust relief (out of play under labor law) are extracted? In the reserve clause era players earned less than twenty percent of revenues, had no mobility rights, and were happy to take it. Labor law allows lockouts and denies antitrust. Lockouts in particular provide owners the means to drive sports right back to those "good ole' days". The solution may be no union, and thus no labor law and no lockouts—putting antitrust relief back into play.

References

Besanko, D. and Simon, D. (1985): Resource Allocation in the Baseball Players Labor Market: An Empirical Investigation. Review of Business and Economic Research, 21, pp. 71–84.
Booth, R. (2005): Comparing Competitive Balance in Australian Sports Leagues: Does a Salary Cap and Player Draft Measure Up? Sport Management Review, 8, pp. 119–143.
Brehm, M. and Allen, K. (2013): NHL Lockout Ends at 113 Days. USA Today January 6. Retrieved from http://www.usatoday.com/story/sports/nhl/2012/09/25/nhl-lockout-timeline/1587675/
Cruise, D. and Griffiths, A. (1991): Net Worth: Exploding the Myths of Pro Hockey. Toronto, Canada: Viking.
Cymrot, D. (1983): Migration Trends and the Earnings of Free Agents in Major League Baseball, 1976–79. Economic Inquiry, 21, pp. 545–56.
Daly, G. and Moore, W. (1981): Externalities, Property Rights, and the Allocation of Resources in Major League Baseball. Economic Inquiry, 19, pp. 77–95.
Dater, A. (2012): NHL Lockout Timeline: Comparing 2004–05 to 2012–13. Sports Illustrated (online content) Retrieved from http://www.si.com/nhl/2012/08/24/nhl-lockout-timeline
Dowbiggen, B. (2007): Money Players: The Amazing Rise and Fall of Bob Goodenow and the NHL Players Association. Toronto, Canada: Key Porter Books.
Fort, R. (2006): Competitive Balance in North American Sports, in: Fizel, J. (ed.): Handbook of Sports Economics Research, Armonk, NY: M. E. Sharpe.
Fort, R. (2014): Rodney Fort's Sports Business Data. Retrieved from https://sites.google.com/site/rodswebpages/codes
Fort, R. and Lee, Y. H. (2007): Structural Change, Competitive Balance, and the Rest of the Major Leagues. Economic Inquiry, 45, pp. 519–32.
Fort, R. and Maxcy J. (2003): Comment: Competitive Balance in Sports Leagues: An Introduction. Journal of Sports Economics, 4, pp. 154–160.
Fort, R. and Quirk, J. (1995): Cross-Subsidization, Incentives, and Outcomes in Professional Team Sports. Journal of Economic Literature, 33, pp. 1265–1299.
Fort, R., Maxcy, J., and Diehl, M. (2016). Uncertainty by Regulation: Is Rottenberg's Invariance Principle Subject to Policy and Circumstance? Research in Economics, 70, pp. 454–467.

Hylan, T., Lage, M., and Treglia, M. (1996): The Coase Theorem, Free Agency and Major League Baseball: A Panel Study of Pitcher Mobility from 1961–1992. Southern Economic Journal, 62, pp. 1029–1042.

Hall S., Szymanski, S. and Zimbalist, A. (2002): Testing Causality between Team Performance and Payroll: The Cases of Major League Baseball and English Soccer. Journal of Sports Economics, 3, pp. 149–168.

Hockey-Reference.com (2014): Retrieved from http://www.hockey-reference.com/

Jones, J.C.H. and Walsh, W.D. (1987): The World Hockey Association and Player Exploitation in the National Hockey League. Quarterly Review of Economics and Business, 27, pp. 87–101.

Kahane, L. (2006): The Economics of the National Hockey League: The 2004–05 Lockout and the Beginning of a New Era, in: Rodríguez, P. Késenne, S. García, J. (eds.): Sports Economics after Fifty Years: Essays in Honor of Simon Rottenberg, Oviedo: University of Oviedo Press.

Késenne, S. (2000a): Revenue Sharing and Competitive Balance in Team Sports. Journal of Sports Economics, 1, pp. 56–65.

Késenne S. (2000b): The Impact of Salary Caps in Professional Team Sports. Scottish Journal of Political Economy, 47, pp. 422–430.

Larson, A. Fenn, A.J., and Spenner, E.L. (2006): The Impact of Free Agency and the Salary Cap on Competitive Balance in the National Football League. Journal of Sports Economics, 7, pp. 374–390.

Lee, T. (2010): Competitive Balance in the National Football League after the 1993 Collective Bargaining Agreement. Journal of Sports Economics, 11, pp. 77–88.

Lee, Y. H. and Fort, R. (2005): Structural Change in Baseball's Competitive Balance: The Depression, Team Location, and Integration. Economic Inquiry, 43, pp. 158–169.

Marburger, D. (2002): Property Rights and Unilateral Player Transfers in a Multi Conference Sports League. Journal of Sports Economics 3, pp. 122–132.

Maxcy, J. (2002): Rethinking Restrictions on Player Mobility in Major League Baseball. Contemporary Economic Policy, 20, pp. 145–159.

Maxcy, J. (2011): The Effect on Player Transfers of a Luxury Tax on Club Payrolls: The Case of Major League Baseball, in: Andreff, W. (ed.): Sports Economics: Participation, Events, and Professional Team Sports, Cheltenham, UK and Northampton, MA: Edward Elgar.

National Labor Relations Board (1935): National Labor Relations Act. Retrieved from http://www.nlrb.gov/resources/national-labor-relations-act

Quirk, J. (1997): The Salary Cap and the Luxury Tax: Affirmative Action Programs for Weak-Drawing Franchises, in: Marburger, D. (ed.): Strike Four! What's Wrong with the Business of Baseball? Westport CT: Praeger Publishing Group.

Rascher, D.A. (1997): A Model of a Professional Sports League, in: Wallace, H. (ed.): Advances in the Economics of Sport, Greenwich, CT: JAI Press.

Richardson, D. (2000): Pay, Performance, and Competitive Balance in the National Hockey League. Eastern Economic Journal, 26, pp. 393–417.

Rottenberg, S. (1956): The Baseball Players Labor Market. Journal of Political Economy, 64, pp. 242–258.

Sanderson, A. and Siegfried, J. (2003): Thinking About Competitive Balance. Journal of Sports Economics, 4, pp. 255–291.

Schmidt, M.B. and Berri, D.J. (2003): On the Evolution of Competitive Balance: The Impact of an Increasing Global Search. Economic Inquiry, 41, pp. 692–704.

Spitzer, M. and Hoffman, E. (1980): A Reply to Consumption Theory, Production Theory, and Ideology in the Coase Theorem. Southern California Law Review, 53, pp. 1187–1214.

Staudohar, P. (2005): The Hockey Lockout of 2004–2005. Monthly Labor Review, December, pp. 23–29.

Weiler, P. and Roberts, G. (2004): Sports and the Law, 3rd Edition, St. Paul, Minnesota: West Group.

Fighting as a Profit-Maximizing Strategy: The American Hockey League

Duane W. Rockerbie

Abstract This chapter tests the argument that fighting in minor league hockey is a profit-maximizing strategy, using the American Hockey League (AHL) as an example. It could be that hockey players in the AHL have differing motivations for aggressive play than players in the senior NHL. Players in the AHL earn much lower salaries than their NHL cousins, so being promoted to the NHL results in significant financial rewards. Some AHL players might use an aggressive style of play as the ticket to the NHL, believing that there is a role in the NHL for tough players to protect the more skilled players from intimidation by other teams. Alternatively, fighting in the AHL could be the result of owners and management encouraging aggressive, physical play to attract fans to games. This chapter attempts to determine why fighting is more commonplace in the AHL than the NHL using an econometric model.

> *I'd like the folks to come down and watch us cream them punks from Syracuse.*
> *Anything new on the sale of the Chiefs?*
> *I think the negotiations are... you know, goin' pretty good. I have a personal announcement, though. I am placing a personal bounty on the head of Tim McCracken. He's the coach and chief punk on that Syracuse team.*
> *Reggie Dunlop (Paul Newman) in the movie Slap Shot (1977)*

The 1977 movie Slap Shot is arguably the most comedic yet accurate portrayal of life for minor league hockey players in the United States. The Charlestown Chiefs play in the fictional Federal League, a minor hockey league one tier below the National Hockey League (NHL). The mill in the town has closed down, the team is performing badly on the ice and attendance is waning. An aging ex-NHL player, Reggie Dunlop, is the player-coach for the Chiefs in what is likely his final season of hockey. To insure jobs for the other younger players on the team, Dunlop needs a quick and effective strategy to bolster the value of the team so that it can find a new owner to keep the team in Charleston or move the team to a better location. The team acquires the three Hansen brothers from a lower-tier league to fill out the

---

D.W. Rockerbie (✉)
Department of Economics, University of Lethbridge, Lethbridge, AL, Canada
e-mail: rockerbie@uleth.ca

roster. Dunlop initially doubts they can play hockey but discovers that their aggressive play is infectious for the other members of the team.

Frequent bloody fights bring fans back to the games and interest in the Chiefs moves outside of small-town Charleston. The team's owner is not impressed with the change in the fortunes of the Chiefs and intends to fold the team at the end of the season to receive a tax write-off that is more profitable than selling the team. The team tries to revert to a clean style of hockey in the league championship game, puzzling and disappointing their fans, but finds this to be a losing strategy and the game ends with a large brawl and the Chiefs are awarded the championship by forfeit.

Slap Shot was a movie that reflected a particularly violent period in professional hockey. The NHL's Philadelphia Flyers won the Stanley Cup championship in the 1975–1976 season by adopting an intimidating, physical style of play that complemented its core of highly skilled players. The most notorious of the Flyers players included Andre ("Moose") Dupont, Bob ("Mad Dog") Kelly, Don Saleski and Dave ("The Hammer") Schultz.[1] The 1974–1975 Flyers team participated in 105 recorded fights on the ice and 106 in the 1975–1976 season, but set an NHL record with 145 recorded fights in the 1977–1978 campaign, only to be eclipsed by the Boston Bruins 150 fights in the 1979–1980 season.[2] The Bruins impressive feat still stands as an all-time NHL record.

The director George Roy Hill (also known for "Butch Cassidy and the Sundance Kid" and "The Sting") intended Slap Shot to be a comedy but the business premise of the movie is very intriguing: encouraging violent play as a means to attract fans to hockey games that might not otherwise pay to attend. In order for the strategy to work, the benefits to violence must outweigh the costs. Back in the 1970s and 1980s, very few professional sports featured the sort of speed and physical contact of hockey. Professional boxing matches drew tremendous interest with the likes of Muhammad Ali, Larry Holmes and Mike Tyson, but these matches were infrequent and often not easily accessible to fans due to their locations and limited television coverage.[3] Other violent television sports that are popular today (particularly mixed martial arts fighting) were not yet invented. NHL hockey was televised by the NBC network in the United States and the CBC network in Canada so North American viewers could enjoy the fights interspersed with skilled hockey play.

Slap Shot portrayed the benefits to hockey violence as largely economic: fighting resulted in higher attendance at the gate that increased revenue, while replacing

---

[1] Dave Schultz accumulated an astounding 472 penalty minutes to lead the team, an all-time NHL single season record. The league average number of penalty minutes per player was just 40 and only 37.9 min excluding the Flyers. Schultz nearly repeated the feat in the 1977–1978 season with 405 penalty minutes, however injuries prevented him from breaking his own record. Taken from www.hockey-reference.com accessed on September 12, 2014.

[2] Taken from www.dropyourgloves.com accessed on September 12, 2014.

[3] Most heavyweight championship fights were not televised on national cable networks, instead they were sold as "closed circuit" broadcasts that were shown in movie theaters or other venues. Some of the larger closed-circuit television networks included MSG, TVS and Sports Network Incorporated.

more highly paid skill players with lower paid "goons" cut payroll costs. The Charleston Chiefs won more games after becoming a fighting team, but movies are fiction and more fighting could just as easily cause a team to lose more games by putting more of its players in the penalty box.

This paper extends the work of Rockerbie (2012) for the NHL to test the argument that fighting in minor league hockey is a profit-maximizing strategy, using the American Hockey League (AHL) as an example. It could be that hockey players in the AHL have differing motivations for aggressive play than players in the senior NHL. Players in the AHL earn much lower salaries than their NHL cousins, so being promoted to the NHL results in significant financial rewards. Some AHL players might use an aggressive style of play as their ticket to the NHL, believing that there is a role in the NHL for tough players to protect the more skilled players from intimidation by other teams. Alternatively, fighting in the AHL could be the result of owners and management encouraging aggressive, physical play to attract fans to games. This paper attempts to determine why fighting is more commonplace in the AHL than the NHL using an econometric model.

Fighting in Ice Hockey

The official tolerance of players engaging in fighting during a game is a distinguishing feature of ice hockey compared to other team sports. Typically, players who fight are immediately ejected from the match in professional and semi-professional sports leagues around the world. However, organized ice hockey leagues impose fewer penalties for fighting that typically remove the guilty players from the ice for a short period of time during the game. Ice hockey is played with five skaters and a goaltender on the ice for each team at any time in the game. If both of the guilty players are penalized for fighting, the number of skaters for each team is not reduced from five, providing only a minor deterrent effect if the penalized players are not the most skilled players on offense or defense. If only one player is penalized, his team must play with only four skaters for the duration of the penalty time (typically 5 min of clock time), placing his team at a disadvantage and potentially negatively affecting the outcome of the game for his team. In other sports, ejection of a player from the game for fighting results in no reduction in the number of players on the field or court (e.g. basketball, American football, baseball) or can result in the inability to replace the player on the pitch (soccer) meaning the team must play a man short.

While fighting is not overtly encouraged in ice hockey, it is tolerated based on the fact that the fighting players are not immediately ejected from the game. The speed of the game and the smaller ice surface in comparison to other sports results in frequent player contact, some of which can be quite violent. Lesser minor penalties for interference, roughing, boarding, tripping and cross-checking occur due to the natural flow of the game and are sometimes unavoidable. Players usually come to fighting as the result of one of two distinct situations. In the first, one player may believe that the physical contact initiated by another player is excessive and an intent to injure one of the players on his team. The unwritten code of behavior in ice hockey is to take matters into your own fists to send the message that excessive contact and intimidation will not be tolerated. Other players on the ice and on the bench respect this code and maintain a safe distance from the fight to allow the issue to be settled. The second situation is less frequent. Two combatants agree to fight to settle a score from a fight or hit that may have occurred earlier in the game or in a previous game. Again the unwritten code of behavior is to allow the combatants some time to fight without interference from any other players.

Sports fans who do not understand the unwritten code of fighting in ice hockey sometimes view fighting in hockey as a primitive method to injure an opponent and advocate that it should be banned. Hockey players do not share this position, despite suffering the possible injuries from fighting. In fact, in a 2011 poll of NHL players, 98% opposed a ban on fighting arguing that fighting makes the game safer by deterring other types of injury-causing violence (e.g. hitting with the stick, hits to the head or violent boarding).[4] Other sports also have unwritten codes of behavior as well that are accepted by players and officials but can serve to make the game less attractive to viewers. The practice of feigning challenges and injuries is very common in European soccer. The objective is either to be rewarded a penalty kick, having an opposing player ejected from the game, or hopefully both. Players who can achieve both objectives by faking fouls and injuries are often congratulated by teammates, knowing that there are no negative consequences to their deception. The term "simulation" is used in soccer to legitimize this tactic. North American sports fans view simulation as "unsportsmanlike" and cowardly, just as soccer fans view fighting in hockey as brutal and barbaric.

Ice hockey leagues have incorporated the unwritten code of behavior developed by players into the formal rules regarding fighting, and severely penalize players who interfere in a fight between two other combatants. Rule 46 in the NHL rulebook outlines the conditions to be granted to players by the officials on the ice to engage in a fight, as well as the penalties that can be imposed for "unsportsmanlike" fighting (e.g. kicking and pulling off an opponent's equipment). This tolerance for fighting can be traced back to the early days of ice hockey in Canada before the inception of the National Hockey League (NHL) in 1917. Beginning in 1893, amateur teams from any part of the country could challenge to win the Stanley Cup in an annual tournament. Players were often unskilled and made up for this by playing a rough game. The winner of the cup kept its possession as long as any "challengers" did not take it away. Up to 1904, players were not penalized for violating the rules of play, instead a guilty player was given two warnings for the same offense before being ejected from the game. The professional National Hockey Association took sole possession of the Stanley Cup in 1910, awarding it to its annual champion. Rules at the time did not significantly punish fighting and players were often injured as a

---

[4] See Whyno, NHL players bristle at fighting debate despite fan support for a ban, National Post, November 7, 2013. http://sports.nationalpost.com/2013/11/07/nhl-players-bristle-at-fighting-debate-despite-fan-support-for-ban/.

result of fights. It was in this early period in hockey history that fighting became ingrained in the sport. The NHL adopted its formal rules regarding fighting in 1922, but fights were still frequent and often bloody.

The American Hockey League

The American Hockey League (AHL) came into formal existence in 1939 with the merging of the International Hockey League and the Canadian-American Hockey League. The AHL has always been considered the top-tier minor hockey league since it supplies a large number of players to the NHL. Other minor hockey leagues in North America include the Canadian Hockey League (CHL) and the East Coast Hockey League (ECHL).[5] The NHL lies at the top of the hockey pyramid in North America, followed below by the AHL in the second tier and the CHL and ECHL in the bottom tier. The number of teams in the AHL fell to a low of only six in the 1976 season, largely due to rapid expansion in the NHL in response to the rival World Hockey Association (WHA) that existed from 1972 to 1979. Currently the AHL boasts 30 teams, 27 in the United States and 3 in Canada. The league underwent a major expansion for the 2001–2002 season when it absorbed six teams from the International Hockey League that failed due to financial losses. Each AHL team plays 76 regular season games from October through April. A total of 16 teams qualify for the Calder Cup playoffs that crown a league champion in June. As such, the AHL schedule closely rivals the NHL for the number of games played (82 in the NHL) and number of months to complete a season with playoffs. Most AHL clubs are located near the eastern seaboard of the United States. Only a few clubs have existed west of Chicago and in Canada, probably due to the higher costs of travel.

The largest recorded attendance for an AHL game was 45,653 for an outdoor game played at Citizens Bank Park in Philadelphia in 2012, however attendances for indoor games average between 2,000 and 5,000 with most clubs in the 2,000–3,000 range. Arenas are much smaller than NHL arenas and attendance is typically less than 50% of capacity. Ticket prices are also much lower than the NHL, ranging from an average of $16.40 for the lowest priced ticket to $35.20 for the highest price ticket in the 2011–2012 season.[6] Assuming an equal number of low and high priced tickets gives a simple average ticket price of $25.80, but this is probably an overestimate. The average ticket price for an NHL game in the same season was $57.49.[7]

Every AHL team is affiliated with a parent NHL club. This agreement allows the NHL club to place its younger players that need further development with the AHL team. These players typically sign two-way contracts that pay the player a higher

---

[5] The CHL is the umbrella organization for three minor hockey leagues in Canada: the Western Hockey League, the Ontario Hockey League and the Quebec Major Junior Hockey League.

[6] See AHL Average Ticket prices, http://www.coppernblue.com/2011/11/1/2518919/2011-12-ahl-ticket-prices sourced on September 3, 2014.

[7] Taken from Rod Fort's Sports Business Data website on September 3, 2014.

salary if he moves to the NHL parent club. Salaries in the AHL are capped at $70,000 with a minimum salary of $40,500 ($42,000 for Canadian clubs). Some older players have two-way contracts that exceed the maximum AHL salary if they have several seasons of NHL service,[8] however most young players in the AHL earn between $55,000 and $65,000. Players signed to one-way contracts by their NHL club receive the same salary whether playing in the AHL or the NHL. To put AHL salaries in perspective, the average NHL salary was $2.3 million for the 2013–2014 season.[9]

Fighting Rules and Penalties in the AHL

Rule 46 of the AHL Rulebook outlines the definitions and penalties for incidences of fighting.[10] Referees are allowed a great degree of latitude in determining penalties to take into consideration the degrees of responsibility in starting a fight and persisting in continuing the fight. Each combatant is assessed a major penalty, typically 5 min in the penalty box, however each team may still play with the full five skaters. An *instigator* is defined as the player that initializes the fight by striking or verbally challenging another player who is otherwise unwilling to fight at that moment. The instigator is penalized with an additional 2 min minor penalty and a major penalty (10 min).[11] His team must play one player short for the 2 min minor penalty. It has become practice for players to avoid the instigator penalty by mutually agreeing to fight, then simultaneously dropping their gloves and engaging in combat. This has proven to be an effective strategy as instigator penalties are very rarely called.

An *aggressor* is defined as a player that continues to throw punches when his opponent is in a defenseless position or is unwilling to continue fighting. The penalties for an aggressor are severe: a major penalty (10 min) and ejection from the game. The unwritten code of conduct among hockey players does not tolerate aggressors. The offense is usually punishable by retaliation in a future match, therefore penalties for being an aggressor are very rare. In most incidences of fighting, each player is assessed a 5 min major penalty with no further punishment. Each of the teams is allowed to play with the full five skaters.

While being deemed an instigator does not expel a player from the game, being deemed an instigator three times in a game does according to Rule 46. This rule was changed prior to the 2014–2015 AHL season so that being deemed an instigator just

---

[8] For instance, Chris Butler (NHL St. Louis Blues) earned $400,000 playing in the AHL in the 2013–2014 season.

[9] Players in the CHL are not paid salaries, but do receive monthly living stipends and are eligible for generous university scholarships. The ECHL has a minimum salary of $415 per week and $460 per week for returning players.

[10] The AHL Rulebook can be found at http://cdn.rapidmanager.com/ahl/files/13_14_AHLRuleBook.pdf.

[11] This rule was established in 1992.

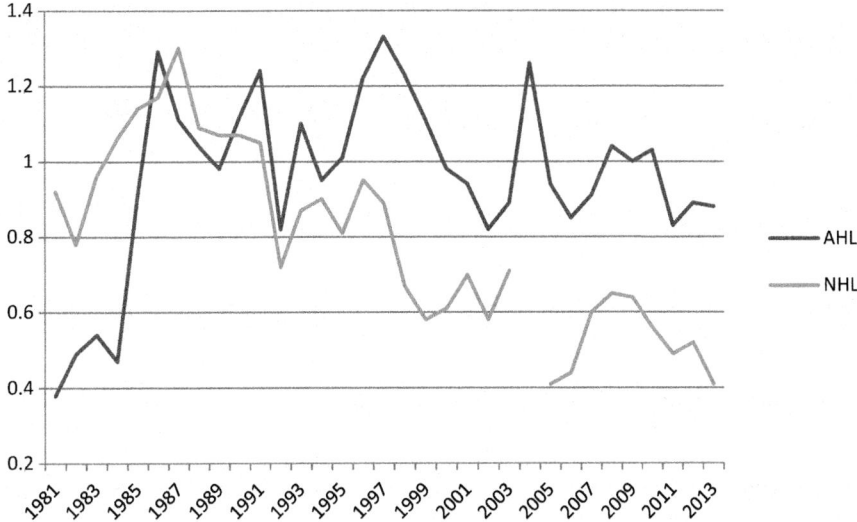

Fig. 1 Fights per game in the AHL and NHL (Source: http://www.dropyourgloves.com)

two times in a game results in expulsion from the game. Rule 46 also specifies that players must cease fighting when they have been separated and are ordered to stop by an official. Failure to do so results in a major penalty (10 min) or expulsion from the game at the discretion of the official. Other penalties can be assessed for removing a helmet before fighting, fighting off the ice surface, being the third player into a fight,[12] fighting before play is started and wearing inappropriate equipment during a fight. Suspensions and fines can be levied to a player who is penalized as an instigator or an aggressor in three or more games during a season, although the fines are modest ($250).

The AHL Rule 46 is identical to the NHL Rule 46 in regards to fighting with the exception that fines for repeated offenses are much higher in the NHL ($25,000). However, when taken as a share of the average player salary, the fines are only slightly higher in the NHL at 1.5% of salary, versus 0.5% in the AHL. Figure 1 plots the number of fights per game from the 1981–1982 season through the 2013–2014 season for each league. Despite the same rules regarding fighting, the AHL has boasted a much higher number of fights per game (averaging 1.016) than the NHL (averaging 0.688) since the 1990–1991 season.[13]

The 1981–1985 period saw fighting more prevalent in the NHL than the AHL, probably due to the large number of players absorbed into the NHL from the WHA with the 1979 merger of the two leagues. In addition, the correlation coefficient between fights per game in the AHL and NHL since the 1990–1991 season is 0.641, suggesting a moderately strong association. Both leagues have experienced a

---

[12] Established in 1977.
[13] The 2004–2005 NHL season was not played due to a player lockout.

downward trend in fights per game since the 1990–1991 season, but more so in the NHL with a 61.7% reduction compared to a 21.4% reduction for the AHL. With much higher salaries, there is less room on NHL rosters for players who specialize in fighting at the expense of more important offensive and defensive skills.

Fighting as a Profit-Maximizing Strategy for the AHL

Since the 1990–1991 season, 55 teams have either expanded into the AHL and continue to exist today (but may have relocated to another city) or have failed. The NHL parents of AHL clubs are not particularly loyal to any city, hence relocations are frequent and swift if the club does not perform well at the box office. Table 1 provides a summary of the wandering path some AHL clubs have taken to where they are today. These relocations have taken place as a result of a private owner or the NHL parent owner club moving or selling the club. In some cases, clubs are suspended by their owner for a season or more, then re-enter the AHL by agreement with the league. Nineteen of the current 30 clubs in the AHL have been relocated from another city, usually after a sale of the club. By way of contrast, only seven NHL teams have been relocated since 1970[14] and only one has relocated twice.[15] Most of the other AHL clubs are new expansion teams that have begun operations within the last 10 years. An exception is the Hershey Bears club that has been operating since the inception of the AHL in 1939. The club was originally established by the Hershey chocolate company as a clever marketing tool (the original name was the Hershey Bars, changed to the Bears after a few seasons). The Bears have never relocated and are still owned by a division of the Hershey company.

On the other end of the spectrum lie the Adirondack Flames who have relocated four times since 2005 with the same parent NHL club as owner (Calgary Flames). The team's last move in 2014 from Abbotsford (British Columbia) was prompted by $12 million in losses since 2010 due to low attendance.[16] Taxpayers agreed to subsidize annual losses up to $5.7 million for 10 years under the deal to move the team from Quad Cities to Abbotsford. The City of Abbotsford agreed to pay the parent NHL Calgary Flames $12 million to be released from the contract and evict the team.

The bottom line is that franchise sales and relocations are far more frequent in the AHL than the NHL and the looming specter of job uncertainty might force management, coaches and players to try the Slap Shot strategy of using fighting and rough play on the ice to maintain the box office. This strategy can have two contrast-

---

[14] These include the Atlanta Thrashers, Colorado Rockies, Kansas City Scouts, Minnesota North Stars, Oakland Seals, Quebec Nordiques and Winnipeg Jets.

[15] The Oakland Seals relocated to become the Cleveland Barons in 1976, then merged with the Minnesota North Stars in 1978. The North Stars moved to Dallas in 1993 to become the Dallas Stars.

[16] http://www.cbc.ca/news/canada/british-columbia/abbotsford-heat-leave-city-with-12m-in-losses-1.2610985. Referenced on September 10, 2014.

Table 1 Franchise relocations of current teams in the AHL

AHL team	Location	NHL parent team	Previous teams
Adirondack Flames (2014)	Glenn Falls, NY	Calgary Flames	Abbotsford Heat (2009–2013)
			Quad City Flames (2007–2008)
			Omaha Ak-Sar-Ben Knights (2005–2006)
			St. John Flames (1993–2003)
Albany Devils (2010)	Albany, NY	New Jersey Devils	Lowell Devils (2006–2009)
			Lowell Lock Monsters (1998–2005)
Binghamton Senators (1992)	Binghamton, NY	Ottawa Senators	
Bridgeport Sound Tigers (2001)	Bridgeport, CT	New York Islanders	
Charlotte Checkers (2011)	Charlotte, NC	Carolina Hurricanes	Albany River Rats (1994–2010)
			Capital District Islanders (1990–1993)
Chicago Wolves (2001)	Chicago, IL	St. Louis Blues	
Grand Rapids Griffins (2001)	Grand Rapids, MI	Detroit Red Wings	
Hamilton Bulldogs (1996)	Hamilton, ON	Montreal Canadiens	Cape Breton Oilers (1988–1995)
Hartford Wolf Pack (1997)	Hartford, CT	New York Rangers	Providence Reds (1926–1976)
			Binghamton Dusters (1977–1996)
Hershey Bears (1938)	Hershey, PA	Washington Capitals	
Iowa Wild (2013)	Des Moines, IA	Minnesota Wild	Houston Aeros (2001–2012)
Lake Erie Monsters (2006)	Cleveland, OH	Colorado Avalanche	
Lehigh Valley Phantoms (2014)	Allentown, PA	Philadelphia Flyers	Adirondack Phantoms (2009–2013)
			Philadelphia Phantoms (1996–2008)
Manchester Monarchs (2001)	Manchester, NH	Los Angeles Kings	
Milwaukee Admirals (2001)	Milwaukee, WI	Nashville Predators	

(continued)

Table 1 (continued)

AHL team	Location	NHL parent team	Previous teams
Norfolk Admirals (2000)	Norfolk, VA	Anaheim Ducks	
Oklahoma City Barons (2010)	Oklahoma City, OK	Edmonton Oilers	Edmonton Road Runners (2005–2006)
			Toronto Road Runners (2003–2004)
			Hamilton Bulldogs (1996–2002)
			Cape Breton Oilers (1989–1995)
			Nova Scotia Oilers (1984–1988)
Portland Pirates (1993)	Portland, ME	Arizona Coyotes	Baltimore Skipjacks (1983–1992)
Providence Bruins (1993)	Providence, RI	Boston Bruins	Maine Mariners (1987–1992)
Rochester Americans (1956)	Rochester, NY	Buffalo Sabres	
Rockford IceHogs (2007)	Rockford, IL	Chicago Blackhawks	Cincinnatti Mighty Ducks (1998–2005)
			Baltimore Bandits (1995–1997)
San Antonio Rampage (2006)	San Antonio, TX	Florida Panthers	
Springfield Falcons (1995)	Springfield, MA	Columbus Blue Jackets	
St. John's IceCaps (2012)	St. John's, NL	Winnipeg Jets	Manitoba Moose (1996–2011)
			Minnesota Moose (1994–1996)
Syracuse Crunch (1995)	Syracuse, NY	Tampa Bay Lightning	Hamilton Canucks (1992–1994)
Texas Stars (2009)	Cedar Park, TX	Dallas Stars	Iowa Chops (2008–2009)
			Iowa Stars (2005–2008)
Toronto Marlies (2005)	Toronto, ON	Toronto Maple Leafs	St. John's Maple Leafs (1992–2004)
			Newmarket Saints (1987–1991)
			St. Catharines Saints (1982–1986)
			New Brunswick Hawks (1978–1981)

(continued)

Table 1 (continued)

AHL team	Location	NHL parent team	Previous teams
Utica Comets (2013)	Utica, NY	Vancouver Canucks	Peoria Rivermen (2005–2012)
			Worcester Ice Cats (1994–2004)
			Springfield Kings (1967–1975)
			Syracuse Warriors (1951–1954)
			Springfield Indians (1936–1946)
Wilkes-Barre/Scranton Penguins (1997)	Wilkes-Barre, PA	Pittsburgh Penguins	Cornwall Aces (1993–1996)
Worcester Sharks (2007)	Worcester, MA	San Jose Sharks	Cleveland Barons (2001–2006)
			Kentucky Thoroughblades (1996–2001)

ing effects on the income statement. Fighting and rough play might attract more fans to games who might not otherwise be interested in hockey. Stewart et al. (1992) referred to this rather dramatically as the "blood-lust" effect. Unfortunately the Slap Shot strategy usually results in more time in the penalty box, forcing the team to play short-handed and potentially lose more games. Fans that value a winning team and do not buy tickets to watch fights will lose interest in the team.

The motivations for a player to fight can be varied. Goldschmied and Espindola (2013) used data from the 2010 to 2011 NHL season to examine whether fighting is just an impulsive action by players due to the physical contact of the game, or if fighting is a calculated action to gain an intimidating advantage over the opponent. Fights were found to be more likely to occur early in regular season games when the apparent costs are lower. Fighting was more frequent in pre-season games when the cost was nil, but almost non-existent in playoff games when the cost could be very large. The authors concluded this was evidence that players consider the benefits and costs of their actions when choosing to fight. They further suggest that raising the costs of fighting by increasing penalty time, fines and suspensions could be an effective deterrent to fighting.

Major penalties, such as fighting, spearing and so on, might respond differently to increased enforcement of the rules than minor penalties, such as interference and tripping. The NHL added an additional on-ice official for the 1998–1999 season which should have increased the likelihood of detection of either type of penalty, thus increasing the probability of incurring the cost of a penalty (but not increasing the cost having committed a penalty and being caught). Allen (2002) found that occurrences of minor penalties decreased with the extra referee, but the occurrences of major penalties *increased* and appeared to be more random. The author attributes this to an *apprehension* effect where the presence of extra policing results in greater frustration for players whose job on the ice is to intimidate the opposition by aggressive play and fighting (so-called "goons") as their offenses are detected more frequently.

Heckelman and Yates (2003) revisited the penalty data for the 1999–2000 NHL season to determine if the addition of a third referee on the ice reduced major penalties, such as fighting. Two effects can result from adding more referees: the *deterrent* effect and the *monitoring* effect. The deterrent effect is observing a reduction in attempts by players to commit major penalties due to the greater likelihood of being caught. The monitoring effect arises from a greater ability by officials to detect penalties resulting in more penalties called, without any increase in attempts to commit penalties. The authors found evidence that the monitoring effect was significant but that there was no deterrent effect. Hence the results suggest again that increasing the costs of committing major penalties could be an effective deterrent.

It could be that the variations in the frequency of fights in the AHL versus the NHL – as displayed in Fig. 1 – are influenced by the talent pool that is available to both leagues. It has already been noted that in the mid-1970s, the NHL competed with the rival World Hockey Association (WHA) for players, resulting in an increase in salaries and the number of player positions to be filled. In the meantime, the AHL experienced a reduction in the number of clubs to just six in 1976. With the NHL-WHA merger in 1978, the large demand and small supply of talented players resulted in many marginal players being employed in the now larger NHL. Some of these players were known to be more prone to fighting, the so-called "goon" players, whose role on the team was to protect the more talented players from physical intimidation. Fighting in the NHL peaked in the late 1980s and has fallen since, while, with far more teams in the AHL today than in 1976, fighting in the AHL is a more common occurrence. With the average salary in the NHL at $2.3 million in 2012, there is no room for "goon" players who are not also talented skaters, shooters or defenders.[17] This sort of specialization has disappeared in the modern NHL, but might remain as a profitable strategy in the AHL.

Owners might encourage fighting as a way to improve their bottom lines. Evidence of the effects of fighting and rough play on attendance is mixed. Jones (1984) estimated a model of NHL attendance that included coefficients for the independent variables that measured violent behavior. The regression model was estimated using individual game data for the 1977–1978 season and used an indicator variable to denote whether the opponent was a fighting team or a skating team. The results suggested that a fighting team could increase ticket demand regardless of type of opponent. Some of the methodological problems in Jones (1984) were addressed in Stewart et al. (1992) where the analysis was refocused to consider the effects of violence on ticket demand more closely than other factors. The paper constructs a model of a profit-maximizing club owner who considers violence to be an important input into the production of wins on the ice. The authors argue convincingly that violence shifts ticket demand through greater on-ice success and

---

[17] See http://www.forbes.com/sites/monteburke/2012/12/07/average-player-salaries-in-the-four-major-american-sports-leagues/ accessed on September 24, 2014.

through the "blood lust" of the fans. This is an important paper since it builds a model of how hockey violence affects attendance through these two channels.

Jones et al. (1993) tested for any difference in fan preferences towards violence between Canadian and American clubs with the argument being that American clubs that operate in weaker markets might promote violence to a greater extent as a way to maintain revenues. American fans were found to respond positively to violence (about 1,500 more fans per misconduct penalty) but Canadian fans responded negatively (about 680 fewer fans per misconduct penalty) using data from the 1983 to 1984 NHL season. Jones et al. (1996) repeated the estimation using a single attendance equation and data from the 1989 to 1990 NHL season and found qualitatively identical results: American fans prefer violence and Canadian fans do not.

Paul (2003) replicated the method of Jones et al. (1996) using the number of fights per game for each club from the 1999 to 2000 NHL season, instead of major and minor penalty minutes. The study found that both American and Canadian fans preferred fighting with American fans somewhat more responsive (about 4,700 more fans per game compared to 3,100 fans per game for Canadian teams). Rockerbie (2012) extended the work of Jones et al. (1993) to include a much longer sample period (1997–2009) and to use fights per game as the measure of violence. Doubling the number of fights per season (a historically large increase) decreased attendance by about 1.63%, so neither fans in the United States nor in Canada were particularly responsive to fighting.

Paul et al. (2013) estimated that fighting increases game day attendance for a single AHL season, when holding constant promotions and other factors that affect game day attendance. This study considers a much longer sample period and utilizes an econometric model derived from profit-maximization. Figure 2 plots a scatter diagram of the number of fights in a season versus the number of points accumulated in the final regular season standings (out of a maximum possible number of 160 points) for all AHL teams that operated in the 2001–2002 through 2013–2014 seasons, including those that relocated or failed. The scatter diagram offers no clear association between fighting and team performance. The correlation coefficient is small at 0.146, but is statistically significant at 95% confidence (t = 2.719). Of course, no other variables that might affect team performance are being held constant so little can be offered in the way of definite conclusions.

The Model

The model of team behavior used here is simpler than the model specified by Stewart et al. (1992) and used in Rockerbie (2012). As will be explained, the simpler model is largely due to data limitations for the AHL. The league is assumed to be composed of N clubs each facing an attendance inverse demand function of the form

$$p_{it} = \delta + \beta v_{it} + b w_{it} + c y_{it} - d A_{it} \tag{1}$$

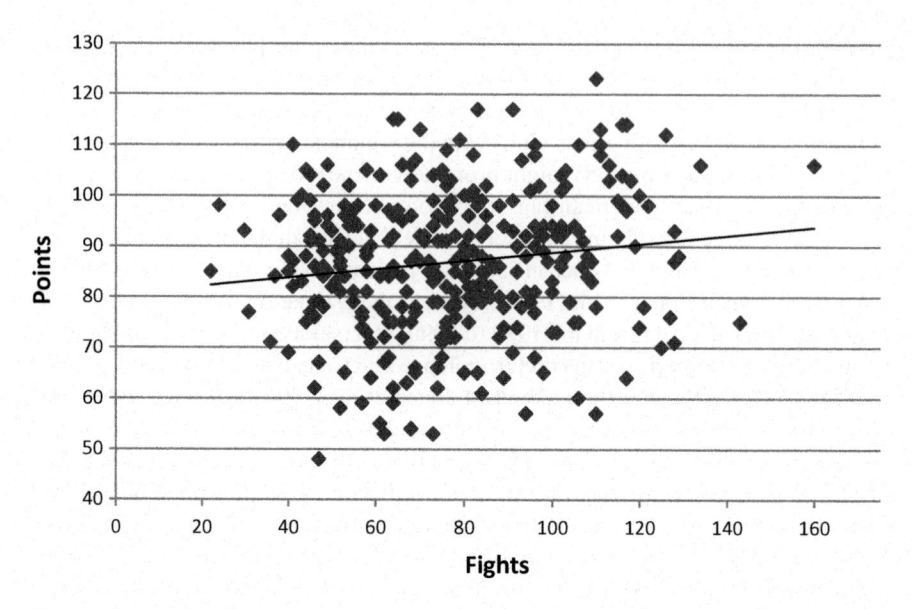

Fig. 2 Number of fights versus total points in the AHL (Source: http://www.dropyourgloves.com and http://www.ahl.com)

Season attendance for club i in year t is given by A_{it}. The variable v_{it} is a measure of violence over an entire season that affects attendance independently of its potential effects on the club's winning percentage. Club success on the ice is measured by w_{it} which is the total points earned during a season divided by the maximum number of points that can be attained. Wins are the direct output of each club that results in greater attendance. The term y_{it} is a vector of independent variables that capture the demographic and economic characteristics of the team location. Finally, p_{it} is the average ticket price for each club.

Increased violence might increase attendance directly through the spectacle of watching two combatants square off on the ice as a form of entertainment, similar to boxing or mixed martial arts fighting. In those sports, greater violence by one opponent often results in a greater chance of victory, however the connection between violence and club success is not so clear in hockey. Violence in hockey often results in one or both participants being penalized, putting their club at a numerical disadvantage on the ice. Frequent violence can result in fewer wins and a lower winning percentage, resulting in lower attendance in (1), ignoring the bloodlust effect. The question of paramount interest here is which effect dominates attendance and to determine that, we need to specify a contest-success function. Many exist in the theoretical sports economics literature with the logistic form being the most desirable in the case of a two-team league. Unfortunately with more than two teams in the league, well-defined functions do not exist, so we specify a linear form. Any probability model that is not a logistic form can suffer from the weakness that the predicted values fall outside the (0, 1) range, however the winning percentages for the AHL clubs in the sample are clustered rather narrowly around 0.5 so a linear form might be a good approximation. Linear contest-success functions have been estimated in the sports economics literature with some examples being Scully (1974) and Krautmann (1999). Generally logistic functions are avoided in empirical work due to the inherent instability of the results.[18] In our case, a non-linear functional form will not allow for identification of the model parameters.

$$w_{it} = \gamma - ev_{it} + gx_{it} \qquad (2)$$

The term x_{it} is a vector of team-specific performance measures that are thought to contribute towards its winning percentage. The last term allows for an interaction between team violence and team measures of performance based on the simple idea that if a team spends a lot of time in the penalty box, the marginal effect of the performance measures could be lower.

We assume that each club maximizes profit and we impose this on the empirical model by deriving a restriction. The assumption is that all costs are fixed costs, that is, costs are independent of the number of fans who attend games when each club has a fixed playing schedule. Maximizing team revenue with respect to A_{it} gives a simple first-order condition which is substituted into (1) to arrive at the optimal attendance level.[19]

$$A_{it}^* = \frac{1}{2d}\left(\delta + \beta v_{it} + bw_{it} + cy_{it}\right) \qquad (3)$$

Maximizing revenue with respect to team violence (v_{it}) results in a simple first-order condition that imposes the restriction that $\beta = be$. Estimating the model is straightforward. The contest-success function (2) can be estimated using least squares to obtain estimates of e and g. Imposing the restriction in the attendance function (3) results in

$$A_{it}^* = \frac{1}{2d}\left(\delta + b\left(ev_{it} + w_{it}\right) + cy_{it}\right) \qquad (4)$$

The restricted attendance function (4) can be estimated using least squares and the estimate of e. Since a time-series of ticket price data for the AHL is not available, (4) will have to be estimated using a grid search method by assuming different values for the inverse price elasticity d. The net effect of increased violence on attendance is $\hat{\beta} = \hat{b} \cdot \hat{e}$.

---

[18] See Peeters (2011) for examples.
[19] We maximize with respect to A_{it} rather than P_{it} due to the lack of availability of a time-series of AHL ticket prices.

Table 2 Variable definitions and data sources for Eq. 2

Variable	Abbreviation	Source
Points (2 points for win, 0 points for loss, 1 point for overtime loss, maximum 152 for regular season)	w_{it}	www.hockeyDB.com
Fights (total per regular season)	v_{it}	www.dropyourgloves.com
Goals allowed (total per regular season)	GA_{it}	www.hockeyDB.com
Power-play percentage (regular season number of power-plays in which goal scored as a percentage of total number of power-plays)	PP_{it}	AHL Yearbook, various issues
Penalty-kill percentage (regular season number of penalties in which goal not allowed as a percentage of total number of penalties against)	PK_{it}	AHL Yearbook, various issues
Number of 20-goal scorers in regular season	TG_{it}	www.hockeyDB.com

Data

The sample period covers the 2002–2003 through 2013–2014 AHL seasons. Not all clubs played in every season in the sample period, in fact, a few played only a single season before moving on to another city. The net sample size was composed of 341 observations for each variable. Three internet sources were used to obtain the necessary data to estimate the contest success function in (2).

The hockeyDB web site contains a variety of time series data for most of the North American hockey leagues that have ever existed, as well as some European leagues. More detailed player statistics for each season were found from the AHL annual Yearbooks. Readers can probably think of other variables that could be included in the estimation to explain the team winning percentages, however it is important not to include variables that merely provide an accounting summary of each team's performance, such as goals scored, lest the specification of (2) become too much like a definition and lose its behavioral qualities.

The specification for the attendance function in (3) included the variables listed in Table 3 below. Arena capacity was included as a scaling variable and to account for the potential of any capacity constraints. This was probably not an issue for the estimation of (3) since the capacity utilization rate (attendance/capacity) did not exceed 85% for any of the clubs over the sample period, and most clubs fell at 50% or less. Population estimates can only be obtained for the county in which each AHL team is located since the U.S. Census Bureau uses the county delineation to define a metropolitan boundary. The FRED2 database maintained by the Federal Reserve Bank of St. Louis was used to download the population figures from Census Bureau files. In most cases, the county boundary enclosed the AHL club's capture area reasonably well, but in a few cases, the county boundary contained an overly large

Table 3 Variable definitions and data sources for Eq. 3

Variable	Abbreviation	Source
Attendance (per game in regular season)	ATT_{it}	www.hockeyDB.com
Fights (total per regular season)	v_{it}	www.dropyourgloves.com
Points (2 points for win, 0 points for loss, 1 point for overtime loss, maximum 152 for regular season)	w_{it}	www.hockeyDB.com
Arena capacity	CAP_{it}	www.hockeyDB.com
Population (annual estimate for county)	POP_{it}	fred.stlouisfed.org/, www.statcan.gc.ca/estat
Real income per capita (annual estimate for county, 2009 dollars)	INC_{it}	www.bea.gov, www.statcan.gc.ca/estat
Unemployment rate (annual estimate by county)	$UNEMP_{it}$	www.bls.gov, www.statcan.gc.ca/estat
Zero-one variable for Canadian clubs	CAN_{it}	

area.[20] Population estimates for Canadian cities were obtained from the Statistics Canada E-Stat website.[21] Real income per capita was obtained also at the county level in 2009 dollars from the U.S. Bureau of Economic Analysis website and E-Stat websites. The county-level unemployment rate was obtained from the U.S. Bureau of Labor Statistics and E-Stat. Finally, a zero-one variable was created to estimate any shift in attendance for AHL clubs located in Canada.

Empirical Results

The attendance function in (4) incorporates the restriction that $\beta = be$ that comes as a result of the assumption of profit-maximization. To test this restriction, (4) was first estimated in unrestricted form as a part of a two-equation system with the contest success function in (2). A weighted least squares procedure was used to correct the coefficient standard errors for heteroskedasticity. Due to the presence of the arena capacity variable, cross-section fixed effects could not be used without incurring perfect multicollinearity, so fixed effects were not included in estimating the

---

[20] Lowel, Massachusetts lies in Middlesex County that contains an area of 2,196 km² and a population of 1.5 million. The city of Lowell had a population of just 108,861 in 2013 (U.S. Census Bureau). For Lowell and two other cases, the county population was ratio-scaled with the 2013 city population and the county population growth rate was then applied to estimate city populations.

[21] Unfortunately for economists interested in economic data for Canada, Statistics Canada has discontinued the E-Stat web portal, although the main STATSCAN web portal is still active and much harder to use.

restricted or unrestricted forms of (4).[22] The restriction $\beta = be$ was tested with a Wald test that is distributed as a chi-squared with a critical rejection value of $\chi^2_{.05,1} = 3.8415$. The restriction could not be rejected with a Wald test value of 0.1175. It is well known that the Wald test can provide differing results if the non-linear restriction is expressed in a different way, such as $e = b/\beta$ or $b = e/\beta$. Fortunately the non-linear restriction could not be rejected in any of the three forms. Having failed to reject the restriction, the two-equation system could be estimated in restricted form and the estimated coefficients for b and e be recovered to compute an estimate for β, the so-called "blood-lust" effect on attendance. These regression results are displayed in Table 4.

The contest success function in (2) fits reasonably well with an adjusted R^2 of 0.674. A one point increase in the team power-play percentage (say from 18% to 19%) increases the team winning percentage by 0.843 points (say from 50.0% to 50.843%) and is statistically significant at the 95% confidence level. Since most penalties are "killed off" in the AHL (average penalty kill percentage over the sample is 82.93%), a one point increase has a much lower effect on the winning percentage than does a one point increase in the power-play percentage (average power-play percentage is just 16.93%) at an increase of just 0.119 points. Reducing the number of goals given up over the season by one goal will increase the club winning percentage by a statistically significant average of 0.189 points. The largest effect on the club winning percentage is the addition of an additional 20 goal scorer at 2.068 percentage points. Twenty goal scorers are surprisingly uncommon in the AHL. Teams averaged less than three in the sample period (2.744) and in only 41 out of a total of 341 club seasons did a team possess more than four. Most clubs experienced far more players moving in and out of the roster in a season than is typical for an NHL club, so scoring is very spread out among players.

The attendance demand function fit only modestly well with an adjusted R^2 of 0.226. Fighting had a positive, albeit small effect on the club winning percentage, contrary to the negative effect found by Rockerbie (2012) for NHL clubs. Recording one more fight in a season increased the team winning percentage by just 0.019 points and was statistically significant at only the 89.25% confidence level. It is probably safe to say that fighting neither improves nor worsens team performance in the AHL.

County population and per capita income are statistically significant factors in average game attendance, however the negative coefficient for per capita income suggests that AHL hockey is an inferior good for consumers. This could be due to the close proximity of NHL teams and other professional sports teams to AHL cities. Higher per capita incomes tend to be observed in the larger urban centers in the sample, where substitute forms of entertainment to AHL hockey are readily available. It is also worth noting that AHL teams tend to be located in areas with lower per capita incomes than NHL cities. Perhaps this a marketing strategy for the owners of the AHL clubs, principally NHL clubs. The unemployment rate is not statisti-

---

[22] Dropping the capacity variable and including fixed effects resulted in many of the statistically significant slope coefficients moving to statistical insignificance.

Table 4 Estimation results of Eqs. 2 and 4

System: VIOLENCE				
Included observations: 341				
Total system (unbalanced) observations 672				
	Coefficient	Std. Error	t-Statistic	Prob.
C(1)	68.46703	7.280195	9.404560	0.0000
C(2)	0.018897	0.011645	1.622786	0.1051
C(3)	0.843547	0.114454	7.370205	0.0000
C(4)	0.119061	0.067312	1.768805	0.0774
C(5)	−0.189335	0.010987	−17.23228	0.0000
C(6)	2.068602	0.187177	11.05160	0.0000
C(7)	1756.895	657.5742	2.671783	0.0077
C(8)	0.000197	7.98E−05	2.463858	0.0140
C(9)	−0.018652	0.006258	−2.980411	0.0030
C(10)	11.99900	33.68128	0.356251	0.7218
C(11)	0.117097	0.024401	4.798873	0.0000
C(12)	54.66719	8.914404	6.132456	0.0000
C(14)	−280.4866	237.2970	−1.182006	0.2376
Determinant residual covariance		49,072,864		
Equation 2: $w_{it} = C(1) + C(2)*v_{it} + C(3)*PP_{it} + C(4)$				
$*PK_{it} + C(5)*GA_{it} + C(6)*TG_{it}$				
Observations: 336				
R-squared	0.679492	Mean dependent var		57.21139
Adjusted R-squared	0.674636	S.D. dependent var		8.753421
S.E. of regression	4.993011	Sum squared resid		8226.951
Equation 4: $ATT_{it} = C(7) + C(8)*POP_{it} + C(9)*INC_{it} + C(10)*UNEMP_{it}$				
$+C(11)*CAP_{it} + C(12)*w_{it} + (C(12)*C(2))*v_{it} + C(14)*CAN_{it}$				
Observations: 336				
R-squared	0.242390	Mean dependent var		5509.704
Adjusted R-squared	0.226222	S.D. dependent var		1635.199
S.E. of regression	1438.397	Sum squared resid		6.79E+08

cally significant suggesting that AHL hockey attendance is acyclical. An increase in arena capacity has a small statistically significant effect on attendance (0.117 seats), however its inclusion was principally to hold capacity constant when considering the effects of the other demand variables. A one point increase in the team winning percentage increase per game attendance by an average of 54.667 seats and was highly statistically significant. Yet the overall modest fit of the attendance demand function suggests that there are many factors other than winning that influence attendance. Having a team located in Canada had no statistically significant effect on attendance, ceteris paribus.

The "blood-lust" effect of fighting on attendance is given by the estimate of $\beta = be$ (C(2)*C(12) in Table 4). Calculating the product gives a value of just 1.033, suggesting that an additional fight during the season increases per game attendance by only one seat. The standard error of the product $\beta = be$ was computed using the delta method (Greene 1997, p. 124) to be 1.678, yielding a statistically insignificant result. Removing the statistically insignificant county unemployment rate and zero-one indicator for a Canadian team resulted in a new system estimate for $\beta = be$ of 1.028, providing some evidence that the result is robust. As a further check, the attendance demand function was estimated without the restriction $\beta = be$ using weighted least squares. The "blood-lust" coefficient was estimated to be 3.3644 and was not statistically significant. Although three times larger than the coefficient from the restricted system estimation, it is only just over three seats per game – not qualitatively different from the restricted estimate.

Conclusions

It has been documented in this paper that fighting has been far more prevalent in the AHL than the NHL since 1990, although movements in both are strongly correlated. The econometric results in this paper suggest that it is not the case that profit-maximizing owners are encouraging greater fighting in the AHL as a means to earn more revenue. Unlike previous results for the NHL (Rockerbie 2012), fighting does not adversely affect a team's winning percentage, but it also does not encourage more attendance. With these results in hand, the greater prevalence of fighting in the AHL cannot be explained by either an intimidation effect on the opponent team or bringing in fans to watch the fights. The recidivism argument for fighting requires that the punishments for fighting in the AHL are not as severe as in the NHL, but that is simply not the case. In fact, the AHL rules regarding fighting are identical to the NHL rules, however the financial penalties in the AHL are smaller than in the NHL when taken as a percentage of the average player salary. However fines for fighting are rarely given in either league.

An alternative argument is that the AHL is a sort of purgatory for semi-professional hockey players. Highly skilled younger players will have a good chance of ascending to the NHL after having been judged by their on-ice statistics. Lesser skilled players might quickly fall out of the AHL after being judged as unworthy of the NHL. But for some players, the judgment takes longer and the AHL can provide a decent living combined with some other off-season employment. A few recent examples of AHL season fight leaders who have had lengthy AHL careers are Zack Stortini (nine seasons), Bobby Robins (nine seasons) and Kyle Hagel (seven seasons). Many more examples exist. There still exists a role for the player who is a known fighter in the AHL that has not existed in the NHL since the rapid increase in NHL salaries in the 1980s. If every other AHL team has one, then your team better have one (or more). There is no strategic advantage to having a player whose main skill is fighting on your team, but if you do not have one, your team could be at a significant disadvantage. Reaching a league-wide agreement to not keep "fighters" on the roster must be difficult in the AHL – for the NHL, no agreement is necessary as high salaries are just as effective.

References

Allen, W.D. (2002): Crime, Punishment and Recidivism: Lessons from the National Hockey League. Journal of Sports Economics, 3, pp. 39–60.
Goldschmied, N. and S. Espindola (2013): Is Professional Hockey Fighting Calculated or Impulsive? Sports Health: A Multidisciplinary Approach, 5, pp. 458–462.
Greene, W. (1997): Econometric Analysis, 3rd ed. Saddle River, NJ: Prentice-Hall.
Heckelman, J. and A. Yates (2003): And a Hockey Game Broke Out: Crime and Punishment in the NHL. Economic Inquiry, 41, pp. 705–712.
Jones, J.C.H. (1984): Winners, Losers and Hosers: Demand and Survival in the National Hockey League. Atlantic Economic Journal, 12, pp. 54–63.
Jones, J.C.H., Ferguson, D. and K. Stewart (1993): Blood Sports and Cherry Pie: Some Economics of Violence in the National Hockey League. American Journal of Economics and Sociology, 52, pp. 63–78.
Jones, J.C.H., Stewart, K. and R. Sunderman (1996): From the Arena into the Streets: Hockey Violence, Economic Incentives and Public Policy. American Journal of Economics and Sociology, 55, pp. 231–243.
Krautmann, A. (1999): What's Wrong with Scully-Estimates of a Player's Marginal Revenue Product? Economic Inquiry, 37, pp. 369–381.
Paul, R.J. (2003): Variations in NHL Attendance: The Impact of Violence, Scoring and Regional Rivalries. American Journal of Economics and Sociology, 62, pp. 345–364.
Paul, R., Weinbach, A., and D. Robbins (2013): American Hockey League Attendance: A Study of Fan Preferences for Fighting, Team Performance and Promotions. International Journal of Sport Finance, 8, pp. 21–38.
Peeters, T. (2011): The Shape of Success: Estimating Contest Success Functions in Sports. IASE Working Paper Series No. 11-08.
Rockerbie, D.W. (2012): The Demand for Violence in Hockey, in: Leo Kahane and Stephen Shmanske (eds.): The Economics of Sport, Vol. 2, Oxford University Press; New York.
Scully, G. (1974): Pay and Performance in Major League Baseball. American Economic Review, 64, pp. 915–930.
Stewart, K., Ferguson, D. and J.C.H. Jones (1992): On Violence in Professional Team Sport as the Endogenous Result of Profit Maximization. Atlantic Economic Journal, 20, pp. 55–64.

Part II
Salary Determination and Player Careers

Returns to Handedness in Professional Hockey

Dennis Coates

Abstract Research in labor economics has examined many determinants of earnings, including whether an individual is left or right handed. Sports economists have recently shown that in the soccer labor market, being able to kick well with both the left and the right foot is rewarded with a salary premium. This paper examines pay and performance for hockey players that shoot left-handed versus those that shoot right-handed. We find that after controlling for goals and assists, time on the ice, player size and age, and team and season fixed effects, players are paid differently by position, and players playing the same position may be paid differently because they shoot left versus right handed. These results suggest that the hockey player labor market is inefficient.

Introduction

Labor economists have studied the determinants of earnings for a very long time, with natural emphasis on the influence of experience and education. Empirical analysis of wages and earnings has also focused on racial and gender differences in compensation (see e.g. Altonji and Blank 1999, for a review). In recent years, analysis has extended to the role of appearance, with better looking (Biddle and Hamermesh 1994) and taller (Heineck 2005) individuals being more highly paid than less attractive and shorter people. Denny and O'Sullivan (2007) and Reubeck et al. (2007) considered the role of handedness in earnings determination. Denny and O'Sullivan (2007) find a premium for left-handed males, with the boost a bit larger for manual laborers, but there is a similarly sized penalty for left-handed females. By contrast, Reubeck et al. (2007) find that college educated, left-handed males earn about 15% more than college educated right-handed males.

Both Denny and O'Sullivan (2007) and Reubeck et al. (2007) examine the extensive literature on differences between right and left-handed individuals. See their discussion for details, but they each cite evidence on intelligence and creativity as well as differences in rates of autism and learning disabilities. Explanations for the

---

D. Coates (✉)
Department of Economics, University of Maryland Baltimore County, Baltimore, MD, USA
e-mail: coates@umbc.edu

differences between left and right-handed individuals run from cognitive to environmental. For example, some evidence suggests that left-handed children make up a disproportionate share of those in the 0.01% of students taking the SAT exam at age 13 (Benbow 1986). Hicks and Dusek (1980) find a lower prevalence of right-handedness among gifted (IQ greater than 131) children. Annett and Manning (1989) find that those with stronger tendencies toward right-handedness scored worse on intelligence tests, and tests of other abilities including language. Left-handers face an environment typically designed for right-handed people. This may be the reason researchers find that left-handers appear to be more accident prone or clumsy than right-handed people. Facing this world, left-handed people may compensate for the situation by working harder to develop skills to cope with their environment than do right-handed individuals, and the result may be better human capital.

Based on their reading of the psychology and neurology literatures, Denny and O'Sullivan (2007) propose three hypotheses related to compensation and handedness. The hypotheses are that (1) left-handers are at a disadvantage in a right-handed world, (2) discrimination against left- handers, possibly related to the cultural view of left-handedness being a sign of evil, and (3) left- handers avoid manual labor jobs where the penalty for being left-handed would be larger because tools are designed for right-handed workers. For males, all three hypotheses are rejected by their data. Instead, they find that left-handers, particularly those in manual labor jobs, earn a premium over right-handers but that left-handed females earn less than right-handed females.

Reubeck et al. (2007) also expect left-handers to suffer a wage loss compared to otherwise identical right-handed workers, for the same reasons given by Denny and O'Sullivan (2007). Their results also contradict that expectation, though they find that college educated left-handed men earn more than similarly educated right-handed men, and that the effect is largest for men with lower earnings levels compared to other men with similar levels of relatively high education. Their results include a weak finding of a higher wage for left-handed laborers than for right-handed laborers. They find no effect for women.

Both papers suffer from similar problems related to the identification of someone as left-handed. For example, Denny and O'Sullivan (2007) count as left-handed people who were reported to be so as 7 year olds. The problem with this, as the authors note, is that children often use both hands at that age and become more one sided only later. The literature on lateralness has developed a continuous scale from right to left in recognition that most people do some activities with each hand. A second difficulty is that there may be unobservable traits for which handedness is merely a proxy. Coren (1995) identifies two cognitive styles, one which is better at using a body of knowledge to produce a known answer, and the other of which is better at extending understanding outside the existing knowledge. Left-handedness is more prevalent among people who are better at the latter; that is, there is some evidence that left-handers are more creative than right-handers. Higher earnings for left handers could be the result of this greater creativity. Another possibility is that left handers make job or occupation choices differently than do right handers. In this case, left-handedness is a proxy for the traits that lead to these different occupational choices, but without detailed occupation data the researchers cannot adequately control for occupational choice.

As is often the case with labor market issues, sports data may be able to shed light on some of these problems. Extensive data on production are connected directly to a specific worker and the industry context is nearly identical. Little has been done with sports data concerning the effects of lateralness on compensation and production. Bryson et al. (2013) considered the value to soccer players of being able to use both the right and the left foot; Bradbury (2006a, b), motivated by the appearance of the Denny and O'Sullivan (2007) and Reubeck et al. (2007) papers, addressed the relationship of handedness and compensation of baseball players on his sabernomics blog.

While controlling for a variety of factors, Bradbury found no statistically significant difference between left-handed and right-handed batters, though the point estimate is for lefties to earn $225,000 less than righties which is about 6% of the average batter's salary. Considering left versus right-handed pitchers, and controlling for innings pitched, the coefficient point estimate is $230,000 for left-handed starters above right-handed starters, but the effect is not statistically significant. However, left-handed relief pitchers are found to earn about $209,000 less than right-handed relief pitchers, a result that is statistically significant. Bradbury points out a number of explanations for his results both for hitters and pitchers. For hitters he notes the lack of inclusion of defensive statistics and no control for lefties being excluded from some positions in the field. For pitchers, he notes there are no controls for relief pitchers known as "LOOGY" (Left-handed One Out GuY) and there are very few "ROOGY" types. Whatever the explanation for Bradbury's results, his findings are not consistent with those of Denny and O'Sullivan (2007) or Reubeck et al. (2007) of premiums for left-handed workers.

Bryson et al. (2013) considered whether soccer players who are adept players with both feet are compensated better than players who have a decidedly stronger side. They find pay premiums for two-footedness, and that the premium is largest for midfielders, and indeed may not exist for either defenders or forwards once performance, e.g. goal scoring, is accounted for. They conjecture that forwards, whose purpose is to score, get compensated for that but not for the other contributions to team success that two-footedness of midfielders provides.

This paper looks at handedness as a potential determinant of compensation in hockey. An interesting phenomenon in ice hockey is that right-handed players tend to shoot left-handed while left-handed players tend to shoot right-handed. The explanation for this is that players tend to hold the end of the stick with their dominant hand. This means they will tend to have better control of the stick when reaching with it but their off-hand will be in the middle of the stick when they go to shoot, and it is this hand that swings the stick. This phenomenon is apparent in the data, as the proportion of players that shoot left-handed is far larger than the proportion of left-handed people in the population.[1]

---

[1] Estimates of left-handedness vary from about 10% to 30%, with the proportion apparently on the rise. In the NHL, 65% of players shoot left-handed. In the Elitserien the proportion is 79%.

The rest of this paper is organized into four sections. In the next section, part two, we provide information about how handedness comes into play in hockey. Part three takes a preliminary look at the data, focusing on means of salary, goals, and assists to determine if there are any differences by handedness among these variables. There are, and these differences lead to an exploration of the determinants of salaries in part four. Part five summarizes our findings.

Handedness and Play in Hockey

In hockey, there are normally five "skaters" (plus one goalie) on the ice for each team. Three of these skaters play forward positions – left-wing (LW), center (C) and right-wing (RW) – while the other two play defense (left or right) positions. As the names suggest, left-wingers and left defensemen line up for the start of play and generally play down the left side of the sheet of ice (when facing the offensive zone), while right-wingers and right defensemen play down the right side, and centers play in the middle.

The relationship between handedness and position is critical in hockey. Handedness in hockey is defined by how a player holds his/her stick. Left-handed shooters are those that place their right hand at the top end of the stick, with their left hand below it, similar to the grip employed by left-handed golfers and left-handed batters in baseball (the opposite grip would occur for right-handed shooters). Historically, players used sticks with straight blades, but over the past decades sticks have evolved so that players now have sticks that are designed with handedness in mind. As a result, a left-handed shooting player, when holding the stick with the blade on the ice, will have a c-shaped blade with the toe of the stick curving to the right. This allows the player to better cradle the puck when holding it on the forehand (when the puck is on the right side of the blade when the left-handed player has the stick facing forward in front of him/her).

Thus, for left-handed shooters, the natural (i.e. forehand) shooting and body motion is from the player's left to right. Players tend to have much more strength and accuracy when shooting or passing on the forehand, as opposed to the backhand. This is similar to other sports that employ both sides of their implements, such as tennis. Backhand passes or shots involve, for left-handed shooters, bringing the stick to the right of the player's body and then passing or shooting across the body to the left, using the opposite side of the stick blade compared to the forehand. Because the player is releasing the puck from the convex side of the curved stick, it is much more difficult to control a backhanded shot or pass compared to the forehand.

A player's handedness often dictates the position played by that player on the ice. Because players are stronger on their forehands, players will tend to play on the same side of the ice that they shoot (a right-handed player will play the right wing or right defense, for example). This allows them to be on their forehand more often for shots and allows them to give and receive passes on their forehand. For wingers playing on their "natural" side – LW for left-handers and RW for right-handers – the player's natural (i.e. forehand) shooting motion is towards the middle of the ice, where the opposition's net is located, and where his teammates are situated. Conversely, if a player plays the "off-wing" position – RW for left-handers and LW for right-handers – the player's natural forehand motion is away from the action in the middle of the ice, and instead is towards the side boards. For this reason, the generally accepted practice in hockey is for players to play on their natural wing, as it allows the player to pass or shoot the puck across the larger portion of the ice using the forehand.

However, there are a number of exceptions to this generalization. First, there are some situations where playing the off-wing gives the player a better angle relative to the opposition's net, and thus is potentially conducive to increased goal scoring. To explain, the optimum area from which to score, all else equal, is the center (middle) of the ice, as opposed to the sides. Shots coming from the sides of the ice surface are less likely to result in a goal, because goalies can "cut down the angle" and give shooters little open space at which to shoot. Thus, in certain game situations it may be advantageous for wingers, if given the opportunity, to cut to the center of the ice from their position on the wing (closer to the boards) to give themselves a better scoring angle. When this occurs, off-wingers are automatically on their forehand. Conversely, when natural wingers cut to the middle of the ice surface, their body angle is not positioned to get off a forehand shot, and they will have to take valuable time and space to get their body turned to allow a forehand shot, or else use their weaker backhand shots. This potential advantage in playing the off-wing must then be weighed against the disadvantages discussed earlier, and the net benefit of playing the off-wing may vary from player to player, depending on their individual characteristics and talents. Similarly, when players start offensive plays from their own end of the rink, it is much easier to play off the natural wing, as the player skating along the boards will receive and give passes on his/her forehand. Where players are on the off wing, they must give and receive passes on their backhands. This requires much greater skill as it is more difficult to play the puck on the backhand due to the curvature of the stick blade and the tendency of players to be weaker on their backhands than forehands.

Further to this, supply imbalances between left-handers and right-handers will necessitate at least some players playing their off-wing. For example, in the NHL approximately 65% (63%, in our data of just free agent forwards) of players shoot left-handed, meaning that some of these left-handed shooters will be forced to play RW. Presumably this positional allocation process is not random, but reflects some type of sorting mechanism based on the various attributes of players – not all players will be equally adept at playing the off-wing, and part of the job of coaches is to determine which players are best suited for such a role.

In addition, the specific needs of individual teams may result in some players playing their off-wing. For example, a team might want to put its three best forwards together on the same line, regardless of the handedness of these players. If all three of these players are, say, left-handed, then one of these players will obviously be required to play the off-wing. In a reversal of the usual scenario, when Ilya Kovalchuk, a right-handed player that had played the off-wing his whole career, went to the New Jersey Devils in 2010–2011, the Devils experimented with switching him to his natural wing so that he could play on the same line as the Devils' two other offensive stars, Zach Parise and Travis Zajac.

A further factor to consider is that within a game, players' positions might be more fluid than what their "official" position would indicate. Power plays are particularly important – teams usually want their four best forwards (along with one defenseman) on the ice at the same time, regardless of handedness. This can then sometimes result in players playing their off-wing on the power play, even though they may play their natural wing at even strength. Playing the off-wing on the power play may not be as disadvantageous to a player as it is at even strength, since the power play allows the player more time and space (given his team's man-advantage) to adjust his body position to get into the best shooting position. In fact, playing the off-wing on the power play may sometimes be directly advantageous, in that it puts a player in a particularly good position to take so-called "one-timers", where they receive a pass and shoot the puck all in one motion. In some cases, forwards may play defense on the opposite side of the ice as well, in order to take advantage of these same shooting angles.

In summary, these types of issues are important to consider because any study of the relationship between handedness and salary must first be cognizant of the relationship between handedness and position-played. Thus, if one were to find, for example, that left-handers on the off-wing were more offensively productive than left-handers on their natural wing, and hence were paid more, the ultimate source of this higher productivity needs to be identified. It may be that playing on the off-wing enables a player to be more offensively productive – thus, positional assignment (LW or RW) drives productivity. If this were true, rational players would lobby coaches to allow them to play the off-wing, for such a positional assignment confers an almost windfall-type benefit to the player. Or, alternatively, it may be the case that offensively-talented players are more likely to be chosen to play the off-wing – under this scenario, offensive talent drives the positional assignment, and not vice-versa. Extending this notion, it may also be that offensively talented players are more talented in other facets of the game (not all of which may be directly observable), and are thus more able to meet the defensive challenges and spatial complexities of playing the off-wing. Thus, disentangling these potential endogeneities is crucial to accurately modeling the salary determination process.

Preliminary Look at the Data

The basic NHL database was provided by Neil Longley and was used by Leo Kahane et al. (2013) in their study of coworker heterogeneity and firm output. The data set covers a number of years (2001 through 2007) and includes information of the position played, whether the player shoots right- or left-handed, the number of goals scored, assists, penalty minutes, time on the ice and plus minus score for each player. The NHL data also includes annual salary. Using a separate data set of those

Table 1 Difference of mean salaries in the NHL

	Right	Left	p-value
	All		
Salary	1,785,682	1,848,398	0.3337
	Center		
Salary	2,076,880	2,016,923	0.6950
	Right wing		
Salary	1,638,163	2,531,296	0.0000
	Left wing		
Salary	1,882,105	1,523,797	0.0428

players who signed free agent contracts puts the focus on those 322 players who have just signed a new agreement.

Using these two datasets, and following the evidence in the broader literature, we look for salary differences between right and left-handed shooting hockey players. Table 1 shows difference in mean salaries of right and left-handed shooters by offensive position in the full sample, not limited to free agents. On average, right and left-handed shooters are paid the same in the full sample and looking only at those playing center. However, right and left handers are paid significantly differently on the wing positions, with pay higher for the right handers on the left wing and for left handers on the right wing; that is, among all players in a given wing position, those playing on their natural side of the ice are paid less than those playing off-wing. That raises the question of whether right-handers are paid differently between the left and right wing positions, and similarly if left-handers are paid differently between the left and the right wings. The mean salary of left-handed shooters on the right wing is $2.53 million while the salary of lefties on the left wing is $1.52 million; right-handed shooters on the right wing are paid $1.64 million while right-handed shooters on the left wing earn, on average, $1.88 million. The difference for the left-handed shooters is quite striking, over a million dollars per season between playing on the left and right wings, but even the nearly $200,000 difference found for right versus left wing right-handed shooters is quite impressive. For the lefties, the difference is statistically significant at the 0.0000 level; the difference for righties is statistically significant only at the 0.10 level. The mean salary of a left-handed shooter at the center position is $2.02 million, for a right-handed center the mean is $2.07 million. The difference between a leftie on the right wing and a leftie at center, about half a million dollars, is statistically significant at the 0.001 level.

That these differences are significant at all is curious. If one is a left-handed shooter, then playing any position other than on the right wing costs you a large amount of money, between a $0.5 and $1.0 million a year. Not all left-handed shooters can play on the right wing, but discrepancies of this size between playing on the right and playing on the left or in the center raise questions about the existence of

Table 2 Difference of mean goals scored by position and shooting hand

	Shoots right	Shoots left	p-value
Goals	12.03	10.93	0.0011
Goals per game	0.1675	0.1533	0.0013
	Center		
Goals	14.9269	14.0034	0.1557
Goals per game	0.2108	0.1933	0.0323
	Right wing		
Goals	15.0505	19.4792	0.0000
Goals per game	0.2075	0.2749	0.0000
	Left wing		
Goals	17.8675	14.5808	0.0069
Goals per game	0.2398	0.2043	0.0215

efficiency gains from reallocating players across positions.[2] Of course, these simple differences in means do not control for other factors.

Before drawing any conclusions about the presence of inefficiencies, it is important to consider whether players on the right, left or in the center are more productive, where we take that to mean produce more goals, or more assists, than other players. To assess this, the first step is a series of difference of means tests in which the average goals by right-handed shooters are compared to average goals by left-handed shooters, both regardless of position played and according to position played. Table 2 shows the means for right-handed and left-handed shooters separately and the p-value for the difference in means test. The first section of the table reports means and p-values simply comparing right and left-handed shooters, without controlling for position. In the full sample, on average, right-handed shooters score more goals and more goals per game played than do left-handed shooters. Right-handers score a bit over one more goal than do the left- handers, and that translates into about 0.014 per game in the NHL. Why this difference occurs is unclear.

Splitting the players by position, the puzzle gets more complex. There is no statistically significant difference in average goals by right versus left-handed shooting centers, but the goals per game averages are significantly different. As in the full sample of players, right-handed shooting centers score more goals per game than do left-handed shooting centers. The difference in goals per game is actually slightly larger than in the full sample. Comparing right and left-handed shooting, average goals and goals per game are both significantly different between right and left-wingers. Moreover, average goals and average goals per game are, for the first time, significantly larger for the left-handed shooters than for the right-handed shooters. In other words, a left-handed shooting right winger in the NHL scores on average

---

[2] Mason and Foster (2007) discuss the possibilities of "Moneyball on Ice", that is, that there is some player input into winning hockey that the hockey world incorrectly values, but all the possibilities discussed involve highly complex data collection and analysis. The beauty and power of the Moneyball hypothesis is that the mispriced attribute was easily observable.

both more goals and more goals per game than does a right-handed shooting right winger. Looking at left-wingers, the opposite is true. Right-handed shooting left-wingers score both more goals and more goals per game played, on average, than left-handed shooting left-wingers.

An alternative measure of success is assists; the ability to make a pass of the puck to a player in a good position to shoot and score. Conducting the same difference in means tests as for goals and goals per game produces similar results as for those variables. Right-handed shooters produce more assists per game than left-handed shooters. Splitting by position, the difference in means tests show that right-handed left-wingers produce more assists on average than left-handed left-wingers. For right-wingers, left-handed shooters produce more assists on average than do right-handed shooters. These results carry over to assists per game, where the differences are significant at the 5% level or better in each case, with right handers on the left wing and left handers on the right wing producing better than lefties on the left or righties on the right. Right and left-handed centers in the NHL do not produce on average a different number of assists, though right-handed centers produce more assists per game than do lefties.

The evidence on production is quite strong that left and right-handed shooters are not equally productive, either in terms of goals or assists. This finding is particularly interesting for players on the wings, because lefties on the right are more productive than righties on the right, while righties on the left are more productive than lefties on the left. Given differential productivity, and the differential in compensation demonstrated above, the next question is whether those differences indicate mispricing of left-handed versus right-handed shooters. To address this issue the next section presents salary regressions. Table 3 provides descriptive statistics for the explanatory variables and for salary and natural log of salary for the sample of free agents between 2001 and 2007.

Salary Determination and Returns to Handedness

Sports economists have long studied the connection between player compensation and player production. Scully (1974) did this for Major League Baseball and found that the reserve system in place at the time his data was drawn from led to substantial underpayment of star players relative to their contributions to team success. Studies of salary determination in the NHL are also numerous (Jones and Walsh 1988; Jones et al. 1997, 1999; Idson and Kahane 2000; Richardson 2000; Lavoie 2000; Longley 1995; McLean and Veall 1992; Lambrinos and Ashman 2007). Many of these are focused on discrimination, particularly discrimination against French-Canadians, or the role of violence in compensation. Kahane et al. (2013) account for composition of the club by national origin and Idson and Kahane (2000) control for the performance of teammates in affecting one's own performance and, therefore, one's salary.

Table 3 Descriptive statistics – free agent forwards only

	Mean	Std. Dev.	Min	Max
Log salary	13.926	0.761	12.766	16.118
Salary	1,539,913	1,488,895	350,000	10,000,000
Goals per game	0.205	0.117	0.000	0.653
Goals per minute	0.939	0.463	0.000	2.422
Assists per game	0.296	0.177	0.013	1.185
Penalty minutes per game	0.738	0.519	0.069	3.434
Assists per minute	1.344	0.704	0.085	4.500
Age	27.099	3.545	21.000	40.000
Age squared	746.889	203.538	441.000	1600.000
Height	72.644	1.988	67.000	80.000
Height squared	5,281.084	289.275	4,489.000	6,400.000
Weight	202.084	14.440	171.000	263.000
Weight squared	41,045.660	5,969.281	29,241.000	69,169.000
Minutes of ice time per game	14.868	3.292	4.267	22.567
Plus minus per game	−0.009	0.162	−0.630	0.435
Shoots left	0.632	0.483	0	1
Right wing	0.282	0.451	0	1
Center	0.427	0.495	0	1
Shoots left*center	0.303	0.460	0	1
Shoots left*right wing	0.071	0.258	0	1

Estimating equations in these papers generally explain the natural logarithm of player salary with an array of player and team attributes, with focus on different attributes depending on the research question. The usual model will include goals and assists per game, or per minute, penalty minutes per game, player age and age squared, and player position. Height and weight of the player are included, along with the square of each. The data we use also include time on the ice per game and "plus/minus" per game. The plus/minus statistic awards a player a + 1 if he is on the ice when his team scores an even-handed goal, that is, when both teams have the same number of players on the ice when the goal is scored, and a − 1 if his team gives up an even-handed goal.

The approach here is to use difference in difference estimation to determine the influence of handedness on salaries. Consider a simple model of salary.

$$\ln Salary_i = X_i\beta + H_i\delta + RW_i\theta + C_i\gamma + \varepsilon_i$$

The vector X includes determinants of salary such as experience, age, age squared, height, height squared, weight, weight squared, goals per game or per minute, assists per game or per minute, time on the ice per game, and penalty minutes per game, H is a dummy variable which takes value of 1 for left-handed shooting players and 0 for right-handed shooters, RW is 1 for a right-winger and 0 otherwise, and C is 1 for a center and 0 otherwise. The δ is the impact of handedness on salary, holding all other variables constant. A positive value of δ indicates that a left-handed shooting player is paid a premium over a right-handed shooting player, all other things held constant. Negative δ means that left-handed shooting players are paid less than right-handers.

To assess whether handedness has different effects for players in different positions, dummy variables for right wing and center are included. The omitted category is left wing. Interacting the handedness dummy with the position dummies produces the difference in difference estimator.

$$\ln Salary_i = \alpha + X_i\beta + H_i\delta + RW_i\theta + C_i\gamma + H_i^*RW_i\pi + H_i^*C_i\mu + \varepsilon_i$$

The α captures the effect of right-handed left-wingers, the omitted category of player type. The effect of a right-handed right-winger is $\alpha + \theta$. The effect of a right-handed center is $\alpha + \gamma$. The coefficients π and μ are the difference in difference estimators for the effects of left-handed right wingers and left-handed centers, respectively. In other words, these two coefficients indicate if there is a difference in compensation between right and left-handed shooters who play the right wing and between left and right-handed shooters that play center.

Table 4 reports log salary regressions for all forwards in the data for the NHL seasons 2001 through 2007. The first column is the baseline regression when goals and assists are measured per game, the third column replaces those variables with their per minute alternatives. The second and fourth columns include the interaction term between left-handed and position dummies. The regressions all include team fixed effects and season dummies which are available upon request.

The results indicate that goals, assists, and more time on the ice lead to a higher salary. Unlike Idson and Kahane (2000), these results do not find more penalty minutes associated with greater pay. Idson and Kahane (2000) argued that more penalty minutes may proxy for more aggressive play, perhaps greater hustle, and determination, as well as willingness to make the sacrifices needed for team success. While this may be true, it is also the case that more penalty minutes leaves a team at a disadvantage and therefore less likely to win which is detrimental to team revenues. Coates et al. (2011) find that more penalty minutes may reduce team points (wins and ties) and are not connected to increased attendance. Actual fights statistically significantly reduce points. However, Coates et al. (2011) also find weak evidence that more penalty minutes are associated with greater revenues in the NHL.

The results here do not find a relationship between plus/minus score and salary, though the point estimate is negative. Idson and Kahane (2000) find a positive coefficient, as would be expected. The negative sign means that the more goals a team gives up, and the fewer it scores, when a player is on the ice the more that player is paid. The negative coefficient would possibly make sense if the variable included time on the ice killing penalties. However, it is calculated only for time when the teams are at equal strength. Consequently, the negative sign is an anomaly, though the estimate is not different from zero. Salary increases with age, but at a decreasing

Table 4 Regression results

	Base per game	DD per game	Base per minute	DD per minute
Goals per game	0.8372**	0.9340**	–	–
	(0.043)	(0.023)		
Assists per game	1.0289***	0.9402***	–	–
	(0.000)	(0.000)		
Penalty min. per game	−0.0212	0.0138	0.0039	0.0401
	(0.718)	(0.814)	(0.949)	(0.504)
Age	0.2026**	0.2202**	0.1548	0.1761*
	(0.038)	(0.022)	(0.118)	(0.071)
Age squared	−0.0024	−0.0027	−0.0017	−0.0020
	(0.158)	(0.105)	(0.336)	(0.228)
height	−0.5051	−0.0635	−0.6931	−0.2226
	(0.516)	(0.935)	(0.387)	(0.781)
Height squared	0.0037	0.0007	0.0050	0.0018
	(0.491)	(0.901)	(0.365)	(0.749)
Weight	0.0353	0.0221	0.0200	0.0065
	(0.385)	(0.584)	(0.629)	(0.875)
Weight squared	−0.0001	−0.0000	−0.0000	−0.0000
	(0.452)	(0.672)	(0.701)	(0.959)
Min. ice time per game	0.1023***	0.1048***	0.1501***	0.1507***
	(0.000)	(0.000)	(0.000)	(0.000)
Plus minus per game	−0.2930	−0.3063	−0.0756	−0.1120
	(0.161)	(0.137)	(0.717)	(0.588)
Shoots left	−0.0107	−0.4836***	0.0085	−0.4814***
	(0.876)	(0.003)	(0.904)	(0.004)
Right wing	−0.0599	−0.5021***	−0.0810	−0.5506***
	(0.489)	(0.002)	(0.360)	(0.001)
Center	−0.2349***	−0.7095***	−0.2641***	−0.7297***
	(0.001)	(0.000)	(0.000)	(0.000)
Shoots left*center	–	0.5757***	–	0.5633***
		(0.002)		(0.004)
Shoots left*right wing	–	0.5797***	–	0.6529***
		(0.004)		(0.002)
Goals per minute	–	–	−0.0068	0.0287
			(0.936)	(0.730)
Assists per minute	–	–	0.1285**	0.1120**
			(0.024)	(0.045)
Constant	21.7424	7.0705	30.4318	14.7631
	(0.417)	(0.792)	(0.269)	(0.592)
Observations	322	322	322	322
R-squared	0.640	0.654	0.622	0.637
Number of Teams	30	30	30	30

p-values in parentheses
***p < 0.01, **p < 0.05, *p < 0.1

rate. Neither player height nor weight is significantly related to pay.[3] The basic model also indicates that centers are paid significantly less, about 20%, than right-handed shooting left wings, but that left-handed shooters and right-wingers are not paid differently than right-handed left wings, all other things constant.

Looking now to the second column of results, the basic implications are the same as in the first column, except the shoots left and right wing variables are statistically significant as are the interactions of shoots left with right wing and center. It is these interaction variables that are of particular interest. Note that both are positive and statistically significant. This means that left-handed shooting right wings are paid more than right-handed shooting right wings, and left-handed shooting centers are paid more than right-handed shooting centers even after holding constant the goals and assists per game, or per minute, time on the ice and other player attributes. The coefficients indicate that left-handed shooters on the left wing are paid about 38% less than right-handed shooters on the left wing, and that left-handed shooters are paid about 44% less than right-handed shooters in the center or right wing positions.

To get a sense of what these percentages mean, in Table 5 are models in which the dependent variables are tens of thousands of dollars of salary per goal scored or per assist rescored. The explanatory variables are as in Table 4 except that the goals and assists variables are omitted. The last two columns indicate that salary per assist does not vary by position or handedness. Indeed, the only factors that seem to matter are height, which seems to reduce salary per assist but at a declining rate, and plus/minus. The latter of these is now significant in determining salary per goal, though with a strong opposite sign.

The coefficients of interest are again the interactions between left-handed shooter and center or right wing. Only the left-handed shooter right wing interaction is statistically significant, and only at the 10% level. This coefficient suggests that a left-handed shooting right wing earns about $88,000 per goal more than a right-handed shooting right wing. Combining coefficients, however, the leftie on the right wing earns about the same per goal as the rightie on the left wing. In other words, off-wing players earn a bit more than on-wing players.

Conclusion

Previous work on the impact of handedness on compensation has been general rather than focused on professional athletes. The evidence there was that left-handers get slightly higher earnings than right-handers. Here, looking at professional hockey players, there is evidence that players that shoot left-handed are paid more than players that shoot right-handed. It is important to note that many right-handed players shoot left-handed, and many left-handed players shoot right-handed. The analysis held constant time on the ice, penalty minutes, player size, the quality

---

[3] Little changes if the body mass index and BMI squared replace the height and weight variables.

Table 5 Salary per goal or per assist ($10,000)

	Salary per goal	Salary per goal	Salary per assist	Salary per assist
Penalty min. per game	−1.003	−0.520	0.721	0.923
	(0.511)	(0.737)	(0.461)	(0.353)
Age	2.334	2.581	0.246	0.388
	(0.338)	(0.289)	(0.877)	(0.808)
Age squared	−0.023	−0.028	0.002	−0.001
	(0.587)	(0.514)	(0.947)	(0.969)
Height	−15.286	−9.767	−38.533***	−36.571***
	(0.439)	(0.625)	(0.003)	(0.005)
Height squared	0.112	0.074	0.272***	0.258***
	(0.411)	(0.589)	(0.002)	(0.004)
Weight	0.874	0.725	0.930	0.856
	(0.389)	(0.475)	(0.163)	(0.200)
Weight squared	−0.002	−0.002	−0.002	−0.002
	(0.384)	(0.472)	(0.175)	(0.216)
Minutes of ice time pg	0.104	0.117	−0.132	−0.138
	(0.679)	(0.645)	(0.418)	(0.399)
Plus minus per game	−15.042***	−15.426***	−5.915*	−6.405**
	(0.002)	(0.002)	(0.067)	(0.048)
Shoots left	−0.754	−7.499*	0.580	−2.179
	(0.668)	(0.070)	(0.612)	(0.423)
Right wing	−1.778	−8.184**	1.059	−1.977
	(0.427)	(0.050)	(0.465)	(0.470)
Center	−1.528	−8.182*	−2.031*	−4.069
	(0.391)	(0.061)	(0.083)	(0.157)
Shoots left*center	–	7.941	–	2.275
		(0.100)		(0.474)
Shoots left*right wing	–	8.847*	–	5.161
		(0.089)		(0.128)
Constant	400.426	216.327	1,268.429***	1,206.298***
	(0.556)	(0.752)	(0.004)	(0.007)
Observations	318	318	322	322
R-squared	0.161	0.171	0.197	0.204
Number of teams	30	30	30	30

p-value in parentheses
***$p < 0.01$, **$p < 0.05$, *$p < 0.1$

of the players on the ice with the individual, and team and season. There is, therefore, a puzzle. Why would players be compensated differently for scoring points for their team based on their handedness?

One possible explanation is that players on the off-wing are inherently more skilled than players in their natural position. That does not explain why they would be paid more per goal, however. Another possible explanation is that the difference is really related to offensive and defensive strategy of the clubs or to coaching and managerial abilities. For example, it may be that some strategies are more advantageous to off-wing players, and that premiums are paid for such players by clubs that employ those strategies. Possible examples of this are the left wing lock strategy and its cousin, the neutral zone trap. Further data collection and analysis are necessary to assess the effect these strategies have in driving the results.

None of the analyses done here is conclusive for inefficiency in the allocation of playing talent. Nonetheless, the fairly substantial pay differentials which arise from playing the same position but shooting with a different hand even after accounting for playing time and points per game are suggestive of a labor market inefficiency. Unlike the esoteric search for a mispriced playing attribute undertaken inside hockey, as described by Mason and Foster (2007), and quite similar to the mispricing of on-base-percentage made famous in Moneyball, this inefficiency, should it stand up to further scrutiny, is easy to observe, and therefore easy to exploit for playing and profitable advantage.

References

Altonji, J.G. and R.M. Blank (1999): Race and Gender in the Labor Market, in: Handbook of Labor Economics, Volume 3c. Amsterdam, New York, and Oxford: Elsevier Science, North Holland.
Annett, M. and M. Manning (1989): The Disadvantages of Dextrality for Intelligence. British Journal of Psychology, 80, pp. 213–226.
Benbow, C. (1986): Physiological Correlates of Extreme Intellectual Precocity. Neuropsychologia, 24, pp. 719–725.
Biddle, J.E. and D.S. Hamermesh (1994): Beauty and the Labor Market. American Economic Review, 84, pp. 1174–1194.
Bradbury, J.C. (2006a): Do Southpaws get a fair shake in MLB? http://www.sabernomics.com/sabernomics/index.php/2006/08/do-southpaws-get-a-fair-shake-in-mlb/
Bradbury, J.C. (2006b): Do Southpaws get a fair shake in MLB? Part 2: pitchers" http://www.sabernomics.com/sabernomics/index.php/2006/08/do-southpaws-get-a-fair-shake-in-mlb-part-2-pitchers/
Bryson, A., B. Frick, and R. Simmons (2013): The Returns to Scarce Talent: Footedness and Player Remuneration in European Soccer. Journal of Sports Economics, 14, pp. 606–628.
Coates, D., M. Battre and C. Deutscher (2011): Does Violence Pay in Professional Hockey?: Cross Country Evidence from Three Leagues, in Violence and Aggression in Sporting Contests, R. Todd Jewell, editor, Springer: New York.
Coren, S. (1995): Differences in Divergent Thinking as a Function of Handedness and Sex. American Journal of Psychology, 108, pp. 311–325.

Denny, K. and V. O'Sullivan (2007): The Economic Consequences of Being Left-Handed: Some Sinister Results. Journal of Human Resources, 42, pp. 353–374.

Heineck, G. (2005): Up in the Skies? The Relationship between Body Height and Earnings in Germany, Labour, 19, pp. 469–489.

Hicks, R. and C. Dusek (1980): The Handedness Distributions of Gifted and Non-Gifted Children. Cortex, 16, pp. 479–481.

Idson, T. and L. Kahane (2000): Team Effects on Compensation: An Application to Salary Determination in the National Hockey League. Economic Inquiry, 38, pp. 345–357.

Jones, J.C.H. and W.D. Walsh (1988): Salary Determination in the National Hockey League: The Effects of Skills, Franchise Characteristics, and Discrimination. Industrial and Labor Relations Review, 41, pp. 592–604.

Jones, J.C.H., S. Nadeau and W.D. Walsh (1997): The Wages of Sin: Employment and Salary Effects of Violence. Atlantic Economic Journal, 25, pp. 191–206.

Jones, J.C.H., S. Nadeau and W.D. Walsh (1999): Ethnicity, Productivity and Salary: Player Compensation and Discrimination in the National Hockey League. Applied Economics, 31, pp. 593–608.

Kahane, L., N. Longley and R. Simmons (2013): The Effects of Coworker Heterogeneity on Firm-Level Output: Assessing the Impacts of Cultural and Language Diversity in the National Hockey League. Review of Economics and Statistics, 95, pp. 302–314.

Lambrinos, J. and T.D. Ashman (2007): Salary Determination in the NHL: Is Arbitration Efficient? Journal of Sports Economics, 8, pp. 192–201.

Lavoie, M. (2000): The Location of Pay Discrimination in the National Hockey League. Journal of Sports Economics, 1, pp. 401–11.

Longley, N. (1995): Salary Discrimination in the National Hockey League: The Effects of Team Location. Canadian Public Policy, 21, pp. 413–22.

Lewis, M. (2003): Moneyball: The Art of Winning an Unfair Game. New York: W.W. Norton and Company.

Mason, D.S. and W.M. Foster (2007): Putting Moneyball on Ice. International Journal of Sport Finance, 2, pp. 206–213.

McLean, R.C. and M.R. Veall (1992): Performance and Salary Differentials in the National Hockey League. Canadian Public Policy, 18, pp. 470–475.

Reubeck, C.S., J.E. Harrington, Jr. and R. Moffitt (2007): Handedness and Earnings. Laterality, 12, pp. 101–120.

Richardson, D. (2000): Pay, Performance, and Competitive Balance in the National Hockey League. Eastern Economic Journal, 26, pp. 393–417.

Scully, G. (1974): Pay and Performance in Major League Baseball. American Economic Review, 64, pp. 915–930.

All-Star or Benchwarmer? Relative Age, Cohort Size and Career Success in the NHL

Alex Bryson, Rafael Gomez, and Tingting Zhang

Abstract We analyze the performance outcomes of National Hockey League (NHL) players over 18 seasons (1990–1991 to 2007–2008) as a function of the demographic conditions into which they were born. We have three main findings. First, larger birth cohorts substantially affect careers. A player born into a large birth cohort can expect an earnings loss of roughly 18% over the course of an average career as compared to a small birth cohort counterpart. The loss in earnings is driven chiefly by supply-side factors in the form of excess cohort competition and not quality differences since the performance of players (as measured by point totals for non-goalies) is actually significantly greater for players born into large birth cohorts. Performance-adjusted wage losses for those born in large birth cohorts are therefore greater than the raw estimates would suggest. Second, career effects differ by relative age. Those born in early calendar months (January to April) are more likely to make it into the NHL, but display significantly lower performance across all birth cohorts than later calendar births (September to December). In short, those in the top echelon of NHL achievement are drawn from fatter cohorts and later relative age categories, consistent with the need to be of greater relative talent in order to overcome significant early barriers (biases) in achievement. We find league expansions increase entry level salaries including the salaries of those born into larger birth cohorts, but they do not affect salaries of older players. Finally we find that the 2004–2005 lock-out appears to have muted the differentials in pay for large birth cohort players relative to their smaller birth cohort counterparts.

Introduction

The magnitude of North America's baby-boom and subsequent baby-bust has been well-documented (e.g. Foot and Stoffman 2001). Between 1957 and 1987 birth rates plunged in Canada from 28 live births per 1000 of the population to 14 births

---

A. Bryson
Department of Social Science, University College London, London, UK
e-mail: a.bryson@ucl.ac.uk

R. Gomez (✉) • T. Zhang
Centre for Industrial Relations and Human Resources, University of Toronto, Toronto, ON, Canada

per 1000 of the population.[1] Research on the labor market effects of those born into historically large birth cohorts suggests this group experiences significant earnings losses over their careers, relative to their luckier counterparts born before or after a baby-boom (Freeman 1979; Welch 1979; Berger 1985, 1989; Bloom et al. 1987; Murphy et al. 1988; Wright 1991; Bachman et al. 2009). A question that surprisingly still remains unanswered is whether, and how, earnings differences across birth cohorts play out amongst professional athletes. This is an interesting question since athletic careers are quite easily mapped and because the limited opportunities available for entry into the professional leagues set up a nice quasi-experiment in which supply of labor can be allowed to vary exogenously, through lagged birth rate fluctuations, while labor demand can be held more or less constant owing to the fixed number of teams in a monopolistically run professional sport setting. This particular feature of pro sport (i.e., strong barriers to entry) turns out to be rather important since a traditional problem in the cohort size literature is that birth rate cycles (the ultimate source of labor market cohort variation) are themselves endogenously determined by economic conditions. Birth rates also change gradually so that by the time a large birth cohort enters the labor market, there may be a derived labor demand side response which serves to offset cohort supply shocks associated with increased births several decades prior (Brunello 2010; Morin 2013).

Research also suggests that professional athletes, in particular, face another demographic determinant of career success; namely their *relative age*. For example in hockey, an early birth month (e.g., being born between January and April) has been found to correlate quite strongly and positively with the probability of playing in professional sports leagues; this despite the fact that most births occur later in the year.[2] It is natural to ask whether, and how, earnings differences across birth months might interact with fluctuating birth rate cycles in a professional sport setting where this may be rather important. What kinds of players (defensive or offensive) are most susceptible to the impacts of cohort size entry conditions? Does a player with a higher relative age (i.e., born in January) who typically has a greater chance of getting into a professional league have a similar advantage in earnings and performance?

Why might professional athletes be particularly sensitive to cohort size effects? As already mentioned, unlike most labor market settings, the positive demand-side effect of a larger birth-cohort (i.e., through potential market size expansion and hence increased derived demand for labor opportunities) is muted in professional leagues which maintain monopoly privileges. This means in practice that league expansion through new team entry – even in the face of substantially larger specta-

---

[1] The baby-boom (and subsequent bust) was felt more in Canada than in the US where birth rates climbed to 25.3 per 1,000 of the population in the 1950s but fell only to 17 per 1,000 of the population in the 1980s.

[2] The actual cut-off dates do vary. This early year bias is of course not true in all sports since it depends on varying school entry date decisions. For example in Britain there is a higher percentage of September to December births in professional soccer because entry conditions into youth sports leagues are tied to the beginning of the school year.

tor demand – is highly restricted.³ In other words, the league's monopsony power can be maintained in the face of potential labor supply increases, ultimately leading to lower entry salaries for large birth cohorts.

Another mechanism is that players born during periods of relatively high birth rates presumably face tougher competition in a variety of amateur settings prior to ever entering the race to become a pro-athlete. This would make pro-athletes born into fat cohorts of greater average quality than those born in smaller cohorts. Other things constant, this should affect earnings in a positive direction.

Ultimately, the question of whether players born into fatter cohorts outperform their skinnier demographic counterparts – in both performance and earnings outcomes – is an empirical one.

Why might the performance of players depend on the relative age of the athlete? First, assuming selection into amateur athletics is conducted according to calendar year conditions,⁴ then those born relatively early (January to April) will face a distinct advantage over those born later (September to December) given the variation in physical and mental development that occurs up to a person's late teens/early 20s (Arnett 2000). These differences could result in a differential opportunity to play with better teams and coaches, which could lead to better athletic career trajectories for early-born athletes. Relative age effects could also counter earnings losses that come from being born into a relatively large birth cohort since being born early could translate into a differential ability to upgrade from poor initial placements into minor leagues, owing to cohort crowding effects.

On the other hand, younger relative age players that make it into the professional leagues may benefit from the positive "peer effects" of playing alongside more mature teammates throughout their amateur careers. They may also have had to be physically capable of keeping up with relatively older counterparts almost from the start of their amateur playing careers.

Does being later-born help players weather the large birth cohort effect? This is still an open question in the literature on relative age effects.

In this paper, we analyze the career outcomes of National Hockey League (NHL) players as a function of relative cohort size at year of birth and relative age (i.e., birth month). We combine information on earnings and player performance for NHL players between the 1990–1991 and 2007–2008 seasons. The data set also merges birth rate information by year of birth for players born across ten major

---

³ There is the special case of competing league formation as occurred in hockey under the banner of the World Hockey Association (WHA) which acted as a competitor for player talent for nearly 10 years from 1971 to 1979. If one imagines a 20 year old entry age for the average hockey player this lines up almost perfectly with the height of the baby-boom in North America, from 1951 to 1959. One could speculate that a supply-side push would allow a competing league to draw near equivalent talent. Once that baby-boom talent pool dries up and wages for marginal players begin to be bid up by rival leagues, the financial viability of the less established franchises in a league is likely to fade.

⁴ Those born during a calendar year January to December are included in the same pool of those eligible to play on the same teams. Despite the potential of playing alongside someone who had almost a full year more of maturation, these systems still prevail in most amateur settings.

countries/regions that are present in the league. The data set yields coverage of multiple birth rate cycles both across time (the baby boom and bust and subsequent echo in North America) and space (birth rate cycles differ across countries). We examine average earnings and performance for differing cohort size groupings – large (above average) versus small (below average) cohort sizes – based on birth rates at time and country of birth. We then identify several experiential phases in a playing career (i.e., rookie, prime age prior to and post free-agency and a veteran stage) and estimate impacts of being born in years with higher than average birth rates, across these experience groupings, for a range of performance outcomes over the length of a playing career.

We address four main questions. First, what is the effect on career performance of being born into a relatively large birth cohort for the average professional hockey player? Second, what is the effect of relative age on the earnings and performance of players in the NHL? Third, how does the effect of cohort size vary by relative age? Fourth, how do the answers to these questions change following the six league expansions (1991–1992, 1992–1993, 1993–1994, 1998–1999, 1999–1900, and 2000–2001) that occurred in our sample period and after the 2004–2005 lockout, which cancelled an entire season of play and imposed the first ever team cap on player salaries?

This paper proceeds as follows. We discuss relevant literature and present a simple framework to guide our analysis in section "Birth Cohort Size, Relative Age Effects and NHL Player Performance". In section "Data and Methods" we introduce our data before describing the methodology. Section "Results" presents our core results on earnings, performance, and career attainment for the average player and discusses how these results differ for players by birth cohort and also by relative age. Section "Relative Age (Birth Month) and Player Outcomes" examines differential effects of being born into a large cohort by relative age. Section "Do Results Differ During League Expansions and in the Post-Lockout Era?" examines the effect of league expansions (positive labor demand shocks) and the 2004–2005 season-ending lockouts on our previous results. Section "Conclusions" concludes.

Birth Cohort Size, Relative Age Effects and NHL Player Performance

Cohort Size and Player Outcomes

There are several reasons why we might expect the size of a birth cohort to affect labor market outcomes for NHL players.

The first explanation is Easterlin's hypothesis. Easterlin (1987) in *Birth and Fortune* argues that the relative size of a cohort can affect individuals' economic and social outcomes including earnings, unemployment, college enrollment, divorce and marriage, fertility, crime, and suicide. Because cohort size determines the amount of competition for job slots (slots that are assumed to be fixed in the short run and/or lagged in relation to cohort entry) this will feed through to a number of outcomes such as family formation. A recent study of marriage rates in the US over the period 1910–2011 found that an increase in cohort size generated a decline in marriage rates and that a reduction in cohort size has the opposite effect, thus confirming Easterlin's hypothesis. Exploiting exogenous variation in birth rates caused by the staggered diffusion of the birth-control-pill across states, the effect of cohort size on marriage patterns is found to be causal.[5]

The second idea that cohort size matters is derived from Welch's (1979) classic paper of the effect of cohort size on earnings, which is more direct than Easterlin's and relies on an adaption of Rosen's optimal life-cycle model.[6] In keeping with this model, we believe the way cohort size affects NHL earnings follows from the notion that player careers consist of three distinct phases. A new entrant into the NHL arrives fresh from the minor leagues and enters his profession as an "apprentice" or "rookie" who learns from his more senior players and coaches. Only rarely – if the player is a superstar or enters the NHL having played in foreign professional leagues – will he immediately become a full-fledged senior member of the team taking on tasks such as penalty killing that are normally assigned to more senior players. Having entered as a rookie, the player gains skills and reaches his *prime* before his performance and learning plateau at which point (after all learning is complete) he achieves *veteran* status in the league.

Just how many career phases there are does not really matter. What does matter is that at each stage players have different skills and, in terms of overall team production, these skills are not perfect substitutes. Each activity is productive and marginal productivities are determined, as for any factor, by numbers of players engaged in these activities. In this view, the NHL is an ordered series of player types/phases/stages (*rookie*, *prime*, and *veteran*) such that at any moment in their career, a member of the NHL is in transit between two of these types and can be viewed as a (convex) combination of them.

As noted by Welch (1979) this view is essentially identical to Rosen's (1972) optimal life-cycle model in which a career consists of a continuum of occupations and a worker solves an optimal occupational sequence by recognizing that each occupation corresponds to learning options that affect performance in subsequent occupations. Rosen allowed productivity in each occupation to depend on the number of workers in that and other occupations, and it is clear that had he considered cohort size, the theory would have predicted that earnings are negatively correlated with cohort size.

To highlight effects of cohort size, we abstract from questions of optimal rates of progression or transit between career phases, and take them as exogenous. We also abstract from depreciation or skill obsolescence which could, nevertheless, be

---

[5] Initially, only indirect evidence in support of the Easterlin hypothesis was advanced and other researchers that attempted to test the general idea behind it found mixed results (Pampel and Peters 1995).

[6] Freeman (1979) published a very similar paper almost simultaneous to the one published by Welch (1979) but it did not include the model provided above.

NHL Player Earnings

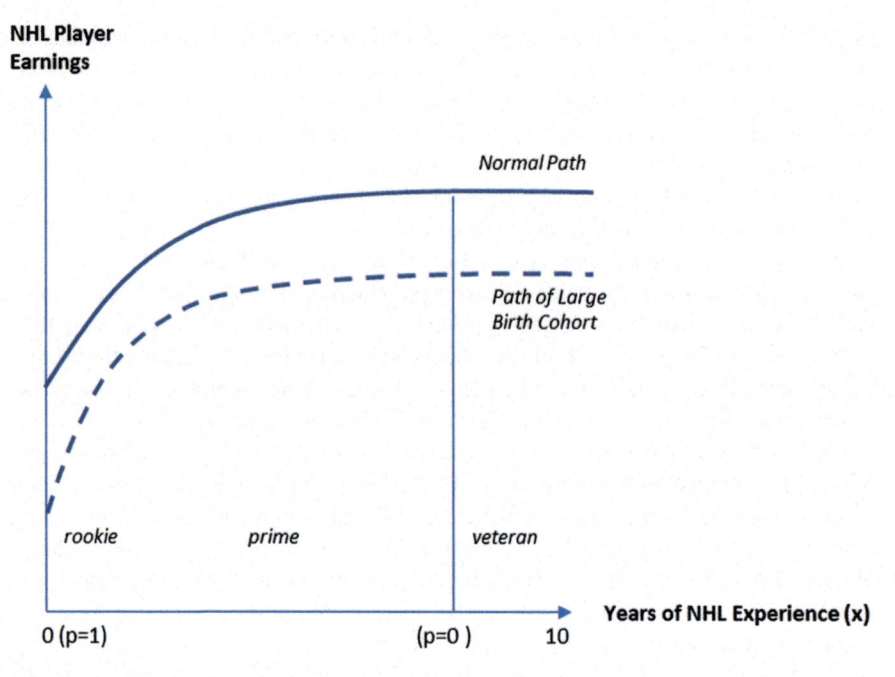

Fig. 1 Hypothetical contrast between career earnings paths of NHL players from normal and unusually large birth cohorts

important if the skills possessed on NHL entry are more conducive to learning about the game (think of the minor leagues or first year in the professional league as learning to play in the NHL) and are depleted as the career progresses, with human capital acquisition focusing on more directly productive on-ice activities. As such, progression is toward higher realized earnings for a given player.

If players substitute perfectly for each other, regardless of experience, the structure of earnings would be independent of cohort size such that the only feasible interpretation of career-earnings-cycle profiles would be one of purely physical aging. The life-cycle investment view, however, argues that age profiles are products of learning and depreciation and therefore suggests that players at different stages of their career do different things for their teams. If so, then the value of each "thing" a player does at each stage or phase of a career would reasonably depend on the number of players potentially doing it, and so cohort size matters and should be inversely related to earnings.

A graphical illustration of this model is provided in Fig. 1 where the difference between the normal earnings profile for an NHL player and that for a player from an illustratively large birth cohort is always negative. In this example, new players are exclusively *rookies* who are learning the "game" (abstracting from the rare cases of superstar talents and more experienced free agents entering the league from other professional leagues) and hence $p = 1$, where $p(x)$ is the fraction of time at "x" experience spent learning the game. At point of entry players not only draw all their earnings as rookie learners, but have the greatest depressing effect on fellow rookie earnings because of their lack of substitutability with prime and veteran player tasks. As experience accrues, a player transits to the prime-age phase, drawing an increasingly larger share of earnings which, for large birth cohort individuals, are being depressed by the large number of competitor players in the same large birth cohort. Earnings grow for large-cohort and average-cohort players as p falls in the early career phase. After the inflexion point the depressant effect of older age on player productivity dominates and earnings growth slows. Finally at the point indicated as $p = 0$ in Fig. 1, when the player has no longer any learning left and instead is fully vested in veteran status, the process is completed. Thereafter, earnings are depressed and the extent of the depression remains constant until retirement.

Several points deserve note. Effects of increased cohort size are inversely proportional to the elasticity of substitution. The substitution elasticity indexes veteran-rookie differences in the nature of roles performed on a team. It is typical for prime-age players to play on specials teams (i.e., appear during penalty killing or power play opportunities) and for veterans to be on the ice in crucial moments of the game. For this reason we feel this aspect of the model to be plausible in the context of the NHL. If, however, a team or coach designs a system of play so that players are more interchangeable, then regardless of career stage/phase, greater similarity of activities implies greater substitutability. It is likely that the substitution elasticity is also related to the transition function, $p(x)$. Rapid transition from learning (rookie) to prime-age playing status implies that rookies can easily adapt to prime-age tasks. We expect that when transition occurs easily, prime-age versus rookie player tasks are more similar, that is, prime-age players and rookies are better substitutes.[7]

This model can be used to explain wage profiles but, in the context of a fixed demand for player talent, it can also be used to explain why average player quality would be expected to be higher amongst those individuals born into large cohorts. This is because those players face tougher competition in a variety of amateur settings prior to ever entering the race to become a professional athlete. Moreover, because the best amateur talent feeds into an essentially static number of professional league openings – owing to the monopoly privileges of the National Hockey League – a large cohort combined with a fixed number of slots makes the lump of labor problem operative (as opposed to fallacious). This would make professional athletes born into unusually large cohorts of greater absolute average quality than those born during smaller cohort years. Other things constant, this should affect absolute performance in a positive direction.

Another consideration is that higher ability players born into fat cohorts could also potentially recover from any early earnings setbacks through free-agency job movement, which kicks in after 7 years in the league, though perhaps more gradually for

---

[7] This leads immediately to predictions across relative age (birth month) in terms of differences in prime-age versus rookie substitution elasticities (discussed in more detail in section "Cohort Size and Player Outcomes" below).

NHL Player Earnings

Path of Large Birth Cohort

Normal Path

rookie | pre-prime | post-prime | veteran

0 (p=1)　　　　7　　(p=0)　　10　　Years of NHL Experience (x)

free-agency

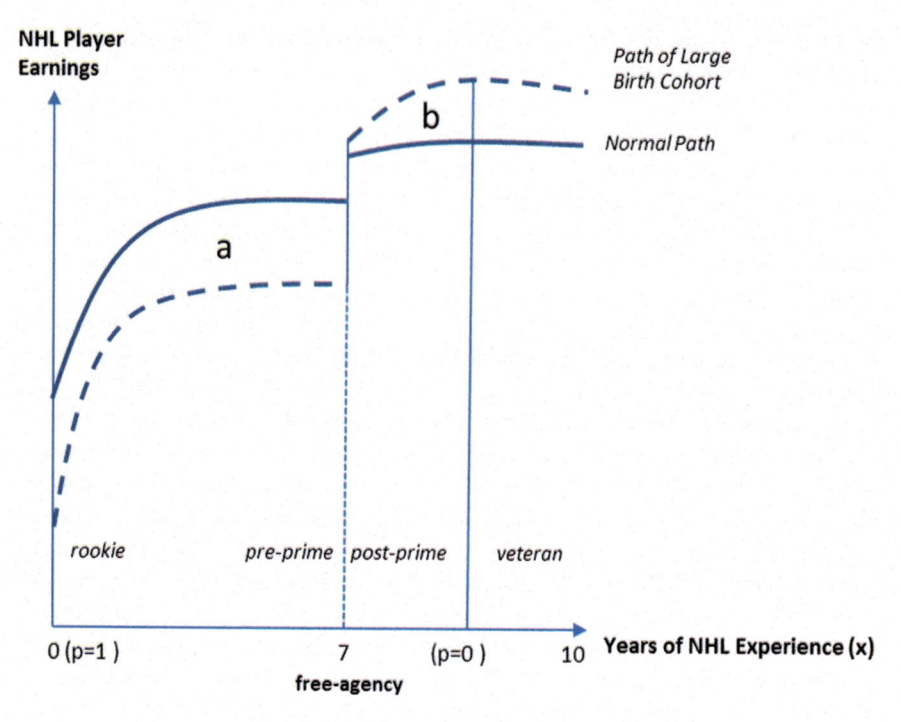

Fig. 2 Hypothetical contrast between career earnings paths of NHL players from normal and unusually large birth cohorts, with free agency occurring after 7 years' experience

large cohorts in the face of fewer vacancies per player.[8] This is illustrated in Fig. 2, where after 7 years' experience – the typical free agency period in the NHL – a jump in the wage profile for both large and small birth cohorts occurs. The large cohort earnings profile jumps higher because presumably this would be a chance for all teams to bid on what is relatively a better quality player. This prime-aged post-free agency period may therefore lead to some catch-up in earnings for the better than average (high birth cohort) player but the question of whether lifetime earnings equalize (i.e., whether the area under b is greater than a) as a result of free-agency is dependent on length of contracts signed and also on ultimate career length in the league.

Finally, one should note that a poor early earnings start for large birth cohort players, possibly also including longer spells spent in minor leagues or playing for lower-ranked teams, could expose these players to lower quality coaching and salary opportunities, resulting in a lasting disadvantage. Ultimately, owing to the competing performance predictions and possibilities for earnings catch-up through

---

[8] The history of unrestricted free agency (UFA) in the NHL begins in 1995. From 1995 to 2004 unrestricted free agency usually began at age 31. Following the season-ending lockout of 2004–2005, a new collective bargaining agreement with a salary cap was implemented, resulting in a gradual lowering of the eligibility age for UFA status from 30 to 27, and the proviso that if a player completed seven full NHL seasons, he would be free-agent eligible prior to age 27 or whichever came first. See: http://spectorshockey.net/blog/is-the-era-of-building-through-unrestricted-free-agency-over/

free-agency, the question of whether players born into larger cohorts outperform their smaller cohort counterparts – in both performance and earnings outcomes – is an empirical one.

Relative Age and Player Outcomes

The literature on relative age and NHL player success goes back to the work of Canadian psychologist Roger Barnsley who in 1985 published one of the first studies to note the effect of relative age in a professional sport setting (Barnsley et al. 1985).[9] His work showing that being born earlier in the year (January to April) resulted in a significantly increased probability of succeeding in all ranks of Canadian hockey, was popularized in the 2008 best-selling book *Outliers: The Story of Success* by Malcolm Gladwell who used these findings and those of others in the field of educational returns to show how seemingly arbitrary eligibility rules – like grouping all individual players by calendar year beginning on January 1st and ending on December 31st – could be important for the future success of individuals.

The argument that early birth dates affect athletic success is a simple one based on the sociological idea of "accumulative advantage" or what economists might label "path dependence". Initial small advantages based, in this case, on relatively greater physical and mental maturity in formative ages for those born early in the year (January to April) as compared to those born late (September to December) build up when coaches spend additional time mentoring the better initial performers. When those initial better performers are further grouped together and are given chances to play alongside other good performers, the performance of the entire early-born group begins to rise and distances itself even further from the later-born group not given these added investments and opportunities. By the time selection into a professional hockey league is possible (late teens) many talented later-born players will never have had the chance to compete let alone be eligible for the NHL draft.

There is now a large body of work – located mostly in the sports science and kinesiology literature – showing the relative age effect (RAE) in sport is real and quite widespread. In a 2001 literature review, nearly 30 studies were surveyed covering 11 sports and the consensus was pretty clear: the relative age effect exists across countries and in most professional sports (Musch and Grodin 2001). Since then an equal if not greater number of papers have emerged showing, in various forms, the same thing (see Deaner et al. 2013 and sources cited therein).

Empirically, however, any claim that cutoff dates in youth leagues is the only factor underlying the skewed birthdate distributions in professional leagues must be defended against possible alternative explanations; such as a skewed distribution of

---

[9] One year earlier a study by Grondin et al. (1984) more or less conforming to the same findings as Barnsley et al. (1985) was published in French and as a result is often neglected by popular English language writers in this field.

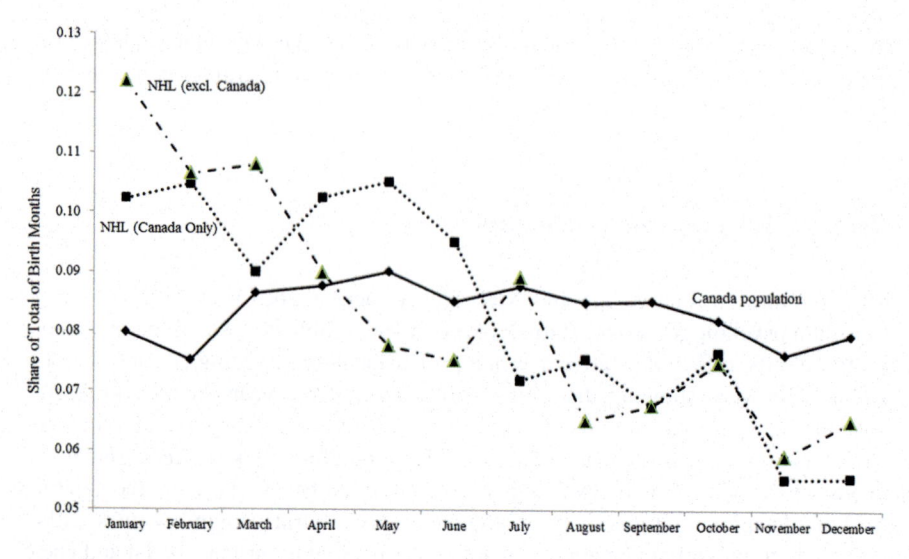

Fig. 3 Seasonality of births for NHL players and Canadian population as a whole, 1991–2008 averages (Sources: NHL player birth month located from official league site: http://www.nhl.com/ice/playerstats.htm. Canadian population birth month data from Statistics Canada, *Live Births, By Month, Canada, Provinces and Territories*: http://data.gc.ca/data/en/dataset/d976763b-5d5e-442e-8f31-48f9102ac66c)

births already present in the non-sport population. For hockey we know this is not the case as taking Canadian births as a representative sample, we see that a comparison of the monthly birthdate distribution for the NHL playing population diverges quite drastically from the general population (see Fig. 3). The fewest births in Canada actually occur between January and February, which are the most prevalent birth months in the NHL.

Further validation of the cutoff date hypothesis has been obtained by observing the consequences of an externally imposed change in eligibility rules in Australia's youth soccer system, whereby the traditional cutoff date of January 1st was replaced by a new cutoff date of August 1st in 1988 owing to a request by FIFA. Musch and Hay (1999) found a corresponding shift in the birth distribution of Australian professional players ten years after the change, providing strong evidence that the cutoff date generates the RAE effect.

In summary, chronological age differences are certainly related to discrepancies in both physical and psychological maturity. For example, in terms of weight and height individual variability is at its maximum between 13 and 15 years of age for boys (Musch and Groding 2001). This is the age-range when players are often selected for college scholarships or junior hockey play (the two most typical feeder systems into the NHL). It therefore seems plausible that a relative age disadvantage can make it harder for a younger born player to compete.

If we assume that there is a similar distribution of latent/true talent for both late- and early- born players, then it is likely that a greater number of below average

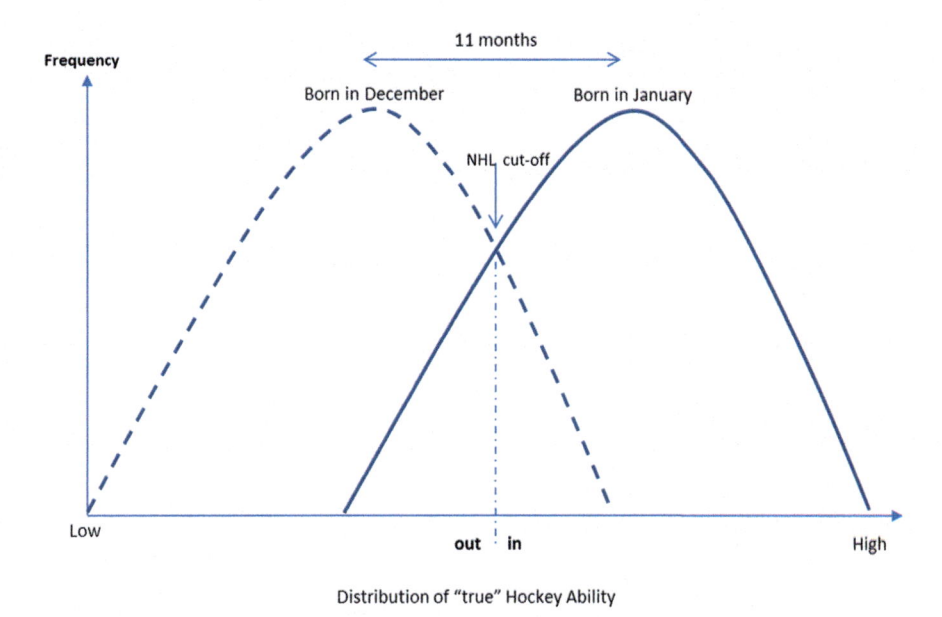

Fig. 4 Illustration of the maturity advantage of youth hockey players born in January versus those born in December in the same calendar year and with similar distribution of ability

quality players from the 'early-born' ranks make it into the league simply because their maturity is masking their true (below average) talent. In contrast, late-born players who overcome the drawbacks of physical and psychological immaturity to enter the ranks of professional hockey are likely to be drawn from the higher part of the ability distribution. We should therefore expect the performance of those with later birth months, conditional on NHL entry, to be greater on average than those with early-year births since the NHL is selecting on observed performance of teenagers whose performance may be due to an 11 month gap in maturation.

This idea that the physical/psychological maturity advantage of children born in January can mask the true ability differences of an early (December) born player is illustrated in Fig. 4. The figure shows that a high ability player born in December and a lower than average ability player born in January will essentially have the same "observed" performance. In other words, an underlying high-ability December born player will appear, at the time of selection into the NHL, exactly the same as an average-to-below average January born player simply because of the 11-month maturity gap. This similarity in performance is misattributed to underlying talent, although the child born in January has an 11-month age advantage over the child born in December. This later-born disadvantage is magnified even further in the teenage years where deviations from the mean physical development are largest. We therefore expect that owing to this selection pressure, any later born entrant into the NHL will be of better than average quality than early born counterparts.

Some evidence for this has already been found by Gibbs et al. (2012) who examined the distribution of birth months for 1109 players who played on major league rosters from 2000 to 2009 and All-Star and Olympic hockey rosters from 2002 to 2010. Their findings illustrate "...how critical it is to define hockey success. When hockey success is defined as playing Major Junior Hockey, the [RAE] effect is strong, as Gladwell reported in the popular press. But the effect diminishes when ....performance and skill are considered. When hockey success is defined as the most elite levels of play, the relative age effect reverses [i.e., later born players outperform their early born counterparts]." Gibbs et al. (2012) only compare means and do not control for individual confounders such as country and team effects; as such, empirically we feel the jury is still out.

Data and Methods

Data Sources and Sample

In order to estimate single season and career effects of cohort size at birth and relative age on the outcomes of NHL hockey players, with coverage over several league expansions and a season-ending lock-out, we draw from multiple online data sources, all of which are listed in the Appendix.

We restrict attention to those players for whom salary data are available, to non-goalies and, in order to limit the pool of players that can be observed only once in a given season, to players who were not traded during the course of a given season. The pooled data therefore contains every player (exclusive of the restrictions mentioned above) who played in the NHL between the 1990–1991 and 2007–2008 seasons. This gives us an unbalanced panel (before missing variables in various specifications) of 8996 player-season observations and 2037 individual players.

To provide a sense of sample coverage, Appendix Tables 12 and 13 present the number of observations in the panel by categorical versions of our two key explanatory variables relative age (birth month) and cohort size – measured against years in the league (hereafter denoted as *experience*). In both cases we have substantial sample sizes at the low and mid-levels of experience but not at the upper end. This is because the average career length in our sample is 4.5 seasons even though the upper range is 17 seasons in the league. This feature of our data leads us to truncate the experience measure and to pool all those players with more than ten seasons of play in the league into a common category called *10 plus*. Since the size of the league (as measured by teams) varies over time, we will also report how the effects on earnings of birth cohort size differ for players in seasons following a league expansion.

In Table 1, we report summary statistics. The table summarizes variables for those players for whom we have earnings in our sample. Average annual earnings in our data are about $1,334,304 in constant USD 2008 dollars. The average number of seasons in the league is 4.4 and the modal season of an earnings observation is 1998–1999 season. As noted above, the pooled sample yields substantial variation

Table 1 Summary statistics for pooled NHL player sample, 1990–2008

Variable	Mean	Std. dev.	Min	Max
Dependent				
1. Salary (2008 US dollars)	1,334,304	1,591,470	16,095.82	2.20e+07
2. Log salary	13.65	0.901	9.68	16.90
3. Player performance:				
Point totals (per season)	24.26	23.77	0	163
Plus/minus (per season)	1.54	10.77	−50	60
Independent				
4. Birth rate (per 1,000 of population)[a]	17.35	3.29	11	28.5
5. Birth month (1–12)	5.84	3.41	1	12
Control variables				
6. Age (years)	27.07	4.36	18	45
7. Birth year	1971.5	6.11	1951	1989
8. Height (inches)	72.85	2.07	61	81
9. Weight (lbs)	200.16	15.56	150	263
10. Body mass ratio (weight/height)	2.74	.169	.233	3.95
11. Experience (years in league)	4.4	3.21	1	17
12. Games played (per season)	47.5	24.04	1	82
Other variables (dummies only)				
13. Experience: rookie <3 years	0.531	0.49	0	1
Early prime 4–6 years	0.256	0.43	0	1
Late prime 7–9 years	0.131	0.33	0	1
[Veteran >= 10 years]	0.075	0.26	0	1
14. Captain	.040	.196	0	1
15. Drafted [non-drafted]	.787	.394	0	1
16. Position				
[Defense]	.315	.464	0	1
Forward	.587	.492	0	1
Goalie	.096	.295	0	1
17. Country of origin				
[Canada]	.598	.490	0	1
United States	.155	.362	0	1
Czech Republic	.059	.237	0	1
Russia	.055	.228	0	1
Sweden	.046	.211	0	1
Finland	.029	.168	0	1
Slovakia	.019	.135	0	1
Former Soviet Republics[b]	.017	.128	0	1
Rest of Europe	.016	.125	0	1
Rest of World	.005	0.125	0	1

The sample is the combined data set described in the text. The sample includes all player positions (including goalies) with potential experience 1 to 17 seasons and with a valid annual earnings observation (>0 in 2008 dollars). The regression samples exclude goalies. Sample sizes vary because of missing variables

[a] Birth rate is crude birth rate measured for every player's birth country and year of birth

[b] These include Latvia, Lithuania, Ukraine, Kazakhstan, and Belarus

in country birth rates ranging from 11 to 28.5 per 1000 of the population. The two most prevalent birth months in the NHL are January and February. By contrast, as we have seen, seasonality of fertility in the population as a whole is skewed towards the spring to early fall. This confirms that the relative age of NHL players is much higher than the population as a whole.

Regression Specifications

There are three estimation equations that we use to answer our major questions in the paper. To estimate the main effect of birth cohort size on the earnings and performance outcomes of NHL players, we use the following specification.

$$Y_{it} = B_1 X_{it} + B_2 Large\,CohortSize_c + \lambda Team + e_{it} \tag{1a}$$

In Eq. 1a, Y_{it} is the outcome (either earnings or point totals) measured for season *t*, for an individual player *i*, in birth cohort country *c* (year), and X*it* is a set of control variables.[10] We also control for team fixed effects (λ *Team*). *LargeCohortSize$_c$* is a birth cohort dummy, defined as an above average crude birth rate in the country of origin at the year of birth for the player *i*. The coefficient B_2 on *LargeCohortSize$_c$* measures the impact of an above average birth cohort size (based on our sample of NHL players) on career outcomes for the average player.

To measure how this impact varies across a career, we interact birth cohort size *LargeCohortSize* with our experience measure *ExperienceCat$_{it}$* in Eq. 1b. We measure *Experience Cat$_{it}$* as a categorical variable capturing four career phases upon entrance to the league – *rookie* <3 years, *prime pre-free-agency* 4–6 years, *prime post-free-agency* 7–9 years and *veteran* 10pls years – rather than actual number of games, which could be endogenously related to seasons shortened by league stoppages observed in our data. Results are robust to including a linear experience interaction and allowing these to interact with *LargeCohortSize$_c$*.

$$Y_{it} = B_1 X_{it} + B_2 Large\,CohortSize_c \bullet ExperienceCat_{it} + B_3 ExperienceCat_{it} \\ + \lambda Team + e_{it} \tag{1b}$$

To estimate the effect of relative age we estimate a second version of (1a, 1b) simply replacing birth cohort with birth month (*BirthMonth*) as below:

$$Y_{it} = B_1 X_{it} + B_2 BirthMonth_c + \lambda Team + e_{ict.} \tag{2a}$$

---

[10]The controls included in X_{it} are *ExperienceCat* as a direct effect, non-goalie forward positional dummy (defensemen as excluded category), a bmi indicator (weight/height) and country of origin dummies.

$$Y_{it} = B_1 X_{it} + B_2 BirthMonth_c \cdot ExperienceCat_{it} + B_3 ExperienceCat_{it} \\ + \lambda Team + e_{ict.} \quad (2b)$$

Finally we add a fourth estimated parameter to (1), B_4

$$Y_{it} = B_1 X_{it} + B_2 Large\,Cohort\,SizeC_c + B_3 Large\,CohortSize_c \cdot ExperienceCat_{it} \\ + B_4 Cohort\,Size \cdot BirthMonth_{it+,} \lambda Team + e_{ict}, \quad (3)$$

which measures the differential impact of birth cohort size across relative age ($LargeCohortSize_c \cdot BirthMonth_{it}$).

For all specifications listed we estimate the differential impact of multiple league expansions and pre versus post-2004–2005 lockout using sub-sample analysis.

Results

Birth Cohort Size and Player Salaries

We begin with visual evidence of the evolution of player salaries. Figure 5 presents log annual compensation in constant 2008 dollars amongst NHL players for seasons 1990–1991 through to 2007–2008. The raw sample is split by those players born into higher and lower than average birth cohorts (i.e., those born when birth rates were above the mean value in our data, which is 17.35 per 1000 of the population, were coded as High Birth Cohorts and those below were tagged Below Average Birth Cohort). Figure 5 also plots the difference in Log Salary between the two groups. Also highlighted in the figure is the typical window for player free agency, which happens after a player has either played seven seasons in the league or has reached the age of 27 (whichever is first).

The pattern of data is consistent with our hypothesized career earnings path in Fig. 2 for normal and high birth rate player cohorts in the presence of free-agency. We see that there is an overall penalty to being born into a large birth cohort of about 12%. This is amplified in the early stages ("rookie" phase) of the career as was suggested by our NHL player earnings model. Then, as anticipated, given an ability to renegotiate contracts with any team, a player from a larger birth cohort can translate his higher than average performance into a higher salary in the free agency window. However, this effect is not large enough to offset the negative impact of being born into a larger birth cohort because free-agency comes relatively late in an NHL career which, on average, only last 4.5 seasons.

We now turn to estimating the average effect of being born into an above average birth cohort for all non-goalies in our sample. Table 2 reports estimates from variants of our base specification in Eq. 1. The controls include a body-mass ratio, a dummy for whether the player is a forward (defenders being the excluded reference category), and country of origin. We also consider specifications where no controls

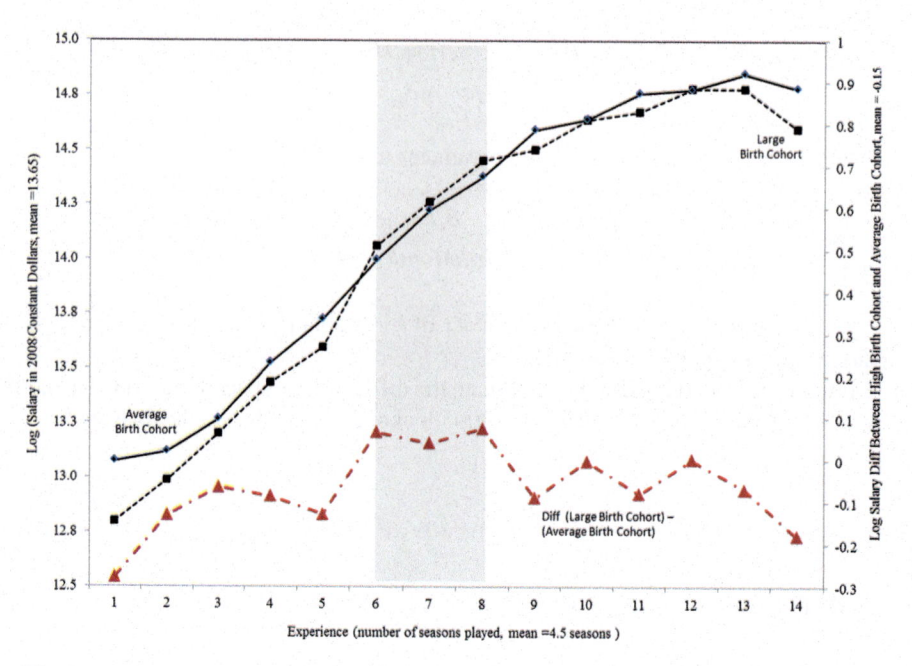

Fig. 5 Unadjusted career earnings paths of NHL players from normal and unusually large birth cohorts, with free agency occurring after 7 years' experience

other than individual points are included (our proxy for observed player ability) in order to see if the effect matches our prediction that adjusting for quality, any large birth cohort earnings losses would be expected to rise in the presence of a player quality control.

The initial parameter of interest is the Large Birth Cohort dummy. Column (1) includes no controls and estimates the panel with a random effects model in which standard errors are clustered on team. The estimated difference in log salary between a Large and Small Birth Cohort player is −0.197. The estimates and significance are largely unaltered when we add a player performance control (column 2) – if anything the negative effect of being born into a large cohort becomes slightly larger in keeping with our hypothesis that large cohorts should produce better than average quality players – when other controls are added (column 3) and when team fixed effects are added (column 4). The estimated large birth cohort effect in the full specification with all controls including player performance and team dummies is a 17.9% reduction in log earnings.

The primary birth cohort size variable in row 1 is estimating the effect over the average career length, which in our data is roughly 4.5 seasons. However, given the hypothetical earnings profile from our player experience model and the actual raw data seen in Fig. 5, there is strong reason to suspect that the cohort effect varies by stage of career. We therefore estimate specification (1b) which disaggregates the cohort effect by years in the league. We highlight four phases: rookie (<3 years), pre-free agency prime age (4–6 years), free agency prime age (7–9 years), and vet-

Table 2 The effect of large birth cohort on NHL player salaries, 1990–2008

	All player observations, 1990–2008			
	Log(salary) Mean = 13.65	Log(salary) Mean = 13.65	Log(salary) Mean = 13.65	Log(salary) Mean = 13.65
	(1)	(2)	(3)	(4)
[Small birth cohort]				
Large birth cohort[a]	−0.197***	−0.209***	−0.184***	−0.179***
(Avg. career length = 4.4 years)	(.029)	(.019)	(.019)	(.019)
By career stage =				
Rookie <3 years	−0.195***	−0.276***	−0.255***	−0.215***
	(.031)	(.023)	(.023)	(.023)
Prime 4–6 years	−0.178***	−0.136***	−0.112***	−0.073**
	(.037)	(.027)	(.026)	(.027)
Prime 7–9 years	−0.169***	−0.077**	−0.043	−0.012
	(.047)	(.035)	(.034)	(.034)
Veteran >=10 years	−0.316***	−0.177***	−0.141***	−0.117***
	(.053)	(.047)	(.044)	(.044)
Player performance[b]	No	Yes	Yes	Yes
Other controls	No	No	Yes	Yes
Team fixed effects	No	No	No	Yes
Between R^2	0.328	0.503	0.555	0.582
Overall R^2	0.409	0.547	0.570	0.587
Total observations	8,992	8,795	8,785	8,785
Number of players	2,036	1,993	1,990	1,990

All regressions are random effect models. Standard errors are in parentheses. The sample is the panel data set described in the text, exclusive of all goalies. Observations are player-season cells. Estimates exclude players without earnings. The controls are a body mass indicator (weight/height), forward dummy and country of origin. In team fixed effects we exclude the team with highest average payroll (New York Rangers)

***p < 0.01, **p < 0.05, *p < 0.1

[a]An indicator coded 1 if crude birth rate is 17.35 or higher in country of origin at time of birth and 0 otherwise – below average Small Birth Cohort size (<17.35) is the excluded reference category. The estimate parameters by career stage are relative to Small Birth Cohort *Rookies <3 years*, Small Birth Cohort *Prime 4–6 years*, etc.

[b]Measured as point totals in a given season

eran status (10 years plus). Each phase is included in the specification as well as the four interaction terms arising from *LargeBirthCohort*ExpereinceCat*. We include these results in row 2 where we see that after adjusting for player quality and other characteristics, there is indeed a differential negative effect that is larger upon entry into the league, narrows considerably in mid-career during the free agency window, and then widens once again in veteran status (columns 2–3). This pattern is almost unchanged with team fixed effects added (column 4). The overall cohort size dummy and the estimates by cohort size interacted with career stage suggest that large birth cohorts do put downward pressure on player wages. This is true despite the fact that hockey ability appears to be higher amongst large birth cohort players, given the larger negative effects seen in column (2) when player performance was controlled for. To see this more clearly we next turn to our player performance estimates.

Birth Cohort Size and Player Performance

A possible concern in interpreting the estimates in Table 2 is that the effects of cohort size might be biased by cohort size effects on player performance. So rather than estimating the effect of large cohort pressure on salaries we are seeing the residual effect of some systematic player performance that matches the salary data. When individual performance was controlled for in Table 2 the negative values for our large birth cohort dummy actually went up, suggesting that large birth cohort players are actually better. Nevertheless there is the possibility that coming of age in a large cohort may lead to a lower likelihood of getting drafted and thus playing for more years in inferior leagues, thus degrading skills.

To test if this is indeed the case, or whether the ability of large cohort players is greater because of added competition throughout a playing career, we use a similar estimating model to that employed in Table 2, only this time the dependent variable used is *season point totals* instead of salary.[11] The results can be seen in Table 3, row 1 where we see that the point estimate of a Large Birth Cohort relative to a Small Birth Cohort varies from 5.21 more (or 20% higher point totals relative to the mean of 25 points) in the unadjusted estimates to 1.89 (or just under 10% higher) when full controls and fixed team effects are added. The big drop in the coefficient occurs after games played is controlled for (see row 1 Column 1 versus Column 2 estimates). The coefficient remains stable thereafter suggesting that large birth cohort players are actually playing more games per season than small birth cohort players. When we checked to see if this is in fact the case, it turns out that the difference is non-trivial and significant. On average large birth cohort players play 52 games per season versus 46 games for small birth cohort counterparts, a difference of 6 games that is significant at the 1% level (p = .000). One interpretation of this finding is that games played per season is capturing yet another dimension of higher player quality (i.e., durability or 'stick-to-it-ness' required to compete in a larger talent pool) that larger birth cohorts possess relative to their smaller cohorts.

When we examine the large birth cohort effect by career stage, essentially replacing our single dummy with four large birth cohort dummies interacted with seasons in the league we find that the positive effect on point totals is confined to the early stage of the career. In fact, for veteran players it appears that small birth cohort size is associated with greater point totals, reversing the trend early in the career. However these estimates need to be taken in context. The majority of players do not reach 10 or even 6 years in the league. As seen in Table 1 row 12, just over half the

---

[11] Total games played is used as an explanatory variable, replacing player performance used in Table 2.

Table 3 The effect of large birth cohort on NHL player performance, 1990–2008

	All player observations, 1990–2008			
	Points (Per season) Mean = 24.6 (1)	Points (Per season) Mean = 24.6 (2)	Points (Per season) Mean = 24.6 (3)	Points (Per season) Mean = 24.6 (4)
[Small birth cohort]				
Large birth cohort[a]	5.21***	1.87***	2.29***	1.89***
(Avg career length= 4.6 years)	(.718)	(.454)	(.457)	(.474)
By career stage =				
Rookie <3 years	9.65***	4.00***	4.41***	3.98***
	(.671)	(.486)	(489)	(.023)
Prime 4–6 years	−1.19	0.326	0.959	0.598
	(.845)	(.613)	(.026)	(.026)
Prime 7–9 years	−5.48***	−4.11***	−3.38***	−3.72***
	(1.06)	(.781)	(.779)	(.708)
Veteran >=10 years	−10.07***	−7.55***	−6.76***	−7.02***
	(0.728)	(1.02)	(1.02)	(.900)
Games played (per season)	No	Yes	Yes	Yes
Other controls	No	No	Yes	Yes
Team fixed effects	No	No	No	Yes
Between R^2	0.058	0.586	0.621	0.623
Overall R^2	0.045	0.474	0.526	0.534
Total observations	12,110	12,110	12,098	12,098
Number of players	2,655	2,655	2,651	2,651

All regressions are random effect models. Standard errors are in parentheses. The sample is the panel data set described in the text, exclusive of all goalies. Observations are player-season cells. Columns 1–4 also include all players regardless of earnings data. In controls we include a body mass indicator (weight/height), forward dummy and country of origin. In team fixed effects we exclude team with highest average payroll (New York Rangers)
***$p < 0.01$, **$p < 0.05$, *$p < 0.1$
[a]An indicator coded 1 if crude birth rate is 17.35 or higher in country of origin at time of birth and 0 otherwise – below average Small Birth Cohort size (<17.35) is the excluded reference category. The estimated parameters by career stage are relative to Small Birth Cohort counterparts; so Small Birth Cohort *Rookies <3 years*, Small Birth Cohort *Prime 4–6 years*, etc.

NHL sample (53%) play only three seasons or less in the league and this rises to 75% when the player sample is on the cusp of free agency at 7 years in the league. In short, given that the clear majority of NHL players spend less than 7 years in the league, the estimated point totals are in accordance with the view that large birth cohorts are, on average, of higher quality than their small birth cohort counterparts.

As a further check Table 4 replaces individual point totals with players' plus/minus record (this is the net point difference based on whether a player was on the ice when a goal was scored for or against) for each player. The results confirm the

Table 4 The effect of large birth cohort on NHL player performance, 1990–2008

	All player observations, 1990–2008			
	Plus/minus (Per season) Mean = 1.54	Plus/minus (Per season) Mean = 1.54	Plus/minus (Per season) Mean = 1.54	Plus/minus (Per season) Mean = 1.54
	(1)	(2)	(3)	(4)
[Small birth cohort]				
Large birth cohort[a]	2.55***	2.21***	2.60***	2.24***
(Avg career length= 4.6 years)	(.718)	(.202)	(.216)	(.220)
By career stage =				
Rookie <3 years	3.53***	3.50***	3.89***	3.55***
	(.266)	(.263)	(.274)	(.277)
Prime 4–6 years	1.77***	1.30***	1.69***	1.34***
	(.344)	(.341)	(.349)	(.350)
Prime 7–9 years	1.09***	0.171	0.586	0.242
	(.999)	(.461)	(.697)	(.465)
Veteran >=10 years	1.83***	.823	1.30**	0.775
	(.622)	(.616)	(.619)	(.618)
Games played (per season)	No	Yes	Yes	Yes
Other controls	No	No	Yes	Yes
Team fixed effects	No	No	No	Yes
Between R^2	0.027	0.083	0.083	0.125
Overall R^2	0.015	0.045	0.051	0.075
Total observations	12,110	12,110	12,098	12,098
Number of players	2,655	2,655	2,651	2,651

All regressions are random effect models. Standard errors are in parentheses. The sample is the panel data set described in the text, exclusive of all goalies. Observations are player-season cells. Columns 1–4 also include all players regardless of earnings data. In controls we include a body mass indicator (weight/height), forward dummy and country of origin. In team fixed effects we exclude team with highest average payroll (New York Rangers)
***$p < 0.01$, **$p < 0.05$, *$p < 0.1$
[a]An indicator coded 1 if crude birth rate is 17.35 or higher in country of origin at time of birth and 0 otherwise – below average Birth Cohort size (<17.35) is the excluded reference category. The estimated parameters by career stage are relative to Small Birth Cohort counterparts; so Small Birth Cohort *Rookies <3 years*, Small Birth Cohort *Prime 4–6 years*, etc.

view that NHL players born when there is more competition in the form of a larger birth cohort tend to be better on average than those born in smaller (less competitive) birth years. The effects relative to the mean plus-minus value of 1.54 are even more impressive than the point totals. Even after adjusting for the full set of characteristics and team effects, there is a near doubling of the overall plus/minus record (2.24) amongst those players born into above average birth cohorts relative to small birth cohort players. This time as well the effect, though it varies across career stage, is always positive.

Table 5 The effect of large birth cohort on other NHL player outcomes, 1990–2008

	All player observations, 1990–2008			
	Pr(drafted)	Pr(drafted)	Pr(captain)	Pr(captain)
	Mean = 0.787	Mean = 0.787	Mean = 0.04	Mean = 0.04
	(1)	(2)	(3)	(4)
[Small birth cohort]				
Large birth cohort[a]	−0.097***	−0.092***	0.028***	0.029***
	(.008)	(.009)	(.004)	(.004)
Other controls	No	Yes	No	Yes
Pseudo R^2	0.027	0.039	0.015	0.161
Total observations	12,369	12,357	12,369	12,179

All regressions are *probit* models reporting the marginal effects. The sample is the panel data set described in the text that includes all non-goalies. Observations are player-season cells. Columns 1–4 include all players regardless of earnings data. In other controls we include body mass indicator (weight/height), country of origin, forward dummy and cumulative experience measure which is a count of seasons in league
***$p < 0.01$, **$p < 0.05$, *$p < 0.1$
[a]An indicator coded 1 if crude birth rate is 17.35 or higher in country of origin at time of birth and 0 otherwise – below average Small Birth Cohort size (<17.35) is the excluded reference category

Added Checks

Further evidence on the possible channels associated with these large and significant salary losses and performance gains comes from Table 5 where we examine the likelihood that a player born into a larger-than-average cohort is drafted into the NHL or becomes a team captain. Essentially most players enter the league via the draft.[12] In the NHL it is particularly large (300 players) and deep in that there are 12 rounds of drafting. If not drafted a player must often play in lower level professional leagues for some time before getting noticed by major league teams. This could perhaps be one mechanism that accounts for the low entry stage (rookie) salaries amongst large birth cohort players. Using only the relevant covariates from the previous analysis – we use characteristics (such as body/mass index, country of origin and forward dummy) that would have been visible to the team at the time of draft – we find that there is a 9 percentage point reduction in the probability of being drafted for players born into larger than average birth cohorts (Table 5 column 2).

When we explore intangible quality or hard-to-observe aspects of a player such as potential leadership skills (Table 5 columns 3 and 4), we find that there is indeed evidence of a large birth cohort effect. Becoming a captain of a team in the NHL is a rare event, only 4% of the sample ever goes on to become a team captain (there is typically only one captain on a team and the average roster on an NHL team is 20 players), yet even after adjusting for player characteristics, a large cohort player is

---

[12] The draft is an annual meeting in which every franchise of the NHL selects players (in ascending order based on past season performance) from the amateur leagues where they meet draft eligibility requirements.

nearly 90% more likely (3.5 percentage points higher relative to the mean probability of 4%) to become a team captain than lower-than-average birth cohort players. This last finding is perhaps not surprising since we anticipate a likely correlation in observed quality to map over into these less visible attributes of player performance.

Relative Age (Birth Month) and Player Outcomes

Models of relative age tend to focus on the probability of entry into the NHL, which is higher for early-born players, in keeping with our earlier theoretical discussion. Instead, we focus here on the prediction that, *conditional on being good enough to enter the NHL*, your overall ability (and hence performance) should be greater the lower your relative age. In other words players born later in the calendar year should display better performance than their earlier-born counterparts because those younger (born later in the year) players are being selected from the top tail of ability whereas those born earlier in the year include both top and mid-to-bottom tail performers (see Fig. 4). This owes simply to the 11 month advantage (at the maximum) that a January born youth has over December born equivalents.

Table 6 reports earnings estimates for the relative age variable (a dummy that takes on the value 1 if a player is born between January and April and 0 otherwise) using a specification identical to the one used in Table 2. We find those who are born later in their cohort suffer a wage penalty of around 3%, but this salary gap widens over the course of the career. This is perhaps reflective of the true ability of an early-born player becoming less noisily visible to teams and coaches. The more time they have to observe an early born player, the less any initial physical or mental advantage becomes relative to their later-born counterparts. Since player free-agency (after 7 years) is often the time when early contracts get renegotiated, this could explain the large negative hit that January-to-April born players take in their late prime and veteran careers in columns 1 through 4.

A more interesting and theoretically consistent set of findings appear in Tables 7 and 8 where point totals and plus/minus records are significantly and consistently lower amongst players with higher relative age (birth months falling between January and April) than amongst those born in May to December. Players born in the early part of the year are drafted on the basis of a potential 11 month calendar advantage in physical and mental development which likely masks a true ability distribution that is drawn from the middle and lower tails. The widening in the point losses the longer a January-to-April born plays in the league may reflect the effects of true underlying quality coming to the fore over time.

Yet in Table 9 column 2 we see that NHL teams are indeed biased in favour of early-birth month players given that the probability of being drafted is 3% higher (2.4 percentage points relative to a mean of 78.7%). Once again, this 'initial' advantage is not seen in a later-stage career outcome such as being awarded the team captaincy. Here we see that (column 4) a player born between January and

Table 6 The effect of relative age (birth month) on NHL player salaries, 1990–2008

	All player observations, 1990–2008			
	Log(salary) Mean = 13.65 (1)	Log(salary) Mean = 13.65 (2)	Log(salary) Mean = 13.65 (3)	Log(salary) Mean = 13.65 (4)
[Low relative age]				
High relative age[a]	−0.073***	−0.032*	−0.029*	−0.027*
(Born Jan-Apr)	(.027)	(.019)	(.017)	(.017)
By career stage =				
Rookie (<3 years)	−0.0288	−0.018	−0.023	−0.020
	(.025)	(.026)	(.021)	(.021)
Prime (4–6 years)	−0.061**	−0.031	−0.039	−0.039
	(.029)	(.026)	(.025)	(.024)
Prime (7–9 years)	−0.124***	−0.089***	−0.097***	−0.096***
	(.035)	(.033)	(.032)	(.031)
Veteran (>=10 years)	−0.086*	−0.053	−0.060	−0.056
	(.044)	(.042)	(.041)	(.045)
Player performance[b]	No	Yes	Yes	Yes
Other controls	No	No	Yes	Yes
Team fixed effects	No	No	No	Yes
Between R^2	0.307	0.452	0.511	0.523
Overall R^2	0.409	0.529	0.558	0.552
Total Observations	8,994	8,797	8,787	8,785
Number of players	2,037	1,994	1,991	1,990

All regressions are random effect models. Standard errors are in parentheses. The sample is the panel data set described in the text, exclusive of all goalies. Observations are player-season cells. Columns 1–4 also exclude players without earnings. In controls we include a body mass indicator (weight/height), forward dummy and country of origin. In team fixed effects we exclude team with highest average payroll (New York Rangers)
***p < 0.01, **p < 0.05, *p < 0.1
[a]An indicator coded 1 if a player is born in the first quarter of the calendar year and 0 for those born between May and December (excluded reference category). The estimated parameters by career stage are relative to earlier born counterparts; so May to December born *Rookies <3 years*, etc. are excluded reference categories
[b]Measured as point totals in a given season

April has a 12% reduced chance (0.5 percentage points less likely to be named a captain relative to the 4% chance observed in the data).

These findings suggest that a higher relative age (being born early in the calendar year), gives players of average or below average quality a greater chance of being drafted and making it into the NHL. But it does not lead to higher earnings and is associated with significantly lower performance that widens as careers progress from rookie to veteran status in the league. Indeed there seems to be a significant realignment of salaries downwards after early born players reach free-agency, perhaps compensating a team for their noisy signal of quality at an earlier age.

Table 7 The effect of relative age (birth month) on NHL player performance, 1990–2008

	All player observations, 1990–2008			
	Points (Per season) Mean = 24.6	Points (Per season) Mean = 24.6	Points (Per season) Mean = 24.6	Points (Per season) Mean = 24.6
	(1)	(2)	(3)	(4)
[Low relative age]				
High relative age[a]	−2.03***	−0.946**	−0.940**	−0.975***
(Born Jan-Apr)	(.718)	(.406)	(.384)	(.387)
By career stage =				
Rookie <3 years	−1.62***	−0.42	−0.41	−0.47
	(.600)	(.431)	(.411)	(.041)
Prime 4–6 years	−2.91***	−1.83***	−1.78***	−1.80***
	(.786)	(.567)	(.550)	(.551)
Prime 7–9 years	−3.31***	−2.34***	−2.32***	−2.33***
	(.786)	(.734)	(.720)	(.721)
Veteran >=10 years	−2.35*	−2.61***	−2.59***	−2.61***
	(1.32)	(.962)	(.950)	(.950)
Games played (per season)	No	Yes	Yes	Yes
Other controls	No	No	Yes	Yes
Team fixed effects	No	No	No	Yes
Between R^2	0.161	0.594	0.629	0.632
Overall R^2	0.035	0.474	0.525	0.539
Total observations	12,113	12,113	12,100	12,098
Number of players	2,657	2,657	2,652	2,651

All regressions are random effect models. Standard errors are in parentheses. The sample is the panel data set described in the text, exclusive of all goalies. Observations are player-season cells. Columns 1–4 also include all players regardless of earnings data. In controls we include a body mass indicator (weight/height), forward dummy and country of origin. In team fixed effects we exclude team with highest average payroll (New York Rangers)
***$p < 0.01$, **$p < 0.05$, *$p < 0.1$
[a]An indicator coded 1 if a player is born in the first quarter of the calendar year (January to April) and 0 for those born between May and December (excluded reference category). The estimated parameters by career stage are all relative to earlier born counterparts; so *May to December born Rookies <3 years*, etc. are excluded reference categories

Does Relative Age (Birth Month) Moderate the Effect of Large Birth Cohort Size?

Next we investigate if downward earnings adjustments owing to large birth cohort size effects are moderated by relative age. If those advantages, already detailed in the text, that come from being born early in the year insulate a January-born player more than one born in December, we should see a smaller negative earnings coefficient on the Large Birth Cohort dummy for player with lower relative ages.

Table 8 The effect of relative age (birth month) on NHL player performance, 1990–2008

	All player observations, 1990–2008			
	Plus/minus (Per season) Mean = 1.54 (1)	Plus/minus (Per season) Mean = 1.54 (2)	Plus/minus (Per season) Mean = 1.54 (3)	Plus/minus (Per season) Mean = 1.54 (4)
[Low relative age]				
High relative age[a]	−0.609***	−0.459***	−0.512***	−0.505***
(Born Jan-Apr)	(.186)	(.184)	(.185)	(.185)
By career stage =				
Rookie <3 years	−0.699***	−0.533**	−0.574***	−0.646***
	(.256)	(.253)	(.361)	(.251)
Prime 4–6 years	−0.494	−0.283	−0.346	−0.273
	(.366)	(.361)	(.361)	(.359)
Prime 7–9 years	−0.712	−0.651	−0.725	−0.542
	(.513)	(.506)	(.506)	(.502)
Veteran >=10 years	−0.097	−0.205	−0.245	−0.252
	(.680)	(.670)	(.670)	(.665)
Games played (per season)	No	Yes	Yes	Yes
Other controls	No	No	Yes	Yes
Team fixed effects	No	No	No	Yes
Between R^2	0.018	0.051	0.056	0.107
Overall R^2	0.013	0.034	0.038	0.075
Total observations	12,155	12,113	12,100	12,098
Number of players	2,655	2,657	2,652	2,651

All regressions are random effect models. Standard errors are in parentheses. The sample is the panel data set described in the text, exclusive of all goalies. Observations are player-season cells. Columns 1–4 also include all players regardless of earnings data. In controls we include a body mass indicator (weight/height), forward dummy and country of origin. In team fixed effects we exclude team with highest average payroll (New York Rangers)
***p < 0.01, **p < 0.05, *p < 0.1
[a]An indicator coded 1 if a player is born in the first quarter of the calendar year (January to April) and 0 for those born between May and December (excluded reference category). The estimated parameters by career stage are all relative to earlier born counterparts; so *May to December born Rookies <3 years*, etc. are excluded reference categories

Table 10 runs the same earnings estimation as was used in Table 2 row 1 column 4, only this time separately by relative age categories, in order to see if there is any differential cohort size effect. The table shows that the earnings losses from being born into a large birth cohort are 10 percentage points lower for those born in January to April than they are for those born in September to December (final column). This means that although an early birth month player still suffers a salary loss if born during a baby-boom birth year, the majority of the overall negative large birth cohort effect is coming from the 'youngest' calendar year months (i.e., those born May to August and September to December).

Table 9 The effect of relative age on other NHL player outcomes, 1990–2008

	All player observations, 1990–2008			
	Pr(drafted)	Pr(drafted)	Pr(captain)	Pr(captain)
	Mean = 0.787	Mean = 0.787	Mean = 0.041	Mean = 0.041
	(1)	(2)	(3)	(4)
[Low relative age] High relative age[a] (Born Jan–Apr)	0.027*** (.007)	0.024*** (.007)	−0.007** (.003)	−0.005* (.003)
Other controls	No	Yes	No	Yes
Pseudo R^2	0.010	0.027	0.015	0.027
Total observations	12,372	12,359	12,372	12,181

All regressions are *probit* models reporting the marginal effects. The sample is the panel data set described in the text that includes all non-goalies. Observations are player-season cells. Columns 1–4 includes all players even those without earnings. In other controls we include body mass indicator (weight/height), country of origin, and forward dummy
***p < 0.01, **p < 0.05, *p < 0.1
[a]An indicator of crude birth rate of 17.5 per 1,000 per population or higher for birth rate, Small Birth cohort size (<17.5) is excluded reference category

Do Results Differ During League Expansions and in the Post-Lockout Era?

Finally in Table 11 we look at how planned league expansions, which exogenously raise the demand for hockey talent as well as the 2004–2005 lockout which imposed the first ever salary cap in the NHL, might have affected salaries for large birth cohort players.

First we divide the sample into the pre and post season-ending lockout periods, 1990–1991 to 2003–2004 seasons and the 2005–2006 to 2007–2008 seasons respectively. Figure 6 charts the evolution of average player salaries over this entire period and we see that the 2004–2005 lockout does indeed produce a reduction in levels of pay but crucially no abatement in the growth trajectory. Collapsing the data into these two periods we then estimate our standard panel data earnings regressions, with full controls, found in column 4 of Table 2. Table 11 columns 1 and 2 show that the lockout served to recalibrate earnings towards large birth cohort players relative to small birth cohort players. There is likely a simple reason for this. In the post lockout aftermath there was a substantial lowering in overall pay levels and in the dispersion of pay. Top salaries were effectively constrained (at least in the three seasons we observed following the lockout) and this is where some of the players facing lower competition due to small birth cohort sizes, were forced to renegotiate salaries with team owners alongside better quality higher birth rate counterparts.

Table 11 also reports the difference (last column) between NHL earnings during seasons in which there were league expansions (six in total) as compared to seasons in which there were none. Based on a labor demand curve which is shifting outward with each league expansion, we would expect any potential negative effects owing to competitive crowding and/or lower bargaining power for players born into large

Table 10 The effect of large birth cohort on NHL player salaries by relative age, 1990–2008

	Dependent variable: log(salary) mean = 13.65				
	By relative age (birth quarter)				
	Born January to April	Born May to August	Born Sep to Dec	Differences (t-stats)	
	(1)	(2)	(3)	(1)–(2)	(1)–(3)
[Small birth cohort]					
Large birth cohort[a]	−0.141***	−0.161***	−0.243***	−0.020	−0.102***
(Avg. career length = 4.4 years)	(.031)	(.035)	(.038)	(0.645)	(2.91)
By career stage =					
Rookie <3 years	−0.128***	−0.177***	−0.185***	−0.049	−0.057
	(.040)	(.047)	(.050)	(1.160)	(1.207)
Prime 4–6 years	−0.034	−0.081	−0.170***	−.047	−0.136***
	(.047)	(.063)	(.057)	(0.903)	(2.72)
Prime 7–9 years	0.010	0.083	−0.215***	−0.073	−0.205***
	(.058)	(.065)	(.070)	(1.211)	(3.36)
Veteran 10 years>	−0.208***	−0.264***	−0.176*	−0.064	0.032
	(.076)	(.077)	(.092)	(0.842)	(0.400)
Player performance[b]	Yes	Yes	Yes		
Other controls	Yes	Yes	Yes		
Team fixed effects	Yes	Yes	Yes		
Between R^2	0.516	0.487	0.533		
Overall R^2	0.522	0.505	0.532		
Total observations	3,520	2,904	2,361		
Number of players	825	638	527		

All regressions are random effect models. Standard errors are in parentheses. The sample is the panel data set described in the text, exclusive of all goalies. Observations are player-season cells. Columns 1–4 also exclude players without earnings. In controls we include a body mass indicator (weight/height), forward dummy and country of origin. In team fixed effects we exclude team with highest average payroll (New York Rangers)

***$p < 0.01$, **$p < 0.05$, *$p < 0.1$

[a]An indicator coded 1 if crude birth rate is 17.35 or higher in country of origin at time of birth and 0 otherwise – below average Small Birth Cohort size (<17.35) is the excluded reference category. The estimate parameters by career stage are relative to Small Birth Cohort *Rookies <3 years*, Small Birth Cohort *Prime 4–6 years*, etc.

[b]Measured as point totals in a given season

Table 11 The effect of large birth cohort on NHL player salaries pre-post lockout and league expansion, 1990–2008

	Dependent variable: log(salary) mean =13.65							
	By lockout and league expansions				League expansion years[a]			
	2004–2005 lockout							
	Pre	Post	Diff		No	Yes	Diff	
	Mean = 13.57	Mean = 14.00	(t-stat) = 0.43		Mean = 13.34	Mean = 14.04	(t-stat) = 0.68	
	(1)	(2)	(2)–(1)		(3)	(4)	(4)–(3)	
[Small birth cohort]								
Large birth cohort[b]	−0.127***	0.470***	0.597***		−0.141***	−0.053*	0.088***	
(Avg. career length = 4.4 years)	(.021)	(.098)	(6.97)		(.028)	(.029)	(3.14)	
By career stage =								
Rookie <3 years	−0.119***	−0.090	0.029		−0.434**	0.025	0.459***	
	(.026)	(.165)	(.966)		(.031)	(.033)	(6.12)	
Prime 4–6 years	−0.050*	0.026	0.076**		−0.124***	−0.161***	−0.035	
	(.029)	(.132)	(2.32)		(.076)	(.039)	(0.777)	
Prime 7–9 years	−0.078**	0.100	0.178**		−0.005	−0.071	−0.066	
	(.058)	(.127)	(2.28)		(.063)	(.052)	(1.10)	
Veteran 10 years>	−0.350***	−0.006	0.344***		−0.044	−0.362***	−0.318***	
	(.052)	(.094)	(3.82)		(.058)	(.089)	(467)	
Player performance[c]	Yes	Yes			Yes	Yes		
Other controls	Yes	Yes			Yes	Yes		
Team fixed effects	Yes	Yes			Yes	Yes		
Between R^2	0.516	0.646			0.633	0.473		
Overall R^2	0.522	0.585			0.599	0.573		

	Dependent variable: log(salary) mean =13.65						
	By lockout and league expansions				League expansion years[a]		
	2004–2005 lockout						
	Pre	Post	Diff		No	Yes	Diff
	Mean = 13.57	Mean = 14.00	(t-stat) = 0.43		Mean = 13.34	Mean = 14.04	(t-stat) = 0.68
	(1)	(2)	(2)–(1)		(3)	(4)	(4)–(3)
Total observations	7,041	1,744			5,330	3,455	
Number of players	1,617	869			1,750	1,250	

All regressions are random effect models. Standard errors are in parentheses. The sample is the panel data set described in the text, exclusive of all goalies. Observations are player-season cells. Columns 1–4 also exclude players without earnings. In controls we include a body mass indicator (weight/height), forward dummy and country of origin. In team fixed effects we exclude team with highest average payroll (New York Rangers)

***$p < 0.01$, **$p < 0.05$, *$p < 0.1$

[a]Six league expansions occurred in total prior to the start of the 1991–1992, 1992–1993, 1993–1994 seasons and again in 1998–1999, 1999–2000, 2000–2001

[b]An indicator coded 1 if crude birth rate is 17.35 or higher in country of origin at time of birth and 0 otherwise – below average Small Birth Cohort size (<17.35) is the excluded reference category. The estimate parameters by career stage are relative to Small Birth Cohort *Rookies <3 years*, Small Birth Cohort *Prime 4–6 years*, etc.

[c]Measured as point totals in a given season

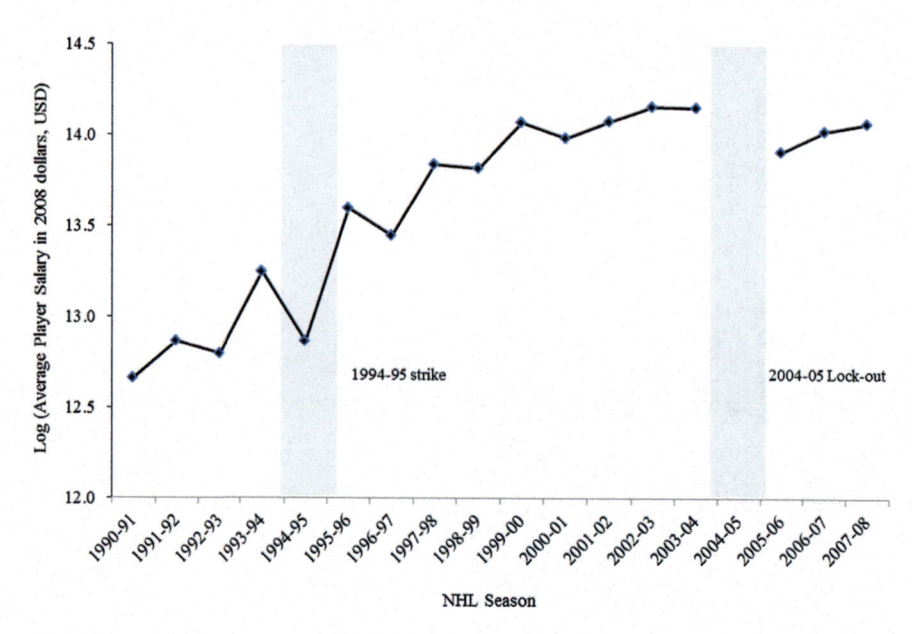

Fig. 6 The evolution of average NHL player salaries, 1990–1991 to 2007–2008 (in 2008 Constant USD dollars)

birth cohorts to be positively moderated. This is borne out for the average large birth cohort player who receives an 8.8% earnings premium if playing in the league during an expansion. For early-career players (less than 3 years in the league) born into large birth cohorts, a league expansion turns into a whopping 45.9% premium. This positive league expansion effect does not seem to carry over into late-stage and veteran salaries: if anything they suffer relatively more perhaps because they are locked into longer term contracts and are not in a position to negotiate freely at such an advantageous time whereas a new entrant into the league is.

Conclusions

Consistent with the previous literature looking at general labor market outcomes, we find that professional hockey players born in times of higher birth rates suffer significant earnings losses relative to those born into smaller birth cohorts. Earnings are roughly 22% lower in the first three seasons for a player born in a higher than average birth rate cohort (>17.35), which is a level much lower than that seen at the height of the largest baby boomers in our sample. This effect persists but narrows from years 4 to 6 and then achieves parity in 7–9 years (the typical free agency window). But this catch-up period is not sufficient to make up for the earnings losses over the average span of a career of 4.5 years which is 18%.

We then examine the channels through which unusually large birth cohorts could potentially affect career outcomes, focusing on career length (games played), performance (point totals for non-goalies) and potential league expansions that occurred post most baby-boom entry into the league. We find that the earnings losses amongst large birth cohorts are accounted for by a combination of reductions in games played and league expansions that improved the bargaining power of player entrants born in years with relatively small birth cohort sizes. As our theoretical intuition would suggest, we find no effect due to lower performance of large birth-cohort players: if anything the opposite was true in that performance was on average higher for players born during these above average birth cohort years.

The answer to our second question runs counter to the thrust of a majority of the literature in this area pointing to significant advantages accruing to higher relative age (i.e., being born later in the year). Whilst our data clearly confirms a higher prevalence of early birth month players in the NHL (far higher than the probability of being born in the general population) the career performance of these players is in fact significantly worse than that of later-birth month players. Though January-to-April born players have about a 2 percentage-point salary advantage in the first part of their career, this effect does not persist past the free agency years, when there is in fact a significant negative relationship between earlier relative age and earnings of 9%. Moreover, relative age is inversely related to point totals for non-goalies and career length as measured by total games played. Beyond this, the probability of captaincy in a team is also inversely related to relative age. A player born in the latter half of the year (from July to December) is 5 percentage points more likely to be a team captain than a player born in the first half (from January to June).

The fact that later born players outperform their early born counterparts is consistent with a number of theories that have been advanced in different contexts such as schooling and educational attainment. Selection into the NHL for those born in younger relative age categories is considerably harder given that these players have had to compete against more physically and mentally mature early born counterparts. Since most hockey players are born in jurisdictions where amateur team play is governed by calendar year births, those with initial physical and mental advantages are given preferential attention and opportunities. If a younger player can not only overcome these initial disadvantages but perhaps gain from having performed alongside more capable peers, then they should be expected to outperform the average player, who is typically drawn from older relative age categories (i.e., born between January and April).

Somewhat surprisingly, given the above findings, we find that those players with higher relative age (born in the first quarter of the calendar year) are relatively sheltered from the negative effects of greater cohort competition. A player that is born early (January to April) experiences significantly lower earnings losses than a player that is born late in the year (September to December) even if both were born in large birth cohorts. This means that players with greater relative age increase their chances of getting into the NHL and also have a slight advantage if born into a large birth cohort over their later born (younger) counterparts.

The final set of results concerns the multiple league expansions that occurred during our sample period and after the 2004–2005-season-ending-lockout. First we find that league expansions are significant predictors of earnings differentials and growth for players. Moreover, these exogenous shifts in demand for player talent benefit early career players (but not veterans) born into larger birth cohorts as one might come to expect, given the opportunity to capitalize in a new negotiation with a new team based on a higher performance record for the average player. Second, we present evidence that the imposition of the first ever salary cap on teams – which would presumably have slowed earnings growth and perhaps muted any differentials noted above – produced a reversal in the sign of the negative association with the large cohort pre-lockout period. We do not think that these changes are associated with an exogenous increase in the underlying demand for professional players since league size remained constant during this period. This may instead be due in part to the decrease in higher birth rate cohorts relative to the average major, although this is probably only part of the story. Therefore, it appears that the lockout was less of an issue overall for all players regardless of birth cohort and relative age, than we would have expected given the salary cap and other concessions players made to ownership in an effort to restrain salaries and ostensibly to improve competitive balance in the league.

Appendix

Table 12 Unweighted sample coverage: birth month and NHL experience (years)

Birth month	Years in league											
	1	2	3	4	5	6	7	8	9	10	11+	Total
Jan–April	584	641	571	484	399	332	270	221	162	122	270	4,056
May–Aug	436	498	455	384	341	280	230	191	147	115	229	3,306
Sep–Dec	361	402	360	314	265	220	181	149	1114	86	165	2,617
Total	1,381	1,541	1,386	1,182	1,005	832	681	561	423	323	664	9.979

An observation here is a player-year. This table includes only valid earnings observations, defined as a player with experience 1 to 17 seasons with positive annual earnings in 2008 constant dollars. Birth month is the month of birth of the player. Experience is a count of number of seasons observed between1990–1991 and 2007–2008 seasons

Table 13 Unweighted sample coverage: birth rate and NHL experience (years)

Birth rate	Years in league											Total
	1	2	3	4	5	6	7	8	9	10	11+	
Low (<15)	490	600	562	472	378	309	254	189	135	93	169	3,651
Avg (15–17.5)	381	449	413	347	316	270	218	199	151	130	309	3,183
High (>17.5)	511	491	411	363	311	253	209	173	137	100	186	3,145
Total	1,380	1,540	1,386	1,182	1,005	832	681	561	423	323	6,664	9,979

An observation here is a player-year. This table includes only valid earnings observations, defined as a player with experience 1 to 17 seasons with positive annual earnings in 2008 constant dollars. Birth rate is the crude birth rate in the player's year and country of birth. Experience is a count of number of seasons observed between 1990–1991 and 2007–2008 seasons

Data Sources

Our key dependent variable is individual player salaries. The USA Today Sports Salaries Database (http://content.usatoday.com/sportsdata/hockey/nhl/salaries/team/) provides player salaries by player by team going back to 2000. For earlier seasons we rely on a time-intensive search of the HockeyZonePlus database which allows one to view the salary history of an individual player since player salaries became public in 1989,[13] by entering the player's last name (http://www.hockey-zoneplus.com/bizdb/nhl-salaries-search.htm). Historical player demographic and performance data was obtained from the official NHL league website (http://www.nhl.com/ice/playerstats.htm).

Birth rate data was obtained from the United Nations Statistics Division's *Demographic Yearbook* (http://unstats.un.org/unsd/demographic/products/dyb/dyb2.htm) which provides crude birth rate data for the countries and the birth years present in our sample of players (1951–1989). Despite having 46 birth countries in our sample of NHL players, we collected birth rate data only for the following countries/regions (Canada, US, Sweden, Russia, Finland, Czech Republic, Slovakia, Former Soviet Republics, and Rest of Europe). A few players born in places like Jamaica or South Korea etc. where there is no history of amateur hockey, were tracked down and found to have been players brought up in Canada or the US and hence assigned birth rates for those countries in the sample period.

---

[13] This was the result of a demand made by the national Hockey League Players Association (NHLPA) in one of the first rounds of bargaining that did not involve Alan Eagleson as head of the NHLPA. Pay secrecy clearly favoured the NHL owners and this move was one reason NHL player salaries began to slowly converge to the rest of the North American player salaries in the 1990s and 2000s. Eagleson was convicted of fraud and collusion with owners in restraining player salary demands.

References

Arnett, J.J. (2000): Emerging adulthood: A theory of development from the late teens through the twenties. American Psychologist, 55(5), pp. 469–480.

Bachman, R., T.K. Bauer and P. David (2009): Cohort Wage Effects and Job Mobility Working Paper 5035, Bonn: Institute for the Study of Labor.

Barnsley, R.H., A.H. Thompson and P.E. Barnsley (1985): Hockey success and birthdate: The relative age effect. Canadian Association of Health, Physical Education and Recreation Journal, 51, pp. 23–28.

Berger, M.C. (1985): The Effect of Cohort Size on Earnings Growth: A Re-examination of the Evidence. Journal of Political Economy, 93(3), pp. 561–573.

Berger, M.C. (1989): Demographic cycles, cohort size, and earnings. Demography, 26(2), pp. 311–321.

Bloom, D.E., R.B. Freeman and S. Korenman (1987): The Labor Market Consequences of Generational Crowding. European Journal of Population, 3, pp. 131–176.

Brunello, G. (2010): The Effects of Cohort Size on European Earnings. Journal of Population Economics, 23(1), pp. 273–290.

Buschemann, A., and Deutscher, C. (2011). "Did the 2005 collective bargaining agreement really improve team efficiency in the NHL?" International Journal of Sport Finance, 6(1), 298–306.

Deaner R.O., A. Lowen and S. Cobley (2013): Born at the Wrong Time: Selection Bias in the NHL Draft. PLoS ONE 8(2): e57753. doi:https://doi.org/10.1371/journal.pone.0057753

Easterlin, R.A. (1987): Birth and Fortune: The Impact of Numbers on Personal Welfare, Chicago: Chicago University Press.

Foot, D. and D. Stoffman (2001): Boom, Bust & Echo: Profiting from the Demographic Shift in the 21st Century, Toronto: Stoddart.

Freeman, R. (1979): The Effect of Demographic Factors on Age-Earnings Profiles. Journal of Human Resources, 14, pp. 289–318.

Frick, B. (2009). "Globalization and Fcator Mobility: The Impact of the "Bosman-Ruling" on Player Migration in Professional Soccer." Journal of Sports Economics, 10(1): 88–106.

Gibbs, B.G., J.A. Jarvis and M.J. Dufur (2012): The rise of the underdog? The relative age effect reversal among Canadian-born NHL hockey players: A reply to Nolan and Howell. International Review for the Sociology of Sport, 47, pp. 644–649.

Gladwell, M (2008). Outliers: The Story of Success. New York: Little, Brown and Company.

Grondin S., P. Deshaies et L.P. Nault (1984): Trimestre de naissance et participation au hockey et au volleyball. Le revue Quebecoise de l'activite physique, 2, pp. 97–103.

Idson, T. and L H. Kahane (2000): Team Effects on Compensation: An Application to Salary Determination in the National Hockey League. Economic Inquiry, 28, pp. 345–357.

Kahn, L (1993). "Free Agency, Long-Term Contracts and Compensation in Major League Baseball: Estimates from Panel Data" The Review of Economics and Statistics, 75(1): 157–64.

Korenman, Sanders and David Neumark. (2000). "Cohort Crowding and Youth Labor Markets (A Cross-National Analysis)" in Youth Employment and Joblessness in Advanced Countries, David Blanchflower and Richard Freeman (eds), NBER: pp 57–106.

Morin, L.-P. (2013): Cohort Size and Youth Earnings: Evidence from a Quasi-Experiment, Working Paper, Vancouver School of Economics.

Murphy, K.M., M. Plant and F. Welch (1988): Cohort Size and Earnings in the United States, in: Economics of Changing Age Distributions in Developing Countries, ed. by R.D. Lee, W.B. Arthur and G. Rodgers, pp. 39–58, Oxford: Oxford University Press.

Musch J. and S. Grondin (2001): Unequal competition as an impediment to personal development: A review of the relative age effect in sport. Developmental Review, 21, pp. 147–167.

Musch, J. and R. Hay (1999): The relative age effecting soccer: Cross-cultural evidence for a systematic discrimination against children born late in the competition year. Sociology of Sport Journal, 16, pp. 54–64.

Nolan J, and G.Howell (2010) "Hockey success and birth date: The relative age effect revisited." International Review for the Sociology of Sport 4(3): 507–512.

Pampel, F.C. and H.E. Peters (1995): The Easterlin Effect. Annual Review of Sociology, 21, pp. 163–194.

Rosen, S. (1972) "Learning and Experience in the Labor Market", The Journal of Human Resources, 7, 3: 326–242.

Welch, F. (1979): Effects of Cohort Size on Earnings: The Baby Boom Babies' Financial Bust. Journal of Political Economy, 87(5), pp. S65–S97.

Wright, R.E. (1991): Cohort Size and Earnings in Great Britain. Journal of Population Economics, 4(4), pp. 295–305.

Wattie N, Baker J, Cobley S, and Montelpare WJ (2007). "A historical examination of relative age effects in Canadian hockey players." International Journal of Sport Psychology 38(2): 178–186.

Part III
Diversity and Discrimination

If You Can Play, You Get the Pay!? A Survey on Salary Discrimination in the NHL

Petra Nieken and Michael Stegh

Abstract The chapter reviews studies investigating salary discrimination in the National Hockey League. The vast majority of studies concentrate on potential discrimination of French-Canadian players compared to English-Canadian players with some also taking salary differences between US and European players into account. The findings presented in the available studies differ considerably and are, therefore, difficult to reconcile. There is limited evidence for salary discrimination of French-Canadian players playing for English-Canadian teams. While some studies do find support for salary discrimination, others fail to find statistically significant salary differences that can be attributed to a player's ethnicity.

> *"Neither the NHLPA, the NHL, nor any Club shall discriminate in the interpretation or application of this Agreement against or in favor of any Player because of religion, race, disability, color, national origin, sex, sexual orientation, age, marital status, or membership or non-membership in or support of or non-support of any labor organization."* (Collective Bargaining Agreement between National Hockey League and National Hockey League Players' Association, September 16, 2012–September 15, 2022, Article 7.2)

Introduction

Issues of labor market discrimination in professional sports have always raised public interest (see for instance Bondy 2014). Typically, professional sports are perceived as offering equal opportunities for minorities and almost every league has adopted a code of conduct which explicitly intends to prevent any form of discrimination against minorities. Nevertheless, incidents of discrimination are manifold

---

P. Nieken (✉)
Karlsruhe Institute of Technology, Institute of Management, Karlsruhe, Germany
e-mail: petra.nieken@kit.edu

M. Stegh
Faculty of Economics and Management, University of Magdeburg, Magdeburg, Germany
e-mail: michael.stegh@gmail.com

and reach from subtle discrimination to open assaults like racial or ethnic slurs or throwing bananas on the field.

Economists have studied labor market discrimination such as salary or hiring discrimination in sport leagues for decades (for an overview see, e.g., Kahn 1991). In contrast to company and firm level data, information on worker productivity, output produced, payroll, and team composition is recorded and easily accessible in sports. Sports data, therefore, are well suited to study issues of discrimination.

In the major US leagues, the share of black players is about 80% in the National Basketball Association (NBA), 67% in the National Football League (NFL), and 8% in Major League Baseball (MLB). However, a high level of minority representation does not automatically rule out possible discrimination against members of minorities in these leagues. Research regarding those three major leagues almost exclusively focuses on issues of racial discrimination. In contrast, studies investigating discrimination in the National Hockey League (NHL) focus on national origin and/or ethnicity as possible sources of discrimination. While the NHL is rather homogeneous with respect to skin tone, the league is nevertheless ethnically more diverse than the other major sports leagues in the US. The majority of players have an English-Canadian background while French-Canadians, US-Americans, and Europeans (including Russians) form the minorities in the league. Players with other ethnic backgrounds are quite rare. Hence, discrimination in the NHL might occur due to cultural, political, or linguistic factors. In his book, former hockey player Robert (Bob) Sirois (2010) has argued that French-Canadian players suffer from various forms of discrimination such as a lower probability to be drafted, lower wages, and shorter careers than similar English-Canadian players.[1]

The literature typically focuses on either entry or salary discrimination. Entry or hiring discrimination means that players belonging to minorities face higher entry barriers making it harder for them to receive a contract. Lavoie et al. (1987), Krashinsky (1989), Lavoie et al. (1989), Walsh (1992), Lavoie (2003), and Longley (2003) as well as Kahane (2005) investigate the issue of entry barriers in the NHL (for a summary see Longley 2012). By contrast, salary discrimination can only occur if the players have already signed a contract. Thus, we speak of salary discrimination only if players are paid less than equally productive other players in the league. In the current survey, we focus on studies investigating salary discrimination in the NHL.

The empirical results regarding salary discrimination are rather ambiguous. While some studies find evidence of salary discrimination, mostly against French-Canadians and especially French-Canadian defensemen, others find none. The results vary by player position, investigated season and the specification of the underlying regression models. There is no consensus about the appropriate empirical model and both, sparse and dense models are used. A possible misspecification of the empirical model might also explain the mixed findings in the literature. The share of French-Canadian and European players, especially in teams located in

---

[1] The book was originally published in French.

English-Canada, is rather low. Thus, the results involving those players are highly sensitive to outliers and the small sample size is especially problematic if the data used to estimate the regression models covers only one season. Therefore, the findings reported in the literature have to be regarded with caution as few outliers (e.g., a French-Canadian superstar) might have a considerable impact on the results.

The dominant empirical approach is to use salary and performance data from one particular season and estimate a Mincer-style earnings function. Typically, the natural logarithm of salary is regressed on various parameters indicating the productivity of a player. The productivity parameters are taken from official game reports and include player attributes such as weight and height as well as career points per game, career penalty minutes per game and/or the draft number. A dummy variable (or a series thereof) indicating the ethnicity of the players usually serves as a proxy for possible discrimination. While the first papers only took the ethnicity of the players into account, later studies focused on the interaction between a player's ethnicity and the location of his team. As Longley (1995) argues, controlling for the players' ethnicity only might yield biased coefficients. If, for instance, one only includes in the estimation a dummy variable indicating whether a player is French-Canadian or not, the underlying assumption is that all teams are equally likely to discriminate against players with that particular ethnic background. However, there is no reason to believe that French-Canadian teams discriminate against French-Canadian players. Therefore, Longley (1995) and others take both into account, a player's ethnicity and the location of the team. However, if the variables used to measure performance do not indicate the player's impact on winning sufficiently, those earnings models might be biased, too (see Kahn 1991; Szymanski 2000 for a detailed discussion). Especially the argument that players coming from a different cultural background simply "do not fit" in a team and therefore ethnicity determines part of the players' productivity is hard to refute.

Another approach is to use a market model instead of an earnings model. The basic idea is that if discrimination occurs, a discriminating team has to pay the price by accepting a lower win percentage for each dollar spent on salaries. Usually a team's productivity is measured by the number of regular season wins divided by the number of matches played which is then regressed on payroll variables as well as the percentage of players from a certain ethnic background relative to the league average. If there is no salary discrimination, the latter variable should not have any impact on the team's win probability. If, however, the ethnicity variable has a positive significant effect, this suggests that increasing the share of players from the respective ethnicity would significantly increase the team's winning probability. While the market-based approach partly overcomes the problems of the earnings based approach, it also has several shortcomings that might bias the results. For instance, the implementation of a salary cap violates the assumption that the teams' payroll can be used as a predictor of their winning probability. While this potential problem can be mitigated by adding further controls, the problem that a particular team's management might be less efficient than others in translating inputs (e.g. player talent) into output (e.g. wins) cannot be accounted for (for a more detailed discussion, see Mongeon 2015).

The remainder of the survey is organized as follows. We discuss the concept of discrimination and its different forms in the section "Discrimination" and provide some background information on the National Hockey League and the players in section "Background and Changes in the NHL." The section "Results" contains the results of our literature survey. Section "Conclusion" concludes with some recommendations for future research.

Discrimination

Before we start investigating possible effects of player discrimination in hockey and especially in the NHL, we need a definition of the term "discrimination." Based on the theoretical work starting with Becker (1957) and Scully (1974), we speak of discrimination if a member of a minority group is treated differently (in general unfavorably) than a member of another (the majority) group if both individuals have the same productive characteristics. Thus, if players in hockey (or any other team sport) with identical productivity are not treated equally by potential employers, team-mates, coaches, and/or fans, we call this discrimination. However, it is difficult to find players who are identical with respect to the relevant productivity characteristics.

Economists typically distinguish between taste-based discrimination and statistical discrimination. Statistical discrimination (see Arrow 1972 for an early contribution) means that an employer has imperfect information about the productivity of potential employees and uses easily observable characteristics such as gender or race to make hiring decisions. In contrast, taste-based discrimination (as for instance discussed by Becker 1957) means that someone has "a taste" for discrimination and requires a compensation for hiring or working with an individual he "dislikes." While both forms of discrimination are not easy to disentangle, the literature discussed in this survey usually focuses on taste-based discrimination. Following Becker (1957), we distinguish between:

- Employer discrimination: The employer has "a taste" for discrimination and tries to avoid employing individuals from certain minorities. Disliked employees either have to "compensate" the employer by accepting lower salaries, or, when earning the same salary, have to display a higher productivity than members of the respective majority group.
- Co-worker discrimination: Co-workers and team-mates do not like to work with individuals from certain minorities and demand a salary premium or other forms of compensation from the employer when working alongside those individuals.
- Customer-based discrimination: Customers, e.g. fans and sponsors, do not like to deal with employees from certain minorities. In hockey, customer-based discrimination means that fans and sponsors dislike watching players from a different cultural and ethnic background.

It is often difficult to identify what form of discrimination is really at work. For instance, employers might be reluctant to hire individuals from minorities simply because potential co-workers dislike working alongside them. Moreover, employers might anticipate the preferences of customers and therefore discriminate against a certain minority to maximize the revenues from ticket sales and merchandising. Thus, in some cases, the first impression that discrimination is employer-based can be misleading and hiding the true sources of discrimination.

The literature discusses several reasons for taste-based discrimination. With respect to hockey, gender or race do not play a (major) role but cultural background and different ethnicities might be an issue. Discrimination by team owners and managers can simply be due to personal prejudices or a reaction to prejudices of fans or media. Based on media reports and the previous literature, we briefly discuss arguments often brought forward to explain salary differences between English-Canadian and players from other ethnic backgrounds. Frequently, prejudices solely refer to French-Canadians which are often called a "nation within a nation." The group of Canadian players is not homogeneous and the French- and the English-Canadian society differ in many aspects such as geography, language, and culture. Roughly 20% of the Canadians belong to the French-Canadian population and most of them live in the province of Quebec. There are a lot of tensions between both groups which have manifested themselves in various attempts of French-Canada to become independent of English-Canada (Longley 2000). In contrast, English-Canadian and US players share the same language and a similar culture even though they live in different nations. Another group suffering from prejudices are Europeans (including Russians) who also do not share the same culture and language.

One potential explanation for performance differences are differences with respect to the style of play (see e.g., Lavoie et al. 1992). When Europeans started to enter the league, the style of North American hockey was usually described as more defensive and physical while the European style was characterized as more offensive. Given the particular emphasis on defense, player attributes such as physical strength, body checking, height and weight were considered important in American hockey while the European style called for skills such as skating and stick-handling. Over time, both styles have converged: American hockey has become more team-oriented and European teams now also emphasize developing physical strength and the defense of the game. However, European players are still believed to be intimidated by the more physical and rough style of play in the NHL. Similar arguments have been brought forward regarding French-Canadian players. They are also perceived as being reluctant to fight and to lack height and weight to engage in defensive work (see e.g., Longley 2000). Those stereotypes regarding style of play are particularly important for defensemen. While the performance of goaltenders and forwards can easily be measured by statistics, there is a higher uncertainty about the quality of defensemen.[2]

---

[2] Potential discrimination of defensemen due to less reliable performance data might therefore also be explained by statistical discrimination (see Kahn 1991).

Another important argument is discussed by the reservation wage hypothesis (Lavoie et al. 1992) which assumes that the fallback option for minorities is less comfortable. For French-Canadians or Europeans it might be harder to find another team that pays an equal or even a higher salary. This, in turn, might induce them to sign contracts including less favorable compensation packages.

Finally, Krashinsky (1989) offers an alternative explanation for the lower salaries of French-Canadians that is based on language skills. While English-Canadians as well as US players share the same language and a similar cultural background, French-Canadians and Europeans speak a different language and come from different cultural backgrounds. This might be a source of discrimination in itself and, in addition, lack of language skills might make it more difficult for the player to communicate and interact with team-mates and to follow the orders of the head coach. Thus, if a player does not "fit" due to language barriers, a lower pay might simply reflect a lower productivity.

Background and Changes in the NHL

In the following, we give a brief overview of the organizational structure of the NHL and its changes over time that might have had an influence on the extent of either entry or salary discrimination such as e.g. changes in draft rules and the entry of new teams in the league.

In the 2013–2014 season the NHL consisted of 30 member teams with 7 teams located in Canada and 23 in the US. The league is divided in two conferences, the Eastern (16 teams) and the Western Conference (14 teams), which are both divided in two equally large divisions. Three out of the seven Canadian teams play in the Atlantic Division of the Eastern Conference (Montreal Canadians, Ottawa Senators, and Toronto Maple Leafs), three play in the Pacific Division of the Western Conference (Calgary Flames, Edmonton Oilers, and Vancouver Canucks) while one team, the Winnipeg Jets, is playing in the Central Division of the Western Conference. Most of the current member teams are located outside Canada. Only one team is located in Quebec and considered French-Canadian, the Montreal Canadians.

When the NHL was founded in 1917 in Montreal (Canada), all teams were located in Canada. The founding teams are the Montreal Canadians, Montreal Wanderers, Ottawa Senators, and Quebec Bulldogs. The latter team did not survive the first season. A new team, the Toronto Arena, was formed to guarantee a balanced schedule. Thus, in the inaugural season in 1917–1918, the league had four members; two of them were located in Montreal, one in Toronto, and one in Ottawa. In 1924, the first US team, the Boston Bruins, joined the league. During the following years the league first grew, but was then reduced again to six teams in 1942–1943. Those six teams continued to form the league for the next 25 years (Boston Bruins, Chicago Black Hawks, Detroit Red Wings, Montreal Canadians, New York Rangers, and Toronto Maple Leafs).

After the mid-1960s, the league grew again, adding six teams, all located in the US, in 1967. In an attempt to balance the number of teams located in Canada and the US, the league added the Vancouver Canucks shortly after that (and the Buffalo Sabres close to the Canadian border as well). Later the league was joined by four other teams raising the number to a total of 18. This number varied over the years. The NHL added teams in the South of the US in the 1990s in an attempt to gain access to new markets, e.g. Anaheim, Atlanta, Miami, Nashville, San Jose, and Tampa. However, the traditional teams are still located in Canada and in the North of the US.

Over the years, the NHL either had one or two teams located in the province of Quebec. Today, the only French-Canadian team is the Montreal Canadians. In the founding year, two teams playing in the NHL were located in Montreal, the Montreal Canadians and the Montreal Wanderers. The latter team only played one season in the NHL and then folded. During the 1919–1920 season, the Quebec Athletics (formerly known as the Quebec Bulldogs) were part of the league. The team was renamed Hamilton Tigers and moved to Hamilton in 1920. Although the Montreal Maroons were founded in Montreal too, they were considered to target the English-Canadian fan base and form a counterbalance to the Montreal Canadians who traditionally target the French-Canadian fans. The Montreal Maroons entered the league in 1924 and left after 1938. The Quebec Nordiques were located in Quebec City and played in the NHL from 1979 to 1995. They have been considered a French-Canadian team until the franchise was sold and relocated to Denver after 1995.

Even though most teams of the NHL are located in the US, players of US origin are a minority in the NHL. In the 2013–2014 season, roughly 25% of the players were from the US (see e.g., quanthockey.com). The NHL is the only major league in the US where players of US origin are not in the majority. Furthermore, the league is rather homogenous with respect to race as the majority of the players are of Caucasian decent while the other US leagues usually employ a larger share of black players with African-American background. During the last 10 years the number of US players has increased rapidly (in the early 2000s the percentage of US players in the NHL was around 15%). The majority of the players are still born in Canada (52%) and they traditionally form the majority in the league. The absolute dominance of Canadians began to crumble during the 1970s when more and more US players entered the league. However, Canadian players still have a dominant position and hockey continues to be an extremely popular sport in Canada. However, the group of Canadian players is not homogeneous in itself; the majority of the Canadian players have an English-Canadian background while a substantial minority has a French-Canadian background (roughly 10 % of the players in the league are French-Canadian). Traditionally, French-Canadian players had a massive influence in the league (e.g. Guy Lafleur or Mario Lemieux). Historically, most of the French-Canadian players played for the only French-Canadian team, the Montreal Canadians. While there was no draft system before 1967, the Montreal Canadians had the first right to choose from the French-Canadian amateur players from the Quebec region. Even after they lost that privilege, the share of French-Canadians playing for the Montreal Canadians remained rather high.

Players from Europe and other parts of the world are still the smallest group on the rosters of the NHL teams. Most European players come from either Finland or Sweden where hockey has a long tradition. Players from Eastern European countries such as the Czech Republic, Slovakia, and the former states of the Soviet Union joined the league in larger numbers after the cold war had ended.

Despite the fact that US players form a large minority in the NHL teams, empirical studies investigating entry and/or salary discrimination focus on the possible discrimination of French-Canadians and (to a lesser extent) Europeans in the league. In contrast to players of US origin, those two groups do not share the cultural background and language with the English-Canadian majority.

Results

In the following section, we summarize selected studies, highlight their findings and discuss their strengths and shortcomings from an economic as well as an econometric point of view (for a synthesis see Table 1).

An early contribution investigating salary discrimination in the National Hockey League is the work of Jones and Walsh (1988) using data from the 1977 to 1978 NHL season with information on 306 players. The dataset includes the players' salaries (as published by the Toronto Global Mail), productivity measures, individual characteristics, and franchise information. Because different positions in hockey require different skills, the authors split the dataset and estimate their models separately for forwards, defensemen, and goaltenders (n = 189 forwards, 89 defensemen, and 32 goaltenders). The productivity measures for the skaters (forwards and defensemen) are their career points per game while those of the goaltenders are the number of career goals received per game. In addition, penalty minutes are used to control for good defense work.[3] The authors also control for weight and height of the players and characteristics of the franchise. The discrimination measure is a dummy variable which equals one if a player was born in Quebec and had a French name indicating that he is francophone. The authors report that differences in individual productivity explain most of the salary variation for all positions. They do not find evidence of salary discrimination against forwards or goaltenders. However, francophone defensemen were found to earn significantly less than other defensemen (however, only 11 out of the 89 defenders in the sample were francophone). Interestingly, the level of statistical significance of that coefficient decreases from 5% to 10% (one-tailed test) if the franchise controls are omitted. The authors admit that the quality of the salary data may be questioned as the figures have been taken from newspaper reports (salary data were not released officially before January 1990) and that, therefore, the results should be regarded with caution. In a second step, the authors argue that salary discrimination against French-Canadians should not occur if the players have signed a contract with a French-Canadian team (only

---

[3] Note that the popular "plus-minus-statistics" have not been available prior to 1977–1978.

Table 1 Overview of studies investigating salary discrimination in the NHL

Authors	Sample years	# FC-teams	Data level	Observations Total	By position	By ethnicity	Discrimination
Jones and Walsh (1988)	1977–1978	1	Player	N = 306	N_F = 185	$N_{F\text{-}nFC}$ = 147 $N_{F\text{-}FC}$ = 38 $N_{D\text{-}nFC}$ = 78 $N_{D\text{-}FC}$ = 11 $N_{G\text{-}nFC}$ = 20 $N_{G\text{-}FC}$ = 12	Yes
					N_D = 89		
					N_G = 32		
McLean and Veall (1992)	1989–1990 performance data	2	Player	N = 510	N_F = 301	$N_{F\text{-}BC}$ = 181 $N_{F\text{-}FC}$ = 36 $N_{F\text{-}US}$ = 53 $N_{F\text{-}EU}$ = 31	No
	1990–1991 salary data				N_D = 159	$N_{D\text{-}BC}$ = 93 $N_{D\text{-}FC}$ = 19 $N_{D\text{-}US}$ = 26 $N_{D\text{-}EU}$ = 21	
					N_G = 50	$N_{G\text{-}BC}$ = 36 $N_{G\text{-}FC}$ = 8 $N_{G\text{-}US}$ = 6 $N_{G\text{-}EU}$ = 0	
Longley (1995)	1989–1990	2	Player	N = 250	N_F = 250	$N_{F\text{-}BC}$ = 172 $N_{F\text{-}FC}$ = 22 $N_{F\text{-}US}$ = 38 $N_{F\text{-}EU}$ = 18	Yes
Krashinsky and Krashinsky (1997)	1989–1990	2	Player	See Longley (1995)			No
Longley (1997)	1989–1990	2	Player	See Longley (1995)			Yes

(continued)

Table 1 (continued)

Authors	Sample years	# FC-teams	Data level	Observations Total	By position	By ethnicity	Discrimination
Jones et al. (1999)	1989–1990	2	Player	N = 431	$N_F = 250$ $N_D = 138$ $N_G = 43$		No
Lavoie (2000)	1993–1994	2	Player	N = 486	$N_F = 308$ $N_D = 178$		Yes
Szymanski and Longley (2001)	1989–1995	2	Team	N = 218		$N_{EC} = 43$ $N_{FC} = 21$ $N_{US} = 154$	Mixed
	1996–1998	1					
Curme and Daugherty (2004)	1999–2000	1	Player	N = 563		$N_{EC} = 266$ $N_{FC} = 62$ $N_{US} = 86$ $N_{EU} = 149$	Yes
Bruggink and Williams (2009)	1999–2002 perf. data	1	Player	N = 439	$N_F = 282$	$N_{F\text{-}EC} = 134$ $N_{F\text{-}FC} = 23$ $N_{F\text{-}US} = 49$ $N_{F\text{-}EU} = 76$	Mixed
	2002–2003 salary data				$N_D = 157$	$N_{D\text{-}EC} = 72$ $N_{D\text{-}FC} = 10$ $N_{D\text{-}US} = 24$ $N_{D\text{-}EU} = 51$	
Mongeon (2015)	2010–2011	1	Game and share of players	N = 1230		$N_{EC} = 49\%$ $N_{FC} = 6\%$ $N_{US} = 23\%$ $N_{INT} = 22\%$	Yes

F Forward, *D* Defender, *G* Goaltender, *EC* English-Canadian, *FC* French-Canadian, *US* US-American, *EU* European, *INT* International

one team was located in Quebec in the respective season) and, therefore, divide their dataset further: Three out of the 11 French-Canadian defensemen played for the Montreal Canadians and the remaining 8 played outside of Quebec. For the former the authors do not find statistical evidence of salary discrimination, but for the latter they observe salaries that are indicative of discrimination. However, due to the very small number of observations the results should be treated with caution as statistical analyses based on such small numbers are known to be sensitive to individual outliers.

McLean and Veall (1992) use performance data from the 1989 to 1990 season to examine entry and salary discrimination of French-Canadians in the NHL. They match these data with salary data from the following season 1990–1991 as salaries usually reflect past performance. Similar to Jones and Walsh (1988) they split their dataset into forwards, defensemen, and goaltenders and control for player attributes such as weight, height, and points scored. For defensemen, they add the individuals' "plus-minus-statistics." Furthermore, they define separate groups of players reflecting their cultural background (English-Canadians, French-Canadians, US-Americans, and Europeans). They only find evidence for salary discrimination of European and US forwards as for these two subgroups the respective coefficients are negative and statistically significant. However, McLean and Veall (1992) are unable to replicate the finding by Jones and Walsh (1988) that French-Canadian defensemen suffer from salary discrimination.

Longley (1995) also uses data from the 1989 to 1990 season and concentrates on forwards. The main difference to previous studies is that he takes both, the origin of the player and the location of the team, systematically into account in his estimation strategy.[4] Assuming that French-Canadians should not be treated as one homogenous group (some of them play for a team located in Quebec, others for a team in the rest of Canada or the US) he argues that French-Canadian players should not be discriminated against if they play for a French-Canadian team. Hence, estimating the models without adequately controlling for the player-team-match might lead to biased coefficients in the sense that the models might fail to document the true extent of salary discrimination against French-Canadians playing for NHL teams located outside Quebec. On the other hand, however, French-Canadian teams might also discriminate against English-Canadian players. Consequently, Longley (1995) includes in his estimations dummy variables reflecting the individual player's region of origin (French-Canadians, Europeans, and US-Americans) as well as dummy variables reflecting the location of the team (Quebec-based, English-Canadian-based, and US-based teams). He also includes interaction terms to control for every possible combination of a player's origin and his current team's location. This results in 12 different categories allowing him to better answer the question if minorities playing for teams that are located outside their own cultural/ethnic sphere are generally discriminated against. For example, Europeans form a minority in all

---

[4] Jones and Walsh (1988) do not consider team location adequately. They only investigate whether French-Canadian defensemen playing outside Quebec are treated differently from those playing in Quebec.

NHL teams. If discrimination is simply based on membership in a minority group one should find salary discrimination against Europeans in all teams. Longley (1995) reports significant salary discrimination against French-Canadian players playing for English-Canadian teams while he does not find robust effects for other minorities. Notably he finds no salary discrimination against French-Canadian players playing for teams located in the US. He conjectures that language or cultural barriers cannot be the source of discrimination because those barriers should also affect the performance of French-Canadian players in the US. The political tension between French-Canada and English-Canada and the resulting social tensions might be a plausible explanation. Longley (1995) suggests that discrimination is likely to be either customer-based, e.g. the fans of English-Canadian teams having a "taste for discrimination" against French-Canadian players (while fans of US teams seem not to discriminate) or employer-based, e.g. coaches and managers having a preference for underpaying French-Canadian players. Again, the results have to be regarded with caution as only 22 out of the 250 players in the dataset are of French-Canadian origin and only 5 of them play for an English-Canadian team.

Krashinsky and Krashinsky (1997) criticize the small sample size of Longley's (1995) study and suggest analyzing data of more than one season to mitigate this problem. They also argue that the causality is not clear and that the findings presented in the literature might suffer from an omitted variable bias, i.e. previous findings might reflect differences in unmeasured player characteristics rather than discrimination due to French-Canadian origin: Four out of five of the French-Canadian players in Longley's (1995) sample were by then quite young and usually young players earn less than they are worth to their clubs. Additionally, four out of the five played for the Toronto Maple Leafs. Thus, even if there is salary discrimination, it might be team-specific rather than a general problem (in the period under investigation the Toronto Maple Leafs had a total payroll well below the average of the other NHL teams).

In his reply, Longley (1997) presents various robustness checks of his initial findings admitting that the Toronto Maple Leafs indeed systematically underpaid their players. After adding dummies for French-Canadians playing for the Toronto Maple Leafs (four players) and for the Non-French-Canadians (eight players), he finds again that the coefficient of the dummy for the French-Canadians playing for the Toronto Maple Leafs is negative and statistically significant while the coefficient of the dummy for the non-French-Canadians is not significant. While this supports Longley's initial results, the problems associated with the small sample size still persists.

Jones et al. (1999) use the same dataset as the authors quoted so far (covering the 1989–1990 season), but add a large set of control variables. They concentrate on forwards and defensemen and control for various player characteristics and skill variables, such as e.g. career goals per game, penalty minutes, weight, height, and the draft number of a player. Moreover, they add controls to capture the market structure of the NHL and use several variables (including interaction terms) reflecting a player's ethnic background to disentangle different sources of discrimination. If, for instance, the language barrier is the underlying cause of salary discrimination, this effect should be stronger for younger (non-veteran) French-Canadian players than for experienced (veteran) players. The latter should have obtained sufficient language skills during their career to pass as bilingual. If, on the other hand, the salary is driven by fan-based discrimination, salaries of players with a different ethnicity than the respective fan base should be lower. Summarizing, the authors do not find significant evidence of salary discrimination against French-Canadians in their data and conclude that salary is basically determined by the skills of a player and respective team's market.

Lavoie (2000) follows the approach adopted by Longley (1995) to investigate salary discrimination with a focus on player ethnicity and team locations. He uses data from the 1993 to 1994 season for forwards as well as defenders. In contrast to Longley (1995), the number of interaction terms in the estimations is reduced, but additional controls such as e.g. all-star-nominations were added. The results obtained for forwards are qualitatively similar to the ones presented by Longley (1995). All coefficients for non-local players (French-Canadian, US, and European players) are negatively signed if the reference category is English-Canadian players playing for English-Canadian teams. However, this effect is only significant for US players, but not for French-Canadian or European players. The findings for defensemen are quite similar. Even though most coefficients in the various regressions fail to reach statistical significance, the overall picture suggests that customer-based discrimination is not only an issue for French-Canadian players in English-Canadian teams, but a more general phenomenon. However, as the authors point out, this conclusion awaits further empirical support as the results of this study are ambiguous and more research using data from several seasons is required to either support or challenge the robustness of the findings.

Szymanski and Longley (2001) use a market- based approach with data from ten consecutive seasons (1989–1998). As the distribution of French-Canadian players across NHL teams is quite uneven with the majority of them playing for French-Canadian teams, the authors test whether the share of French-Canadian players affects a team's performance. Team performance is measured by the win percentage during the regular season, which is regressed on a team's wage bill and player composition. The wage expenditures are calculated by a team's payroll relative to the league's average payroll. Discrimination is measured by the number of games played by French-Canadian players in the respective team's roster relative to the average in the NHL. If there is salary discrimination against French-Canadian players, teams with an above average share of French-Canadian players would perform better than teams with a below average share, given an identical payroll. The authors estimate OLS- and Fixed Effects models and find mixed results. While the OLS- and Fixed Effects models fail to show signs of discrimination against French-Canadians, estimations with region-specific fixed effects reveal evidence of (potential) discrimination. Hence, even using data covering various seasons does not lead to clear-cut results.

Curme and Daugherty (2004) again use an earnings model and follow Longley's (1995) approach to include both, player ethnicity and team location. They conjecture that salary discrimination should be absent (or at least lower) for players who have become free agents by discussing a number of reasons for salary discrimination in a non-competitive labor market where teams have monopsony power. However, with increasing tenure in the NHL, players are likely to become free agents enabling them to sell their services to the highest bidder (e.g. the best paying team). Thus, younger players should be more likely to suffer from salary discrimination than more experienced ones with longer tenure. The analysis with salary data from the 1999 to 2000 season including skaters only reveals that French-Canadian players earn 37% less than their English-Canadian teammates in English-Canadian teams. Those findings are similar to Longley's (1995) and Lavoie's (2000) results. After further dividing the dataset into "older" and "younger" players, the authors find the opposite of what they expected. Salary discrimination seems to be larger for "older" French-Canadian players in English-Canadian teams than for "younger" ones. Hence, free agency does not help to reduce salary discrimination. However, the authors admit that splitting the dataset results in two rather small databases and remind the reader to treat the results accordingly.

While the focus of the studies quoted so far is on salary discrimination of French-Canadians, Bruggink and Williams (2009) focus on European players. Following the estimation strategy developed by Curme and Daugherty (2004), they use salary data from the 2002 to 2003 season for skaters and regress the log of annual salary on dummies reflecting the players' place of birth, team location and various controls for physical attributes, individual performance, and team revenues (the performance information is averages from the 1999 to 2002 seasons). The authors estimate regressions for the pooled data as well as for forwards and defensemen separately. Their results show little evidence of salary discrimination in the NHL against European players.

In a recent paper, Mongeon (2015) uses a market-based approach similar to Szymanski and Longley (2001) to investigate potential salary discrimination of French-Canadian, European and US players playing for teams in different locations. He uses data from the 2010 to 2011 season and a game-level panel data approach to estimate different specifications. The observation unit in this study is a game for a respective team (game-team-combination) and the dependent variable is either binary, indicating if a team won or lost, or continuous (two if a team won during regular time, one if there was a draw after regular time, and zero if the team lost in regular time). Mongeon (2015) estimates Weighted Least Squares, Instrumental Variable, and Random Effects models to document the robustness of his results. He uses two different measures of player input. The first is game-level information, namely the relative share of game-team players on the starting roster. The second uses within-game information, i.e. the relative share of game-team player time on ice, to account for changes that occur during a game. Furthermore, Mongeon (2015) adds controls for e.g. the share of the payroll, the share of rookies, and remaining contract length. He first presents the results of estimations not controlling for region-specific effects and then estimations using data disaggregated by region. To avoid perfect multicollinearity, one interaction of player ethnicity and team location has to be omitted. None of the ethnic group dummies are significant in the non-region specific regressions. In contrast, in the regressions where the reference group is

English-Canadian players playing for an English-Canadian team, the coefficient of the dummy for French-Canadian players is positive and significant for both player input variables, the relative share of game-team players on the starting roster as well as for the relative share of game-team player time on ice. Moreover, the dummy for US players on English-Canadian teams is positive and significant as well. These results indicate that increasing the share of French-Canadian and US players on English-Canadian teams would increase their win probability significantly. However, as the author admits, labor market restrictions such as the salary cap and restricted free-agency might bias the coefficients because the market model relies on the assumption that the payroll is directly linked to a team's win probability. The author discusses this and other potential limitations of his approach such as the small number of French-Canadian players on English-Canadian teams or the potential inefficient use of labor inputs in the league.

Conclusion

The question whether members of ethnic minorities suffer from salary discrimination in the NHL is not easy to answer and the discussion is often very passionate. The available evidence is difficult – if not impossible – to reconcile as some studies do find evidence of salary discrimination while others (using the same data from the same season(s)) fail to do so. The relatively small share of French-Canadian and/or European players in English-Canadian teams is a major problem in most of the datasets that have been used so far. Extending the observation period by including multiple seasons to produce a larger dataset is, therefore, urgently required. However, even a larger dataset covering more than two or three seasons can at best mitigate the problem, because changes of rules, labor market restrictions, and lockouts make it difficult to compare data across seasons. The results, therefore, have to be interpreted with caution.

If there is robust evidence for salary discrimination, the important next step is to identify the underlying sources. Different causes of discrimination call for different actions to prevent it. If, for instance, discrimination is employer-based, the organizational structure of the labor market, e.g. draft rules and policies governing free agency, needs to be changed. If there is evidence that co-workers are the source of discrimination, changing the organization of the labor market will not solve the problem. Instead, the aim then has to be to reduce prejudice and resentment for instance with the help of team-building workshops. Customer-based discrimination might be the form of discrimination that is hardest to overcome. If fans dislike players coming from a different ethnic background, it is reasonable for profit-maximizing employers to anticipate and to react to that taste. Fan-based discrimination will lead to both, entry and salary discrimination, as a managerial response to lower revenues from ticket sales and merchandising. To change the perception of ethnic minorities in the eyes of fans is difficult. However, cleverly targeted public relations and media coverage can help to change the public opinion and reduce potential prejudice.

References

Arrow, K. J. (1972): Models of Job Discrimination, in: Racial Discrimination in Economic Life (A.H. Pascal ed.), Lexington, MA: D. C. Heath, pp. 83–102.

Becker, G. S. (1957): The Economics of Discrimination. Chicago: University of Chicago Press.

Bondy, F. (2014): 10 Places Where Racism is Still a Major Issue in Sports, NY Daily News, 03.05.2014.

Bruggink, T. H. and D. Williams (2009): Discrimination Against Europeans in the National Hockey League: Are Players Getting Their Fair Pay? The American Economist, 54 (2), pp. 82–90.

Curme, M. A. and G. M. Daugherty (2004): Competition and Pay for National Hockey League Players Born in Québec. Journal of Sports Economics, 5 (2), pp. 186–205.

Jones, J. C. H., Nadeau, S. and W. D. Walsh (1999): Ethnicity, Productivity and Salary: Player Compensation and Discrimination in the National Hockey League. Applied Economics, 31 (5), pp. 593–608.

Jones, J. C. H. and W. D. Walsh (1988): Salary Determination in the National Hockey League: The Effects of Skills, Franchise Characteristics, and Discrimination. Industrial and Labor Relations Review, 41 (4), pp. 592–604.

Kahane, L. H. (2005): Production Efficiency and Discriminatory Hiring Practices in the National Hockey League: A Stochastic Frontier Approach. Review of Industrial Organization, 27 (1), pp. 47–71.

Kahn, L. M. (1991): Discrimination in Professional Sports: A Survey of the Literature. Industrial and Labor Relations Review, 44 (3), pp. 395–418.

Krashinsky, M. (1989): Do Hockey Teams Discriminate against French Canadians? A Comment on "Discrimination and Performance Differentials in the National Hockey League". Canadian Public Policy, 15 (1), pp. 94–97.

Krashinsky, M. and H. A. Krashinsky (1997): Do English Canadian Hockey Teams Discriminate Against French Canadian Players? Canadian Public Policy, 23 (2), pp. 212–216.

Lavoie, M. (2000): The Location of Pay Discrimination in the National Hockey League. Journal of Sports Economics, 1 (4), pp. 401–411.

Lavoie, M. (2003): The Entry Draft in the National Hockey League: Discrimination, Style of Play, and Team Location. American Journal of Economics and Sociology, 62 (2), p. 383–405.

Lavoie, M., Grenier, G. and S. Coulombe (1987): Discrimination and Performance Differentials in the National Hockey League. Canadian Public Policy, 13 (4), pp. 407–422.

Lavoie, M. Grenier, G. and S. Coulombe (1989): Discrimination versus English Proficiency in the National Hockey League: A Reply. Canadian Public Policy, 15 (1), pp. 98–101.

Lavoie, M., Grenier, G. and S. Coulombe (1992): Comment: Performance Differentials in the National Hockey League: Discrimination versus Style-of-Play Thesis. Canadian Public Policy, 18 (4), pp. 461–469.

Longley, N. (1995): Salary Discrimination in the National Hockey League: The Effects of Team Location. Canadian Public Policy, 21 (4), pp. 413–422.

Longley, N. (1997): Do English Canadian Hockey Teams Discriminate Against French Canadian Players? A Reply. Canadian Public Policy, 23 (2), 217–220.

Longley, N. (2000): The Underrepresentation of French Canadians on English Canadian NHL Teams: Evidence from 1943 to 1998. Journal of Sports Economics, 1 (3), pp. 236–256.

Longley, N. (2003): Measuring Employer-Based Discrimination versus Customer-Based Discrimination: The Case of French Canadians in the National Hockey League. American Journal of Economics and Sociology, 62 (2), pp. 365–381.

Longley, N. (2012): The Economics of Discrimination: Evidence from Hockey, in: The Oxford Handbook of Sports Economics, Volume 2 (S. Schmanske & L. H. Kahane eds.), Oxford University Press, New York, pp. 55–72.

McLean, R. C. and M. R. Veall (1992): Performance and Salary Differentials in the National Hockey League. Canadian Public Policy, 18 (4), pp. 470–475.

Mongeon, K. (2015): A Market Test for Ethnic Discrimination in the National Hockey League: A Game-Level Panel Data Approach. Journal of Sports Economics, 16 (5), pp. 460–481.

Scully, G. W. (1974): Pay and Performance in Major League Baseball. American Economic Review, 64 (6), pp. 915–930.

Sirois, B. (2010): Discrimination in the NHL: Quebec Hockey Players Sidelined. Quebec Canada: Baraka Books.

Szymanski, S. (2000): A Market Test for Discrimination in the English Professional Soccer Leagues. Journal of Political Economy, 108 (3), pp. 590–603.

Szymanski, S. and N. Longley (2001): A Market Test for Discrimination in the National Hockey League, Working Paper.

Walsh, W. D. (1992): The Entry Problem of Francophones in the National Hockey League: A Systemic Interpretation. Canadian Public Policy, 18 (4), pp. 443–460.

The Source of the Cultural or Language Diversity Effects in the National Hockey League

Kevin P. Mongeon and J. Michael Boyle

Abstract This chapter reexamines the impact of cultural and language diversity on the production of winning hockey games to discern the underlying source(s) driving the effects. It makes inferences based on various analyses of micro-level data that include information relating to player interactions, which suggest that the diversity effects are a result of lower off-ice communication costs rather than reduced cultural dominance of the domestic group or on-ice synergies amongst homogeneous players. The inferences are of general interest to managerial economists who can increase firm-level productivity by hiring employees that speak similar languages and share ideas regardless of their cultural background.

Introduction

The relationship between workers in a team and productivity is a central issue in labour and managerial economics. An important aspect of team production is that the intra-team effects outweigh the organizing and information costs to yield outputs larger than the sum of the separable inputs (Alchian and Demsetz 1972). While the labor aspect of the process is generally concerned with the impact on productivity levels, the managerial aspect is concerned with bridging the economic concept with practical application by creating information that can be used to enhance managerial decision making (e.g., Baumol 1962; Allen et al. 1988).

Theoretical frameworks suggest teams of workers can impact firm productivity through the learning and/or sharing of complementary information/skills amongst heterogeneous workers (Lazear 1999a, b; Prat 2002), or through partnerships (Kandel and Lazear 1992) and social ties (Spagnolo 1999) among homogenous workers. A substantial portion of the diversity literature is related to the impact of

K.P. Mongeon (✉)
Department of Sport Management, Brock University, St. Catharines, ON, Canada
e-mail: kmongeon@brocku.ca

J. Michael Boyle
Department of Operations & Information Systems, David Eccles School of Business, University of Utah, Salt Lake City, UT, USA

cultural and language diversity on output/production. The impact of cultural and language diversity is a relevant area of study because a diversity of cultural mixes introduces both benefits (e.g., heterogeneity in abilities and experiences) and costs (e.g., reduced communication and instances of prejudice) into the production process (Alesina and Ferrara 2005).

Two studies by Ottaviano and Peri (2005, 2006) use 1970–1990 U.S. Census data to measure the economic value of diversity, examining cultural and language diversity effects on productivity of U.S. residents. The earlier study found that wages and employment density were higher in cities with greater linguistic diversity among its residents. In real terms, a change in a linguistically homogeneous city, like Pittsburgh, to a more linguistically heterogeneous city, like Los Angeles, would increase the average real wage rate of U.S.-born workers by 13%. The later study found that cultural diversity, measured both by the number of foreign-born resident groups, as well as by the distribution of the individuals across foreign-born resident groups, increased the average wage rate and rent paid of U.S.-born residents. In real terms, the approximate increase of ethnic diversity of Los Angeles from 1970 to 1990 increased the average real wage and rents by 13% and 19%, respectively.

Examining data from a garment manufacturing facility in California, Hamilton et al. (2012) found some evidence that teams composed of entirely Hispanic workers were more productive than ethnically diverse teams.[1,2] In their examination of production levels in a number of German manufacturing plants (which collectively comprise a firm), Trax et al. (2012) found that regional, rather than within plant, cultural diversity effects increased production. An inference can be made from their finding that the gains from cultural diversity are externalities that likely originate from more frequent face-to-face interactions with diverse people outside the workforce rather than through learning and/or sharing of complementary information/skills amongst heterogeneous workers within the plant.

A recent article by Kahane et al. (2013) analyzed 6 years of a team's annualized winning percentages to examine the impact of intra-team dynamics, in terms of cultural and language diversity, on production. They claim that the National Hockey League (NHL) is a good environment to test the impact of cultural and language diversity on production because many NHL players originate from different European countries (i.e., primarily Russia, Sweden, Czech/Slovak Republic, and Finland), each having distinct cultural and language backgrounds. However, European players in general have similar skill sets that are on average somewhat different from those of North American players.[3] While the gains in production from

---

[1] There is also a diversity literature that is unrelated to cultural diversity. Hamilton et al. (2003) examined the production efficiency of 288 garment company workers involved in a change from a primarily individual to a team environment, and found that, in terms of ability, more heterogeneous teams of workers were more productive than less heterogeneous teams. Leonard and Levine (2003) found that retail sales were lower among teams with diverse age range.

[2] See Alesina and Ferrara (2005) for a summary of additional studies analyzing the impact of cultural diversity on economic output.

[3] In general, European players are trained to focus more on basic skill development as compared to North American players who are trained more typically through playing games. While European

the different skill sets yield a testable hypothesis, heterogeneity in terms of culture and language across European countries increases the communication costs to teams that hire European players originating from various countries.

Kahane et al. (2013) found that teams consisting of a more homogeneous group of European players had increased productivity levels in comparison to teams consisting of a more heterogeneous group of European players, and that European players playing on these teams had better individual performance statistics. The researchers hypothesized a number of potential underlying source(s) causing the gains and the effects, such as greater on-ice synergies or reduced cultural dominance of the domestic group (i.e., North American players). The primary reason for the inability of the research to discern the underlying source causing the diversity effects is the fact that the data are aggregated beyond the within game on-ice player interaction level. Information relating to on-ice player interactions is important because it can be used to discern whether or not the diversity effects are a result of on-ice player synergies amongst a homogeneous group of players. Consequently, their estimated diversity effects contain the (weighted) average of the within (including both on-ice and off-ice player interactions) and across game effects.

This chapter builds on the work of Kahane et al. (2013) with the purpose of inferring the underlying source(s) driving the cultural and language diversity effects on production. The current chapter also analyzes the intra-team dynamics of NHL teams, however various analyses are performed using more micro-level data that includes information relating to on-ice player interactions captured at important points during the production process of winning. It is important to note that the inferences presented in this article are based on a comparison of the results across various levels of analysis from both previous and current research, rather than from the findings of one particular analysis or hypothesis test. In this sense the current chapter is similar in scope to Trax et al. (2012), which used micro, rather than aggregated, data to discern that the diversity gains were generated from out-of-plant externalities rather than within plant effects.

The inferences relating to the underlying source(s) of the diversity effects are of interest to managerial economics/economists. Depending on the underlying source(s) causing the gains, managers can alter their composition of their workforce to increase productivity. For example, if the productivity gains derive from learning new skills, then optimal decision-making managers will create teams/departments in which diverse groups of people work closely together. On the other hand, if the productivity gains are invariant to the learning of new skills and are instead originating from a broader factor, such as reduced cultural dominance, then managers can benefit from increased productivity by hiring a diverse workforce. Further, if the productivity gains derive from reduced communication costs and not reduced cultural dominance, then managers can hire workers than can speak similar languages regardless of their cultural background.

---

players on average are considered to have better individual skills, North American players are considered to be better at physical play.

The remainder of this chapter will present this examination as follows: section "The NHL and the Game of Hockey" discusses relevant details relating to the game of hockey and the production of winning games. Section "Data and Empirical Model Motivation" presents the data and motivation for the forthcoming empirical models. Section "Empirical Models, Estimation Results, and Inferences" presents a number of empirical models, puts forth the estimation results and discusses the inferences relating to the underlying sources driving the cultural and language diversity effects. Concluding remarks are presented in section "Empirical Models".

The NHL and the Game of Hockey

The NHL is the premier professional hockey league in the world consisting of 30 teams disseminated throughout the United States and Canada. Each team plays 82 regular-season games amounting to 1230 season-games. Teams play each game with 20 skaters and two goaltenders on their rosters. The majority of regulation time is played at even-strength with each team competing for goals with five skaters and one goaltender. The game of hockey is known for its fast play in which skaters make frequent changes (approximately every 45 s) for more well-rested players. As a result, throughout the game, players from each team play with many different teammates and against many different opposing team players.

The winner of the game is declared to be the team that scored the most goals at the end of 60 min of regulation time. If the score is tied at the end of regulation time, 5 additional minutes of sudden death overtime is played, and if still tied, each team participates in a shoot-out until a winner is decided.[4] If the game is won during regulation play, the winning team is awarded two points and the losing team is not awarded any points in terms of their league standing. However, if the game is won in overtime or after a shoot-out, the winning team is still awarded two points, but the losing team is then awarded one point towards its league standing.

Data and Empirical Model Motivation

The data that is available dictates the potential analyses that can be completed. The NHL disseminates game and within game information through game summary and play-by-play reports. The game summary reports contain associated information on the game number, the identities of the home and visiting team, the identity of the winning team, and each team's game specific roster as well as their game time on ice. The play-by-play reports contain the additional associated information on the game-goal number, the period and score margin of the game, and the identity of each player on the ice for each goal event. Both sets of reports were obtained for

---

[4] Regular season overtime is played 4-on-4 compared to 5-on-5 during regulation play.

every game played during the 2010–2011 season. Each player's salary and their country of origin were also obtained from nhl.com.[5]

Since games are a result of net goals scored, the empirical models test for diversity effects on production at both the season-game (henceforth called game) and season-game-goal (henceforth called goal) levels rather than the season level as in previous research. While there are advantages to utilizing game and goal level information compared to season level information, such as accounting for dynamic game rosters (i.e. team roster changes throughout the seasons or across games) and opposing team effects, which if not accounted for can potentially contaminate hypothesis tests. Documenting these effects is, however, not the purpose of the following analyses. Kahane et al.'s (2013) results are robust and this paper assumes that they are valid. The purpose of the analysis is to estimate the diversity effects at two additional, and equally important, units of observation, and then collectively compare the three sets of results to discern the underlying source(s) driving the diversity effects.

The game level analysis estimates the impact of diversity on game outcomes (i.e., winning games or the probability of a win) based on the (relative) ethnic composition of each team's game specific roster and their game time on ice. The game level analysis is similar to the season level analysis (presented in Kahane et al. 2013) in that game specific rosters (or game time on ice) does not contain information relating to within game ethnic specific player interactions. Similar to the season level analysis, the estimated diversity effects obtained from the game level analysis potentially contain both on-ice and off-ice player effects. However, comparing the magnitudes of the diversity effects across the season and game levels will provide the necessary information to make inferences relating to how much of the diversity effects are generated across or within games.

The goal level analysis estimates the impact of diversity on net goal outcomes (i.e. the probability of a net team goal) based on the (relative) ethnic composition of each team's players on the ice when the goal was scored. The goal data offers a different perspective, in terms of identifying the players, than do the season and game data. The goal information identifies each player on the ice for the various goal events, rather than all of the players that played between subsequent goal events (which would be analogous to the season and game data). This is an important distinction because the estimated diversity effects obtained from the goal level analysis contain the effects generated from on-ice player interactions. Since the game level analysis contains both on-ice and off-ice effects, it is reasonable to extrapolate how much of the effects can be attributed to on-ice and off-ice player interactions.

The following example illustrates the potential benefits of analyzing diversity effects with both the game and goal models as described above: A team's game roster can be comprised of a number of Russian players, one of whom is low quality while the others are high quality. When the former is on the ice for more goals

---
[5] Only one season of each player's salary and their country of origin were obtained. One season of data provides a sufficient amount of observations to test the various hypotheses and to make inferences.

Table 1 Distribution of ethnic specific players based on game rosters, total game time on ice, and player on the ice for each goal event

Player ethnic group	Game roster (%)	Total game time on ice (%)	Players on the ice for each goal event (%)
North American	84	77	77
Czech/Slovakian	4	8	7
Swedish	5	7	7
Finnish	3	3	3
Russian	3	4	5
Other	1	1	1

scored against his team than scored for his team as compared to his high quality Russian teammates, the low quality Russian player would contribute relatively less to winning (or more to losing) than his high quality Russian teammates even in the absence of any diversity effects. However, the low quality Russian player is part of the team's cultural mix, and potentially contributes to winning through its effect: The low quality Russian player's presence on the bench could reduce the cultural dominance of the North American players and indirectly improve the performance of the high quality Russian players, resulting in increased team production.

Empirical Models, Estimation Results, and Inferences

Empirical Models

Based on their country of origin, the ethnicity of a player is placed into one of six ethnic categories defined by[6]

$$E_P = \begin{Bmatrix} North\,American(N), Czech/Slovakian\,(C), \\ Swedish(S), Finnish(F), Russian(R), and\,Other(O) \end{Bmatrix}.$$

According to these categories, Table 1 presents the distribution based on game rosters, total game time on ice, and players on the ice for each goal event. The distribution of players based on the proportion of ethnic specific players on the game roster is different than both the proportion of players' total game time on ice and players on the ice for each goal event. North American players comprise 84% of teams' starting rosters, but only comprise 77% of teams' total game time on ice and total number players on the ice for each goal event. The main discrepancy is from

---

[6] Player ethnic categories are defined identically to those of Kahane et al. (2013). Players originating from the following countries are categorized as originating from Other countries: Austria, Denmark, France, Germany, Italy, Norway, Poland, and Switzerland.

Czech/Slovakian players who comprise 4% of teams' game roster, play 8% of the total game time on ice, and represent 7% of players on the ice for each goal event.

The analysis uses two measures of cultural and language diversity, both of which are based on the player's country of origin. The first diversity measure is the Herfindahl–Hirschman Index (HHI). As noted by Kahane et al. (2013), the HHI is heavily dominated by North American players. Therefore, a European Share (i.e., the share of players not originating from North America) diversity measure is included as a second diversity measure. Collectively, the two diversity measures indicate the impacts of having a higher concentration of non-North American players, and having these players originate from the same country (relative to their opponent). Specific examples of the HHI and European Share variable derivations are provided below in the description of the empirical model.

Two categories of models are specified. The first category of models analyzes observations at the game (g) level, which is henceforth called the Game Model (GM). The second category of models analyzes observations at the game(g)-goal(l) level, which is henceforth called the Goal Model (LM). The models are defined below, with the GM defined by eliminating the goal reference ($i.e., l = \emptyset$), as well as the **PSMX** terms:

$$Home_{g,l} = \alpha + \beta_1 DHHI_{g,l} + \beta_2 DEUR_{g,l} + \theta_1 \ln DPAY_{g,l} + \mathbf{TFX}_{g,l}'\Phi + \mathbf{PSMX}_{g,l}'\Omega + \varepsilon_{g,l} \qquad (1)$$

In the GMs, the dependent variable $Home_g$ takes a number of forms. In some specifications, it equals 2 for a home team regulation win, 1 for a home team overtime loss, and 0 for a home team regulation loss (i.e., continuous win); in other specifications it is a binary variable equaling 1 for a home team win and 0 for a home team loss (i.e., binary win); and in other specifications we only analyze games that ended in regulation time and use a binary dependent variable equaling 1 for a home team win and 0 for a home team loss (i.e., regulation win). The $DHHI_g$ and $DEUR_g$ variables are the HHI and European Share team differences (home minus visiting team) based on both the team specific proportion of ethnic specific players on the game roster and their proportion of total game time on ice.[7,8] The $lnDPAY$-

---

[7] The ethnic specific player groups are defined by E_P.

[8] Based on game rosters, a (home or visiting) team consisting of ten North American, five Russian, three Finnish, and two Swedish players would have a HHI of $0.345 \left(= \left(10/20\right)^2 + \left(5/20\right)^2 + \left(3/20\right)^2 + \left(3/20\right)^2\right)$. The European Share would be $0.50 \left(= \left(5/20\right) + \left(3/20\right) + \left(3/20\right)\right)$. Based on total game time on ice, a (home or visiting) team in which the North American, Russian, Finnish, and Swedish players played 130, 85, 60, and 25 min of the total game time (300 min) would have a HHI of $0.315 \left(= \left(120/300\right)^2 + \left(85/300\right)^2 + \left(60/300\right)^2 + \left(25/300\right)^2\right)$. The European Share would be $0.567 \left(= \left(85/300\right) + \left(60/300\right) + \left(25/300\right)\right)$. Total game time on ice is the sum of the game time of the individual players. Deviations in the total game time on ice from 300 min (= 60 min × 5 players) exists from short-handed situations and overtime play.

$_g$variable is the log differences (home minus visiting team) of the collective team's player (i.e., skater) salaries on the game roster, and the vector **TFX**$_g$ are team specific two-sided indicator variables identifying which of the 30 NHL teams is the home team (1) and visiting team (−1).

In the LMs, the dependent variable $Home_{g,l}$ is an indicator variable equaling 1 if the gl^{th} goal was scored by the home team and 0 if it was scored by the visiting team. The *DHHI* and *DEUR* variables are the HHI and European Share team differences (home minus visiting team) based on the proportion of ethnic specific players on the ice for each goal event.[9] The $lnDPAY_{g,l}$ variable is the log differences (home minus visiting team) of the collective team's player salaries that were on the ice for each goal event. The vector **TFX**$_{g,l}$ are team specific two-sided indicator variables identifying which of the 30 NHL teams is the home team (1) and visiting team (−1), and the vector **PSMX**$_{g,l}$ are period and score margin specific (relative to the home team) fixed effects interactions identifying period-score margin specific game state when the gl^{th} goal was scored.[10] There are three period fixed effects each identifying the first, second, and third/overtime periods and nine score margin fixed effects that identify home team leading by greater than four goals through home team trailing by greater than four goals.

In both the GMs and LMs, the indicator variable identifying the team Washington Capitals, as well as in the LMs, the third/overtime period – tied game score margin game state interaction, were dropped to avoid perfect multicollinearity. A number of variables are included in Eq. 1 to account for factors that can potentially impact winning or net goals beyond team diversity. The constant controls for home advantage effects. The variable $lnDPAY_{g,l}$ controls for relative team quality at the game or game-goal levels. The vector **TFX**$_{g,l}$ controls for relative season-level team quality beyond game or game-goal levels.[11] In the LMs, the vector **PSMX**$_{g,l}$ controls for within game heterogeneity affecting net goals scored across periods and score margin game states.

The GMs encompassed 1230 observations, and the LMs encompassed 4734 even-strength observations.[12] Home teams won approximately 53% (639 out of

---

[9] Based on players on the ice for each goal event a (home or visiting) team that had two North American, two Russian, and one Finnish player on the ice for a goal event would have a HHI of $0.360 \left(= \left(\frac{2}{5} \right)^2 + \left(\frac{2}{5} \right)^2 + \left(\frac{1}{5} \right)^2 \right)$. The European Share would be $0.600 \left(= \left(\frac{2}{5} \right) + \left(\frac{1}{5} \right) \right)$. Only even-strength observations in which each team has five players on the ice are included in the analysis.

[10] The score margin fixed effects identify the score margin state of the game prior to the goal being scored (e.g., home team leading by two goals, home team leading by one goal, etc.).

[11] The majority of team season-games are played with one or two goaltenders. As a result, goaltender quality in both GM and LM is accounted for with the team fixed effects. Kahane (2005) does not find that goaltender quality metrics (i.e., save percentage) impacts winning beyond team effects, a finding that he attributes to increased goaltender quality across the league over time.

[12] We omit man-advantage observations from the analyses. Results that include man-advantage scenarios (i.e., power-player goals) that are controlled for with fixed effects are similar and support identical inferences.

1230) of the games, and scored approximately 52% (2449 out of 4734) of the even-strength goals. Home and visiting team specific summary statistics of the diversity variables are presented in Table 2. Table 2 includes three horizontal panels that categorize the summary statistics across the data categories (i.e., the proportion of players on the game roster, total game time on ice, players on the ice for each goal event). While there is little discrepancy across home and visiting team HHI and European Shares, there are discrepancies across the three categories. The home and visiting team HHI is greatest based on game rosters, followed by goal events, and then by total game time on ice.

With the exception of the GM with the continuous win dependent variable, the GM and LM were estimated with weighted least squares to account for heterogeneity inherent in the Bernoulli win or goal scored processes models, respectively. The semi-parametric linear model was chosen to avoid a possible misspecification of the probability distribution that can occur for a specific parametric functional form.[13] The GM with the continuous win dependent variable was estimated with ordinary least squares.

Estimation Results

The estimation results are presented in Table 3. Columns (1)–(3) present the GM results in which the diversity variables are based on the (relative) proportion of number of players on the starting rosters, and columns (4)–(6) present the results from models in which they are based on the (relative) proportion of total game time on ice. Denoted by the column headers, columns (1) and (4), (2) and (5), and (3) and (6) were estimated with the continuous win, binary win, and regulation win as dependent variables, respectively. All GM model specifications included both the game payroll variable and the vector of team fixed effects. The LM results are presented in columns (7)–(8). Column (7) presents the LM results from the specification that includes the payroll variable and the vector of team fixed effects. Column (8) presents the results from a specification that adds the period-score margin interaction fixed effects to the specification presented in column (7).[14]

---

[13] We note the coefficients of the marginal effect obtained from a logit regression model are similar and support identical conclusions to the coefficients and inferences presented in this paper.

[14] We note that team quality is controlled for by both payroll/player salaries and team fixed effects. Since we are using one season of data and team rosters are fairly constant throughout the season, team fixed effects provide for a strong control variable in terms of accounting for factors that can impact the likelihood of game outcomes beyond diversity. The lower R-squared values compared to previous research based on season games is a function of the more micro unit of observation rather than poorer model fit. Variations in game outcomes are more easily explained at the season level compared to the game level.

Table 2 Summary statistics across data categories

Data categories	Diversity variable	Game rosters			Total game time on ice			Players on the ice for each goal event		
		Number of observations	Mean	Standard deviation	Number of observations	Mean	Standard deviation	Number of observations	Mean	Standard deviation
All games								All goal events		
	Home team HHI	1230	0.7150	(0.1597)	1230	0.5959	(0.1316)	4734	0.6928	(0.2220)
	Visiting team HHI	1230	0.7134	(0.1588)	1230	0.5959	(0.1310)	4734	0.7023	(0.2223)
	Home team European share	1230	0.1642	(0.1175)	1230	0.2317	(0.1159)	4734	0.2330	(0.2004)
	Visiting team European share	1230	0.1639	(0.1188)	1230	0.2307	(0.1150)	4734	0.2248	(0.1988)
Home team game wins								Home team goals		
	Home team HHI	639	0.7153	(0.1634)	639	0.5967	(0.1325)	2449	0.6900	(0.2221)
	Visiting team HHI	639	0.7151	(0.1526)	639	0.5983	(0.1303)	2449	0.7057	(0.2232)
	Home team European share	639	0.1640	(0.1167)	639	0.2315	(0.1141)	2449	0.2354	(0.2012)
	Visiting team European share	639	0.1617	(0.1140)	639	0.2290	(0.1126)	2449	0.2224	(0.2003)

	Visiting team game wins				Visiting team goals			
Home team HHI	591	0.7148	(0.1558)	591	0.5950	(0.1308)	2285	0.6958	(0.2220)
Visiting team HHI	591	0.7116	(0.1654)	591	0.5934	(0.1318)	2285	0.6986	(0.2214)
Home team European share	591	0.1643	(0.1184)	591	0.2319	(0.1180)	2285	0.2305	(0.1995)
Visiting team European share	591	0.1662	(0.1238)	591	0.2325	(0.1177)	2285	0.2275	(0.1972)

Table 3 The impact of diversity on winning and net goals scored

	(1)	(2)	(3)	(4)	(5)	(6)	(7)	(8)
	Game models						Goal models	
	Starting roster			Game time on ice			Players on ice	
	Continuous win	Binary win	Regulation win	Continuous win	Binary win	Regulation win	Goal event	Goal event
Diversity variables								
Difference in HHI	0.7705*	0.2630	0.4804*	1.5003***	0.5572*	0.9756***	−0.09084	−0.09065
	(0.4446)	(0.2432)	(0.2800)	(0.5750)	(0.3187)	(0.3610)	(0.06636)	(0.06647)
Difference in European share	1.0663	0.4334	0.6961	1.4021*	0.5474	0.9723**	−0.04928	−0.05083
	(0.6908)	(0.3775)	(0.4297)	(0.7658)	(0.4223)	(0.4753)	(0.07769)	(0.07784)
Game or goal level control variables								
Log difference in payroll	0.4547***	0.2428**	0.3108***	0.4548***	0.2534**	0.3144***	0.07740***	0.07860***
	(0.1753)	(0.1005)	(0.1146)	(0.1735)	(0.09967)	(0.1135)	(0.01409)	(0.01410)
Constant	1.1609***	0.5150***	0.5310***	1.1611***	0.5150***	0.5319***	0.5156***	0.5106***
	(0.02575)	(0.01410)	(0.01604)	(0.02569)	(0.01408)	(0.01601)	(0.007236)	(0.02718)
Model	OLS	WLS	WLS	OLS	WLS	WLS	WLS	WLS

Control variables included							
Team fixed effects included:	Yes	Yes	Yes	Yes	Yes	Yes	Yes
Score margin and period fixed effects interactions	No	No	No	No	No	No	Yes
Observations	1230	1230	934	1230	1230	934	4734	4734
Adjusted R-squared	0.0405	0.0267	0.0498	0.0440	0.0282	0.0545	0.0149	0.0166

***, **, * , indicates statistical significance at the 1%, 5%, and 10% levels, respectively. Team fixed effects are two-sided indicator variables

We note that the GM results presented in columns (1) and (4), from the specifications in which the dependent variable was continuous, are on a different scale than the results presented in the other specifications in which the dependent variable was a binary variable. Based on the specifications in which the dependent variable was a binary variable, the estimates are given in terms of their impact of a probability team win/goal, which can be directly compared with the estimates presented by Kahane et al. (2013) that are based on their impact on a team's annualized winning percentage. Therefore, we only discuss the estimates based on specifications in which the dependent variable was a binary variable. After accounting for winning across teams with team fixed effects, each of the payrolls coefficients are positive and significant at the 0.01 level in all specifications, and the coefficient of the constant indicates a home team advantage in terms of both game and goal outcomes.

In general, the diversity measures have an impact on winning games, but not on net goals scored. The coefficients of the HHI and European Share are positive across all GM specifications. Based on starting rosters, the coefficient of the HHI variable is approximately 0.26 and not significant in the binary win specification, and is 0.45 and significant at the 0.10 level, in the regulation win specification. The European Share coefficients are 0.43 and 0.70 and not significant in the binary and win specifications, respectively. Based on game time on ice, the coefficient of the HHI variable is approximately 0.56, and significant at the 0.10 level, in the binary win specification, and 0.98, and significant at the 0.01 level, in the regulation win specification. The European Share coefficient is 0.55, and not significant, in the binary win specification, and 0.97, and significant at the 0.05 level, in the regulation win specification. Both of the HHI and European Share coefficients are small in magnitude and not significant across the LM specifications.

Since the proportion of North American players is being accounted for by both the HHI and European Share variable, teams that have a number of European players would benefit most, in terms of increasing the likelihood of game wins, if those player originated from the same country. A team having a roster comprised of 14 North American players and six European players originating from the same country has a HHI of 0.580, while a team comprised of 14 North American players and six European players originating from six different countries has a HHI of 0.505, resulting in an HHI difference of 0.075 (=0.580–0.505). In real terms, Kahane et al.'s (2013) finding suggested that this HHI difference results in approximately 3.5 more season-game wins. The diversity effects presented in this paper are relative to a team's opponent. Using the GM game roster HHI coefficients of 0.2630 and 0.4804 (i.e., columns [2]–[3]), an HHI difference of 0.075 results in associated increments of win probabilities of 0.0197 (=0.2630 * 0.075) and 0.3600 (=0.4805 * 0.075) or 1.62 (=82 * 0.0197) and 2.95 (=82 * 0.3600) season-games, respectively. Using the GM game time on ice HHI coefficients of 0.5572 and 0.9756 (i.e., columns [5]–[6]), an HHI difference of 0.075 results in associated increments of win probabilities of 0.0418 (=0.5572 * 0.075) and 0.0732 (=0.9756 * 0.075) or 3.43 (=82 * 0.0418) and 6.00 (=82 * 0.0732) season-games, respectively.

Inferences

There are no diversity effects in the LM based on the proportion of ethnic specific players on the ice for each goal event. This finding suggests that the diversity effects can be attributed to off-ice rather than on-ice (ethnic specific) player interactions, such as familiarity in playing styles or reduced on-ice communication costs across players as underlying sources driving the effects. This finding is particularly interesting because Kahane et al. (2013) found that European players on teams that have a more homogenous group of European teammates have better individual performance statistics.

The GM game time on ice diversity effects are strongest, in terms of both magnitude and significance, as compared to both the GM game roster presented and the season model presented by Kahane et al. (2013). The GM starting roster results are similar to the results presented by Kahane et al. (2013). Therefore, an inference would suggest that the diversity effects are being generated *within* rather than across games, potentially ruling out reduced cultural dominance of the domestic group as an underlying source. Reduced cultural dominance would most likely not require game time on ice to generate the effects. For example, an larger ethnic specific group of European players on a team would (most likely) be able to reduce the cultural dominance of the domestic group during team meetings, dinners, or in the dressing room, regardless of their game time on ice.

The GM game time on ice findings provides additional information relating to the underlying source of the diversity effects. With both on-ice ethnic specific player interactions and reduced cultural dominance of the domestic group eliminated as potential underlying sources, it is highly likely that the underlying source of the diversity effects are reduced within game, but off-ice, communication across homogeneous groups of European players. For example, European players originating from the same country could share information in their native language relating to within game dynamics such as effective game strategies. This explanation also supports Kahane et al.'s (2013) finding that a more homogeneous group of European players increases the individual performance statistics of similar ethnic specific European players. The increase in the performance statistics is a result of the off-ice externality of lower communication costs rather than on-ice synergies amongst a homogenous group of players.

Conclusion

Prior research examined the effects of cultural and language diversity on the production of winning hockey games to find that a more homogeneous group of European players increases a team's production as well as the individual production of European players. However, the analyses were undertaken using aggregated data preventing the researcher from discerning the underlying source causing the effects.

The current article attempts to discern the underlying source(s) of the diversity effects by analyzing various sets of more micro-level data that includes information relating to on-ice player interactions, and it makes inferences based on the collective findings.

While none of the potentially underlying sources driving the diversity effects are mutually exclusive, the collective results relating to the impact of ethnic diversity on the production of winning suggest that the underlying source of the diversity effects is related reduced communication costs. More specifically, it is highly likely that the diversity effects are from reduced off-ice, but within game communication costs amongst a homogenous group of European players that speak the same language and can more easily share within game information and strategies amongst themselves.

Understanding the underlying source driving the diversity effects is of general interest to managerial economists who can potentially generate productivity gains from optimally designing workforces. While globalization and teamwork amongst workers has increased in recent years, firm managers can benefit from gains in productivity by lowering communication costs amongst employees. Hiring employees that speak similar languages and can effectively communicate and share ideas within the workforce may be more important than hiring workers with similar cultural backgrounds.

References

Alchian, A.A. and Demsetz, H. (1972): Production, Information Costs, and Economic Organization. American Economic Review, 62 (5), pp. 777–795.
Alesina, A., and Ferrara, E. L. (2005): Ethnic Diversity and Economic Performance. Journal of Economic Literature, 43, pp. 762–800.
Allen, B. T., Doherty, N., Weigelt, K., and Mansfield, E. (1988): Managerial Economics. New York, NY: Harper & Row.
Baumol, W.J. (1962): On the Theory of Expansion of the Firm. American Economic Review, 52 (5), pp. 1078–1087.
Hamilton, B.H., Nickerson, J.A. and Owan, H. (2003): Team Incentives and Worker Heterogeneity: An Empirical Analysis of the Impact of Teams on Productivity and Participation. Journal of Political Economy, 111 (3), pp. 465–497.
Hamilton, B.H., Nickerson, J.A. and Owan, H. (2012): Diversity and Productivity in Production Teams. Advances in the Economic Analysis of Participatory & Labor-Managed Firms, 13, pp. 99–138.
Kahane, L. H. (2005): Production Efficiency and Discriminatory Hiring Practices in the National Hockey League: A Stochastic Frontier Approach. Review of Industrial Organization, 27 (1), pp. 47–71.
Kahane, L., Longley, N. and Simmons, R. (2013): The Effects of Coworker Heterogeneity on Firm-Level Output: Assessing the Impacts of Cultural and Language Diversity in the National Hockey League. Review of Economics and Statistics, 95 (1), pp. 302–314.
Kandel, E. and Lazear, E. P. (1992): Peer Pressure and Partnerships. Journal of Political Economy, 100 (4), pp. 801–817.
Lazear, E.P. (1999a): Culture and Language. Journal of Political Economy, 107 (6), pp. S95–S126.

Lazear, E.P. (1999b): Globalisation and the Market for Team-Mates. Economic Journal, 109 (454), pp. 15–40.
Leonard, J. and Levine, D. (2003): Diversity, Discrimination, and Performance. Institute of Industrial Relations Working Paper No. iirwps-091-03.
Ottaviano, G.I. and Peri, G. (2005): Cities and Cultures. Journal of Urban Economics, 58 (2), pp. 304–337.
Ottaviano, G.I. and Peri, G. (2006): The Economic Value of Cultural Diversity: Evidence from US Cities. Journal of Economic Geography, 6 (1), pp. 9–44.
Prat, A. (2002): Should a Team be Homogeneous? European Economic Review, 46 (7), pp. 1187–1207.
Spagnolo, G. (1999): Social Relations and Cooperation in Organizations. Journal of Economic Behavior & Organization, 38 (1), pp. 1–25.
Trax, M., Brunow, S. and Suedekum, J. (2012): Cultural Diversity and Plant-Level Productivity, Working Paper No. 1223, Centre for Research and Analysis of Migration, Department of Economics, University College London.

Team-Level Referee Discrimination in the National Hockey League

Kevin Mongeon and Neil Longley

Abstract Previous research on referee discrimination in penalty calling has been based on relative comparisons across race/ethnic groups, and does not discern whether the findings are based on players of a different or the same race/ethnicity. This paper tests for team-level discrimination amongst professional hockey referees, and finds that French-Canadian referees favor teams, in the form of fewer penalty calls, that have more French-Canadian players. The analysis is undertaken at penalty level to account for additional within-game referee biases and varying costs of player infractions across score margin game states.

Introduction

The production of winning in professional sporting contests is somewhat unique in that games involve referees that act as impartial arbiters to ensure that the winner of the game is determined in a manner that is consistent with its rules. A recent line of research has emerged that examines whether or not referee adjudicators exhibit discrimination against players in their penalty calling decision-making based on the relative race/ethnicity of the players and referees.[1]

Referees have been found to exhibit discrimination in professional basketball, baseball, and hockey. Price and Wolfers (2010) examined the foul calling rates of National Basketball Association (NBA) referees to find that referees call more fouls both on players of opposite race and on teams comprised of more players of opposite

---

[1] The majority of the literature examining discrimination in sports has focused on racial discrimination, and has examined the extent to which black players may suffer from discrimination at the hands of consumers (fans), team management, and/or co-workers (teammates). See Kahn (1991) for a summary of the discrimination literature based on professional sports labor markets.

K. Mongeon (✉)
Department of Sport Management, Brock University, St. Catharines, ON, Canada
e-mail: kmongeon@brocku.ca

N. Longley
Department of Sport Management, Isenberg School of Management, University of Massachusetts, Amherst, MA, USA

race to their own race.[2] Studying the ball and strike calling of Major League Baseball (MLB) umpires, Parsons et al. (2011) found that the probability that pitches were called strikes was greater when the umpire and pitcher shared the same race/ethnicity. Mongeon and Longley (2015) found that French Canadian National Hockey League (NHL) referees call more penalties against English Canadian players than do English Canadian referees.

There is a subtlety in the analysis of discrimination that involves referees calling players' discretionary infractions as fouls or penalties, such as in basketball and hockey. The accuracy of referees' penalty calls in relation to whether or not players' infractions are indeed penalty events are not available for analysis purposes. As a result, researchers have no base of comparison in their analysis and have been forced to test for discrimination by making relative comparisons in penalty rates across opposite referee-player race/ethnic groups. This chapter uses an innovative identification strategy to test for team-level discrimination in terms of both, a referee's propensity to call more penalties against teams that are represented by relatively more players of a different ethnicity than their own ethnicity, and fewer penalties against teams that are represented by relatively more players of the same ethnicity as their own.

The remainder of the chapter is organized as follows. Section "The NHL, the Game of Hockey, and Related" briefly describes the NHL and the game of hockey including the infraction and penalty calling processes. Moreover, section "The NHL, the Game of Hockey, and Related" also summarizes related ethnic discrimination research. Section "Empirical Methodology" presents the empirical methodology including model motivation, the data, and empirical specifications. Section "Estimation Procedure, Discrimination Tests and Results" discusses the estimation procedure, presents the discrimination hypothesis tests, and discusses the results. Concluding remarks are presented in section "Concluding Remarks".

The NHL, the Game of Hockey, and Related

The NHL and the Game of Hockey

The NHL is the premier professional hockey league generating substantial revenues. During the 2010–2011 NHL seasons, League revenues were approximately $2.9 billion.[3] The league consists of 30 teams disseminated through the United States and Canada. Team rosters are generally comprised of 18 skaters and two goaltenders that remain relatively constant within seasons; and, in many cases, across subsequent seasons. The majority of game-time is played with five skaters and one goaltender on each team competing to score own team goals while not

---

[2] Mongeon and Longley (2013) re-estimated Price and Wolfers (2010) game-player-level analysis to find that only black players were discriminated against.

[3] http://www.nhl.com/ice/news.htm?id=559630

allowing opposing team goals. A unique aspect of hockey is that skaters make frequent changes (approximately every 45 s) for rested players far more often than in many other sports (e.g., basketball).

The NHL player and referee labor markets are characterized by considerable ethnic diversity. Players originating from English Canada represent approximately 40% of the total distribution of players. European, American, and French Canadian players each represent approximately 30%, 20%, and 10% of the distribution, respectively. The ethnic composition of the league's referees is also dominated by English Canadians who represent approximately 64% of all referees; followed by French Canadians with 18%; Americans with 16%; and Internationals with 2%.

Each game is officiated by two referees who call player infractions as penalties. In general penalties can be considered as either discretionary (e.g., tripping, slashing, and hooking) or non-discretionary (e.g., fighting) in nature. In the case of discretionary penalties, referees exhibit judgment in discerning whether or not the player infraction warranted a penalty call, whereas non-discretionary penalties calls are obvious. Most penalties are discretionary in nature and result in a 2-min penalty in which the player's team must play with one player less. On average, a penalty increases the probability of an opposing team goal by approximately 15%.[4]

Related Literature

Beyond hockey, French and English Canadians have many differences. One primary difference is the language they speak. However, these differences extend well beyond the language to include discrepancies in cultural and social norms to the extent that they have historically contributed to political tensions between the two groups.[5] As a result, much of the discrimination literature relating to the NHL has focused on French and English Canadians.

Early work by Jones and Walsh (1988) and Lavoie and Grenier (1992) had conflicting results related to salary discrimination toward French Canadian players: while the former study found evidence of discrimination, the latter did not. Longley (1995) found that French Canadian players were discriminated against when playing for teams located within the region of English Canada, a finding that he attributed to the broader historical tensions between English and French Canadians. Longley's results were later challenged (Jones et al. 1999) and subsequent related findings have been mixed. While some researchers have documented that French

---

[4] During the 2009–2010 NHL regular season, a discretionary penalty on average increased the net probability of an opposing team goal by 14.7 %. Assuming two teams are of equal ability, the expected scoring differential over any fixed period of time is zero when the teams are at equal strength. During the 2009–2010 season teams scored on the power-play an average of 18.2% of the time compared to 3.5% while short-handed. Therefore, the average cost of a penalty is 18.2%–3.5% = 14.7%.

[5] See Longley (2012) for a discussion of discrimination in the NHL within the broader framework of French-English relations in Canada.

Canadian players have suffered from salary discrimination (Mongeon 2015, Lavoie 2000; Curme and Daugherty 2004; Szymanski and Longley 2001), others have failed to do so (Bruggink and Williams 2009).

Other forms of discrimination have also been examined. Lavoie et al. (1987) and Lavoie (2003) found that players from minority groups suffer from entry discrimination and Longley (2000, 2003) documented that not only French Canadian players, but also managers and coaches are underrepresented on English Canadian NHL teams. Moreover, Kahane (2005) found potential discrimination in hiring practices relating to French Canadian players. Finally, a book by a former French Canadian player (Sirois 2010) titled "Discrimination in the NHL: Quebec Hockey Players Sidelined" also claims that French Canadian players suffer from both salary and entry discrimination.[6]

Empirical Methodology

Empirical Model Motivation

Our empirical models test for discrimination at the season-game-penalty level (i.e. penalty level) rather than at the season-game level (i.e. game level) used by Price and Wolfers (2010). The penalty level analysis used in this paper will estimate the relative probability of a team compared to the opposing team penalty conditioned on the relative ethnic composition of the players on the ice, which serves as a proxy for the ethnic composition of each team. This is employed instead of the game level analysis that estimates the team-game penalty rates conditioned on the ethnic composition of each team's roster across games.[7] We suggest that the penalty-level analysis has both theoretical and empirical advantages that should be considered for analysis purposes.

First, the penalty level analysis provides much more variation across player ethnic groups than does the game level analysis, leveraging the frequent within-game player changes. Given that there are multiple penalties across games, the penalty level analysis requires fewer season games to obtain a sufficient amount of data for reliable hypothesis tests.

Second, the game level analysis requires the model specification to hold constant a referee's propensity to call infractions as penalties (usually with referee fixed effects), while the penalty level analysis presented in this chapter does not. As a result, the penalty level model is more parsimonious than the game level model and does not require the multi-stage estimation procedure to test for discrimination

---

[6] The book was originally released in French and called *Le Quebec mis en echec*.
[7] The penalty level analysis is similar to the pitch level analysis conducted by Parsons et al. (2011) who tested for discrimination based on the relative probability of a strike compared to a ball rather than based on aggregated strike calling rates.

Table 1 2008–2010 Unconditional score margin specific mid-game probability of a home team win and the changes in the probability of a win given a visiting team goal

Mid-game score margin (relative to the home team)	Sample average probability of a home team win	Change in probability of a home team win given a visiting team goal	Sample frequency
6	1	0	3
5	1	−0.016	16
4	0.984	−0.057	63
3	0.928	−0.019	207
2	0.909	−0.185	438
1	0.724	−0.193	862
0	0.531	−0.225	1098
−1	0.306	−0.17	735
−2	0.136	−0.092	361
−3	0.043	−0.043	115
−4	0	0	34
−5	0	0	17
−6	0	0	1

across discrete referee ethnic groups (e.g., two English Canadian referees, one English Canadian and one French Canadian referee).[8,9]

Third, there is literature suggesting that referees exhibit various biases in penalty calling beyond discrimination, some of which can be accounted for with penalty level information. Early research suggests that referees may be subject to social pressures that cause them to call fewer penalties against home than visiting teams (Dohmen 2008; Garicano et al. 2005; Pettersson-Lidbom and Priks 2010).[10] However, more recent research finds evidence of close-game and balanced penalty calling biases (Abrevaya and McCulloch 2006; Mongeon and Mittelhammer 2012; Price et al. 2012). The former bias is a phenomenon in which officials make calls to ensure scores in games to not get too one-sided, and the latter is where officials balance the penalty calls between the two teams in order to promote the perception of fairness in officiating. While game level analyses can account for home team biases in penalty calling, both close-game and balanced penalty calling biases are based on within-game penalty level information, which if aggregated over and/or not

---

[8] See Mongeon and Longely (2013) and Mongeon and Mittelhammer (2013) for the multi-stage estimation procedure to test for discrimination across discrete referee ethnic groups.

[9] Including referee fixed effects in the penalty level analysis presented in this chapter would hold constant an individual referee's bias across home and visiting penalty calls rather than preferences to call player infractions as penalties.

[10] See also Balmer et al. (2001, 2003), Buraimo et al. (2010), Boyko et al. (2007), Dawson et al. (2007), Mohr and Larsen (1998), and Sutter and Kocher (2004) as well as Witt (2005) for evidence relating to home team biased officiating.

controlled for in the econometric specification, can potentially result in contaminated hypothesis tests.[11]

Finally, in hockey, as well as in many other sports, within-game score margin (i.e. the difference in the number of goals of the two competing teams) can alter the costs of an opposing team goal. The various costs of opposing team goals create discrepancies in a player's incentive to commit infractions resulting in differences in the number of team penalty events. The data presented in Table 1 demonstrates these various costs of opposing team goals across score margin states. Column (1) presents the score margin game state (relative to the home team), and column (2) presents the associated unconditional probability of a home team win, which is taken at the midpoint of the game. Column (3) presents the changes in the probability of a home team win given a visiting team goal, or the costs of conceding a goal. The costs of an opposing team goal is greater during closer games (e.g., 0.225 points during tied games) compared to games with a larger score differential (e.g., 0.057 during leading by four goals). A penalty level model lends itself to a straightforward way to account for varying costs of opposing team goals with score margin fixed effects.[12]

The Data

Our base data covers all discretionary penalties called during all regular season games in the 2008–2009, 2009–2010, and 2010–2011 seasons as well as the identities of the two referees who officiated the game. The data identifies only the referees who officiated the game and does not provide the identity of the specific referee that called the penalty.[13,14]

Some adjustments are made to the data. First, there was only one international referee who officiated a limited number of games. Therefore, we discard all games officiated by the international referee. Second, some penalties are coincidental in nature (i.e., simultaneously called on players from both teams) and do not result in a man-advantage situation, and therefore, probabilistically they do not alter the

---

[11] Garrett (2003) derived the theoretical conditions under which the magnitudes of the estimates and the standard errors can be different when the regression analysis uses aggregated versus disaggregated data.

[12] Parsons et al. (2011) used the within-game information to test for discrimination amongst MLB umpires and controlled for pitch count in the empirical analysis.

[13] Discretionary penalties are those that involve a judgment call on the part of the referee as whether to call, or not to call, a penalty. We consider the following penalties to be discretionary penalties: checking from behind, closing hand on puck, cross checking, delaying the game, diving, elbowing, holding, holding the stick, hooking, instigating, interference, interference on goalkeeper, slashing, and tripping. Henceforth, we refer to all discretionary penalties as, simply, penalties.

[14] All data are available from NHL.com. The penalty data are obtained from the NHL's play-by-play reports and the game summary reports to ascertain the names of the two referees that worked each game.

Table 2 Games and penalties across refereeing ethnicity mixes

Referee ethnicity	Games (% of total)	Penalties called (% of total)
2 English Canadian	1483 (41.88)	5985 (40.66)
1 English Canadian and 1 French Canadian	867 (24.48)	3714 (25.23)
1 English Canadian and 1 American	803 (22.68)	3336 (22.67)
2 French Canadians	125 (3.53)	531 (3.61)
1 French Canadian and 1 American	196 (5.54)	871 (5.92)
2 Americans	67 (1.89)	281 (1.91)
Total	3541 (100.0)	14,718 (100.0)

outcome of the game. As a result, we have discarded all coincidental discretionary penalty calls.

Our final data set consists of 3541 games and 14,718 penalty events. For each penalty event there is associated information on the season, the game number, the team that was called for the penalty, the identity of the home and visiting team, the score of the game, the identity and ethnicity of both referees and the ten skaters (i.e. players) on ice.[15] The ethnicity of a player is placed into one of the following four ethnic categories: English Canadian (born in Canada, but outside of the province of Quebec [English or E]), French Canadian (born in Quebec with a French-sounding surname [French or F]), American [A], or International [I]. In the same manner as players, referees are categorized as English, French, or American.

Table 2 provides summary data on the number of games refereed and the corresponding number of penalties called for each ethnicity combination of referee crew. English Canadians are the dominant group, with about 89% of the games in the data set having at least one member of the referee crew who is English. Table 3 presents some summary statistics in the form of the means and standard deviations of the number of ethnic specific players on the ice, categorized by whether or not the team was called for the penalty, and further categorized by the various referee ethnicity mixes. Table 3 also presents summary statistics relating to the difference in the means of the number of ethnic-specific players on teams that were, and were not, called for the penalty.

As noted by Price and Wolfers (2010), the assignment of refereeing crews to games does not literally need to be random to test for discrimination. The racial/ethnic mix of the refereeing crews must be unrelated to the racial/ethnic characters of the teams that they officiate. The p-values resulting from chi-square tests for independence between the number of referees of a given ethnicity in a game and the number of same ethnicity players in that game are presented in Table 4. The null hypothesis of independence was not rejected in 32 of the 36 cases, providing a general assurance that referee assignments are random.

---

[15] Goaltenders are rarely replaced during the course of a game and are, therefore, omitted from the analysis.

Table 3 Summary statistics of the number of ethnic specific players across penalized and non-penalized teams categorized by the various referee ethnicity mixes

Referee ethnicity mix	Summary statistic	Number of players on the ice across player ethnic categories			
		English	French	American	International
Penalized team					
Two English	Mean	2.346	0.301	0.999	1.355
	Std. dev.	(1.171)	(0.551)	(0.905)	(1.099)
One English and one French	Mean	2.322	0.32	1.05	1.308
	Std. dev.	(1.182)	(0.556)	(0.920)	(1.072)
One English and one American	Mean	2.336	0.316	1.032	1.316
	Std. dev.	(1.162)	(0.541)	(0.915)	(1.075)
Two French	Mean	2.384	0.299	1.006	1.311
	Std. dev.	(1.225)	(0.541)	(0.924)	(1.109)
One French and one American	Mean	2.31	0.326	1.056	1.308
	Std. dev.	(1.142)	(0.554)	(0.945)	(1.053)
Two Americans	Mean	2.466	0.281	0.961	1.292
	Std. dev.	(1.230)	(0.537)	(0.935)	(1.062)
Non-penalized team					
Two English	Mean	2.260	0.303	1.029	1.408
	Std. dev.	(1.179)	(0.547)	(0.931)	(1.110)
One English and one French	Mean	2.289	0.315	1.04	1.355
	Std. dev.	(1.160)	(0.567)	(0.920)	(1.060)
One English and one American	Mean	2.324	0.305	1.019	1.353
	Std. dev.	(1.173)	(0.548)	(0.932)	(1.086)
Two French	Mean	2.284	0.394	0.979	1.343
	Std. dev.	(1.144)	(0.628)	(0.889)	(1.022)
One French and one American	Mean	2.295	0.3	1.048	1.357
	Std. dev.	(1.155)	(0.548)	(0.936)	(1.077)
Two Americans	Mean	2.577	0.285	0.872	1.267
	Std. dev.	(1.269)	(0.539)	(0.951)	(1.104)
Difference in means (penalized minus non-penalized teams)					
Two English	Mean	0.086	−0.002	−0.030	−0.053
One English and one French	Mean	0.032	0.005	0.010	−0.047
One English and one American	Mean	0.012	0.012	0.013	−0.037
Two French	Mean	0.100	−0.094	0.026	−0.032
One French and one American	Mean	0.015	0.026	0.008	−0.049
Two Americans	Mean	−0.110	−0.004	0.089	0.025

Standard deviations are in parentheses

Table 4 Chi-squared tests for independence (p-values) between the number of ethnic specific players and referees

Season	Number of English Canadian starters	Number of French Canadian starters	Number of American starters	Number of International starters
English Canadian referees				
2008	0.221	0.833	0.001	0.013
2009	0.225	0.445	0.782	0.511
2010	0.833	0.312	0.18	0.779
French Canadian referees				
2008	0.29	0.206	0.041	0.308
2009	0.611	0.343	0.647	0.979
2010	0.201	0.611	0.032	0.517
American referees				
2008	0.035	0.81	0	0.595
2009	0.55	0.677	0.676	0.954
2010	0.767	0.314	0.256	0.962

The cells contain p-values of the null hypothesis that number of ethnic specific players and referees are independent

Empirical Model Specifications

The empirical specification needs to interact both the ethnicities of the referees that officiated the game and the relative ethnic composition of the players on the ice at the time of the penalty event across competing teams variables. We use a discrete variable approach to identify each of the six referee ethnic groups (i.e., RR ∈ {E ∧ E, E ∧ F, E ∧ A, F ∧ F, F ∧ A, A ∧ A}). Since only even strength penalty events are analyzed, representing the relative ethnic composition of the players on the ice as a continuous variable (e.g., the differences in the number of [or proportion of] English, French, American, and International players on the ice across competing teams, respectively) results in perfect multicollinearity across each of the six referee ethnic groups. The avoidance of perfect multicollinearity through the omission of a continuous variable across each of the six referee ethnic groups results in analyzing relative probabilities across ethnic player groups (as in previous research) and mitigates the possibility to test for a referee's propensity to call more penalties against teams with more different ethnic-specific players, and fewer penalties against teams with more same ethnic-specific players. Therefore, to avoid perfect multicollinearity we use a two-sided indicator variable that identifies which of the two competing teams has a greater, same, or lesser amount of players across each of the four ethnic specific player groups as a proxy to represent the relative ethnic composition of the players on the ice across competing teams.

A number of empirical models are nested within the following saturated specification:

$$HP_{s,g,p} = \alpha + \left(X_{s,g,p}^{RRXP}\right)' B \ STX_{s,g,p} + PV_{s,g,p} + SMX_{s,g,p} + PPX_{s,g,p} + \varepsilon_{s,g,p} \quad (1)$$

where subscripts s, g, p denote a season, game, and penalty event, respectively. The unit of observation is a discretionary penalty event.

The dependent variable HPs,g,p is a home team penalty indicator equaling one if the s, g, pth penalty call was against the home team and zero if the penalty call was against the visiting team. The vector $X_{s,g,p}^{RR \times P}$ is a collection of 24 (6 referee ethnic mixes × 4 player ethnic groups) two-sided indicator variables determined through interacting each of the four ethnic player group two-sided indicator variables identifying whether the home (1), neither (0), or visiting team (−1) had more ethnic specific players on the ice at the time of the penalty event each interacted with the six indicator variables identifying referee ethnic mixes that officiated the game. The superscript $RR \times P$ denotes the referee mix and player ethnic interactions. The vector STXs,g,p is a collection of season-specific team two-sided indicator variables identifying which of the 30 teams is the home team (1) and which is the visiting team (−1). The vector PV$s,g,p$ is a collection of player variable effects and contains the log differences of the collective home and visiting players' ages (in years relative to the start of each season), heights (in inches), and weights (in pounds) of those that were on the ice when the penalty was called. The vector SMXs,g,p is a collection of ten score-margin fixed effects identifying the score-margin of the game relative to the home team (i.e., home team leading by greater than or equal to five goals through home team trailing by greater than or equal to five goals). The vector PPXs,g,p is a collection of two-sided indicator variables identifying whether the home (1) or visiting (−1) team was called for the previous and second previous penalty event.[16] The α and the ε terms represent the constant and the residual of the specifications, respectively. To avoid perfect multicollinearity the two-sided indicator variable identifying the 2008-Anaheim Ducks team, as well as the tied game score margin state were dropped from the specifications in which they were included.

The constant controls for home team biased officiating. The vectors STXs,g,p and PV$s,g,p$ control for heterogeneity in teams' propensity to engage in discretionary play and for player characteristics that contribute to discretionary infractions, respectively. The vector SMXs,g,p controls for the relationship between within game score margin and a player's propensity to engage in discretionary play across score margin game states as well as the potential for close game biased officiating, and the vector PPXs,g,p controls for referee biases related to balanced penalty calling.

---

[16] The two-sided indicator variables are equal to zero for the first and second penalties of the game.

Estimation Procedure, Discrimination Tests and Results

Estimation Procedure

Equation 1 was estimated using weighted least squares to account for variance heterogeneity inherent in the Bernoulli process. The standard errors of the estimates were clustered by season-game. The coefficients of control variables are similar across specifications and support similar inferences as the previous research. For brevity we do not present the coefficients of the control variables in table format and discuss the results based on the most saturated model specification, assuming all else constant (the complete presentation of the control variable estimates is available from the authors upon request).

The coefficient of the constant is approximately 0.47, which suggests that the probability that a penalty is called on the home team is approximately −0.03 (=0.47−0.50) less than the visiting team. The difference is significant at the 0.01 level. Many of the score margin fixed effects are significantly different from one another and support the finding that referees exhibit a close-game bias and call more penalties on teams that are leading compared to those that are trailing by similar score margin states. For example, the difference in the coefficients (which are associated increments in penalty probabilities) of the home team leading and trailing by one, two, and three goals are approximately 0.90, 0.12, and 0.10, respectively, with each of the differences significant at the 0.01 level. The coefficients of the previous and second previous penalty call two-sided indicator variables are approximately −0.07 and −0.04, respectively, and are significant at the 0.01 level, suggesting that referees balance their within-game penalty calling across competing teams.

The coefficients of the log differences in heights, weights, and ages of players on the ice during penalty events are approximately 0.96, 0.35, and 0.19, respectively; the coefficients of the heights and weights are significant at the 0.05 level and the coefficient of ages is significant at the 0.01 level. At the sample means of height (366 in.), weight (1026 lb), and ages (138 years) of the collective five players on the ice during penalty events, a 12-in., 50-lb, and 20-year increase results in associated increments in penalty probabilities of approximately

$$0.03 = \left(0.96 \times \ln\left(\frac{366+12}{366}\right)\right), 0.02\left(0.35 \times \ln\left(\frac{1026+50}{1026}\right)\right), 0.03\left(0.19 \times \ln\left(\frac{138+20}{138}\right)\right),$$

respectively. A number of the season-team two sided indicator variables are significantly different from zero.

Discrimination Tests

We test the discrimination hypotheses in terms of the sign and significance of the estimates contained within B, which are changes in the probabilities of a team penalty call based on which of the two competing teams has more ethnic-specific players on the ice across the various referee ethnic mixes. The null hypothesis of no discrimination in terms of calling more penalties against teams that are represented by relatively more players of a different and same ethnicity than their own are as follows:

$$H_o(No\,discrimination): B \leq 0 \forall P = R \wedge R = R \quad (2)$$

$$H_o(No\,discrimination): B \geq 0 \forall P = R \wedge R = R \quad (3)$$

Both Eqs. 2 and 3 test for discrimination based on homogeneous referee pairings (i.e., $R = R$). Equation 2 is based on different player and referee ethnic interactions (i.e., $P \neq R$) and Eq. 3 is based on same and referee ethnic interactions (i.e., $P = R$). The former and latter tests reject the null hypothesis if the coefficients are significantly negative and positive, respectively. Equation 1 includes the interaction of mixed ethnicity referee pairings (i.e., $R \neq R$) both to provide more accurate control variables estimates through utilizing an increased amount of data, as well as to provide the information relating to patterns in penalty calling across the referee-player ethnic interactions.

Test Results

Table 5 presents the discrimination test results obtained from Eq. 1. The column headers indicate the model specification implemented. Column (1) presents the results obtained from the parsimonious specification, column (2) from the intermediate specification, and column (3) from the saturated specification. The table footer identifies the control variables included in each model specification. Table 5 has two horizontal and vertical panels that categorize the results across player ethnic groups. The referee mixes are identified in the left hand column. The standard errors are in parentheses. Equations 2 and 3 are specified such that one-sided significance is appropriate to reject the null hypothesis of no discrimination. Therefore, asterisks that denote one-sided statistical significance in the direction of rejecting the appropriate null hypothesis are included for the homogeneous referee mixes.

The discrimination test presented in Eq. 3 rejects the null hypothesis of no discrimination amongst French Canadian referees. The coefficient of the interaction of two French Canadian referees and more French Canadian players on the ice variables is approximately −0.09 across all specifications. Each of the coefficients has an associated one-sided significance level of 0.01. The coefficients are straightforward to interpret in terms of the impact on the relative probability of a team penalty. During games officiated by two French Canadian referees, teams that have more French Canadian players on the ice than the opposing team are approximately 9% less likely to be called for a penalty than their opponent.

Table 5 Changes in probability of a team penalty based on the team that more ethnic specific players on the ice across referee ethnic mixes

Referee ethnic mix	(1)	(2)	(3)	(1)	(2)	(3)
	English Canadian players			French Canadian players		
Two English	0.0284	0.029	0.027	−0.00623	0.000337	0.00264
	(0.0125)	(0.0125)	(0.0123)	(0.0117)	(0.0117)	(0.0118)
One English and one French	0.0133	0.0137	0.0129	0.00601	0.0105	0.0148
	(0.0149)	(0.0148)	(0.0149)	(0.0146)	(0.0145)	(0.0146)
One English and one American	0.0166	0.0182	0.0208	0.0211	0.0299	0.0285
	(0.0156)	(0.0155)	(0.0152)	(0.0150)	(0.0149)	(0.0150)
Two French	−0.0443	−0.0472	−0.0364	−0.0944***	−0.0879***	−0.0879***
	(0.0384)	(0.0387)	(0.0388)	(0.0358)	(0.0358)	(0.0356)
One French and one American	−0.00174	−0.00212	−0.00655	0.027	0.0276	0.0246
	(0.0315)	(0.0310)	(0.0309)	(0.0338)	(0.0337)	(0.0341)
Two American	0.0122	0.0179	0.00828	0.00937	0.0183	0.0123
	(0.0556)	(0.0546)	(0.0560)	(0.0449)	(0.0439)	(0.0447)
	American players			International players		
Two English Canadian	−0.00171	0.00201	0.000416	−0.0134	−0.0153	−0.0148
	(0.0111)	(0.0111)	(0.0110)	(0.0122)	(0.0123)	(0.0122)
One English and one French	0.00508	0.00841	0.0102	−0.0141	−0.0168	−0.014
	(0.0141)	(0.0140)	(0.0140)	(0.0149)	(0.0148)	(0.0149)
One English and one American	0.0153	0.0212	0.0249	0.00134	−0.000158	0.00681
	(0.0148)	(0.0147)	(0.0148)	(0.0151)	(0.0150)	(0.0149)
Two French	−0.0359	−0.0325	−0.0143	−0.0656	−0.0725	−0.0532
	(0.0360)	(0.0358)	(0.0352)	(0.0370)	(0.0371)	(0.0364)
One French and one American	0.0101	0.0138	0.00469	−0.0126	−0.0167	−0.0219
	(0.0282)	(0.0279)	(0.0282)	(0.0295)	(0.0292)	(0.0296)

(continued)

Table 5 (continued)

Referee ethnic mix	(1)	(2)	(3)	(1)	(2)	(3)	(1)	(2)	(3)
	English Canadian players			French Canadian players					
Two American	0.0511	0.0567	0.0573	0.0494	0.0563	0.0471
	(0.0487)	(0.0483)	(0.0496)	(0.0449)	(0.0449)	(0.0469)
Adjusted R-squared	0.0024	0.0074	0.0335	0.0024	0.0074	0.0335
Control variable included						
Season-team effects	Yes	Yes	Yes	Yes	Yes	Yes
Player variable effects	No	Yes	Yes	No	Yes	Yes
Score-margin effects	No	No	Yes	No	No	Yes
Balanced penalty calling effects	No	No	Yes	No	No	Yes

***, **, * , indicate one-sided statistical significance in the direction of rejecting the appropriate null hypothesis at the 1%, 5%, and 10% levels, respectively. Asterisks denoting significance are only included in homogeneous referee mixes. The standard errors are in parentheses and clustered by season-game

Number of observations is 14,721 across all specifications

We note that although the previous statement is an exact interpretation of the results, there is potential for more general inferences based on the notion that the two-sided ethnic specific indicator variables are intended to be proxy variables for the amount of ethnic specific players on a team. French Canadian players that play on teams with more, compared to less, French Canadian players on their roster, will more than likely, be on the ice more for penalties. Therefore, the possibility exists that French Canadian referees are favoring teams with more French Canadian players on their roster as opposed (or in addition) to basing it on the relative number of French Canadian players on the ice.

The panel relating to English Canadian players presented in Table 5 shows that English Canadian referees call more penalties on teams that have more English Canadian players on the ice. This could be considered an anti-discrimination finding. However, both the magnitudes of the coefficients (approximately 0.03 across all model specifications) and the associated t-values (ranging from 2.20 to 2.32, indicating a two-sided significance at the 0.10 level) are relatively small/low.[17] This level of significance is considered to be relatively low considering almost half of the games (41% or 1483 games) were officiated by two English Canadian referees. As a result, this finding is a potential result of a spurious correlation rather than anti-discrimination in penalty calling bias. None of the other player ethnic and referee ethnic mix interactions are significant.

Concluding Remarks

This chapter tests for team-level discrimination among professional hockey referees. The analyses use real-time penalty level data to control for additional within-game referee biases as well as for the changing costs of player infractions (and therefore penalties) across score margin game states. The null hypothesis of no discrimination among French Canadian referees is rejected. During games officiated by two French Canadian referees, teams that have more French Canadian players on the ice than the opposing team are approximately 9% less likely to be called for a penalty. While the estimation procedure uses the number of ethnic players on the ice as a proxy for the ethnic composition of teams, the results are potentially generalizable beyond the game-team-penalty level to the game-team level.

Given that discrimination manifests beyond the most obvious entity to a broader group there exists a productive area of future research beyond exclusively testing for various forms of discrimination. Discrimination can potentially result in a positive externality in terms of favorable treatment to people belonging to a different ethnic group, and in a negative externality in terms of unfavorable treatment to people belonging to a same ethnic group.

---

[17] Asterisks denoting levels of significance are not included in the table because the signs of the coefficients are in opposition to rejecting the null hypothesis of no discrimination.

In the case presented in this chapter, discrimination is manifesting towards the team rather than towards the player in the form of French Canadian referees favoring teams with more French Canadian players. Players of a different ethnicity (e.g., English Canadian) relative to the referees exhibiting a same-ethnicity bias potentially benefit in terms of fewer penalty calls, providing the player has teammates who are of the same ethnicity as the referee (e.g., French Canadian). This idea that discrimination that manifests beyond the most obvious entity can result in externalities among other people/groups associated with the discriminated groups extends well beyond the context for sports. It is reasonable to consider the team as a firm and the players as employees. Suppliers that discriminate at the firm level can unintentionally affect a firm's employees of a different race toward which the discrimination is based.

References

Abrevaya, J. and McCulloch, R. (2006): Reversal of Fortune: A Statistical Analysis of Penalty Calls in the National Hockey League. Working Paper, Department of Economics, University of Texas, Austin.

Balmer, N.J., Nevill, A. and Williams, M. (2001): Home Advantage in the Winter Olympics (1908–1998). Journal of Sports Sciences, 19 (2), pp. 129–139.

Balmer, N.J., Nevill, A. and Williams, M. (2003): Modeling Home Advantage in the Summer Olympic Games. Journal of Sports Sciences, 21 (6), pp. 469–478.

Boyko, R.H., Boyko, A.R. and Boyko, M.G. (2007): Referee Bias Contributes to Home Advantage in English Premiership Football. Journal of Sports Sciences, 25 (11), pp. 1185–1194.

Bruggink, T.H. and Williams, D. (2009): Discrimination Against Europeans in the National Hockey League: Are Players Getting Their Fair Pay? American Economist, 54 (2), p. 82.

Buraimo, B., Forrest, D. and Simmons, R. (2010): The 12th Man? Refereeing Bias in English and German Soccer. Journal of the Royal Statistical Society: Series A (Statistics in Society), 173 (2), pp. 431–449.

Curme, M.A. and Daugherty, G.M. (2004): Competition and Pay for National Hockey League Players born in Quebec. Journal of Sports Economics, 5 (2), pp. 186–205.

Dawson, P., Dobson, S., Goddard, J. and Wilson, J. (2007): Are Football Referees Really Biased and Inconsistent? Evidence on the Incidence of Disciplinary Sanctions in the English Premier League. Journal of the Royal Statistical Society: Series A (Statistics in Society), 170 (1), pp. 231–250.

Dohmen, T.J. (2008): The Influence of Social Forces: Evidence from the Behavior of Football Referees. Economic Inquiry, 46 (3), pp. 411–424.

Garicano, L., Palacios-Huerta, I. and Prendergast, C. (2005): Favoritism under Social Pressure. Review of Economics and Statistics, 87 (2), pp. 208–216.

Garrett, T.A. (2003): Aggregated Versus Disaggregated Data in Regression Analysis: Implications for Inference. Economics Letters, 81 (1), pp. 61–65.

Jones, C.H., and Walsh, W.D. (1988): Salary Determination in the National Hockey League: The Effects of Skills, Franchise Characteristics, and Discrimination. Industrial and Labor Relations Review, 41 (4), pp. 592–604.

Jones, C.H., Nadeau, S. and William, W.D. (1999): Ethnicity, Productivity and Salary: Player Compensation and Discrimination in the National Hockey League. Applied Economics, 31 (5), pp. 593–608.

Kahane, L.H. (2005): Production Efficiency and Discriminatory Hiring Practices in the National Hockey League: A Stochastic Frontier Approach. Review of Industrial Organization, 27 (1), pp. 47–71.

Kahn, L.M. (1991): Discrimination in Professional Sports: A Survey of the Literature. Industrial and Labor Relations Review, 44 (3), pp. 395–418.

Mohr, P.B, and Larsen, K. (1998): Ingroup Favoritism in Umpiring Decisions in Australian Football. Journal of Social Psychology, 138 (4), pp. 495–504.

Lavoie, M., and Grenier, G. (1992): Discrimination and Salary Determination in the National Hockey League: 1977 and 1988 Compared, in: Advances in the Economics of Sport, Volume I (ed. G. Scully), Greenwich, CT: JAI Press.

Lavoie, M. (2000): The Location of Pay discrimination in the National Hockey League. Journal of Sports Economics, 1 (4), pp. 401–411.

Lavoie M. (2003): The Entry Draft in the National Hockey League: Discrimination, Style of Play, and Team Location. American Journal of Economics and Sociology, 62 (2), pp. 383–405.

Lavoie, M., Grenier, G. and Coulombe, S. (1987): Discrimination and Performance Differentials in the National Hockey League. Canadian Public Policy/Analyse de Politiques, 13 (4), pp. 407–422.

Longley, N. (1995): Salary Discrimination in the National Hockey League: The Effects of Team Location. Canadian Public Policy/Analyse de Politiques, 21 (4), pp. 413–422.

Longley, N. (2000): The Underrepresentation of French Canadians on English Canadian NHL Teams. Journal of Sports Economics, 1 (3), pp. 236–256.

Longley, N. (2003): Measuring Employer-Based Discrimination Versus Customer-Based Discrimination: The Case of French Canadians in the National Hockey League. American Journal of Economics and Sociology, 62 (2), pp. 365–381.

Longley, N. (2012): The Economics of Discrimination: Evidence from Hockey, in: The Oxford Handbook of Sports Economics (eds. Stephen Schmanske and Leo Kahane), New York, NY: Oxford University Press.

Mongeon, K. (2015): A Market Test for Ethnic Discrimination in the National Hockey League: A Game-Level Panel Data Approach. Journal of Sports Economics, 16 (5), pp. 460–481.

Mongeon, K. and Longley, N. (2013): A Methodology for Identifying the Impacted Groups in Referee Discrimination Studies. Applied Economics Letters, 20 (5), pp. 416–419.

Mongeon, K. and Longley, N. (2015): Testing for Ethnicity Discrimination among NHL Referees: A Duration Model Approach. Eastern Economic Journal, 40 (1), pp. 86–101

Mongeon, K., and Mittelhammer, R. (2012): Existence and Economics of Rationally Biased Officiating. Working Paper, Brock University.

Mongeon, K., and Mittelhammer, R. (2013): To Discriminate or Not to Discriminate: Is Data Aggregation the Question? Applied Economics Letters, 20 (16), pp. 1485–1490.

Parsons, C.A., Sulaeman, J., Yates, M.C. and Hamermesh, D.S. (2011): Strike Three: Discrimination, Incentives, and Evaluation. American Economic Review, 101 (4), pp. 1410–1435.

Pettersson-Lidbom, P. and Priks, M. (2010): Behavior under Social Pressure: Empty Italian Stadiums and Referee Bias. Economics Letters, 108 (2), pp. 212–214.

Price, J., and Wolfers, J. (2010): Racial Discrimination among NBA Referees. Quarterly Journal of Economics, 125 (4), pp. 1859–1887.

Price, J., Remer, M. and Stone, D. F. (2012): Sub-perfect Game: Profitable Biases of NBA Referees. Journal of Economics & Management Strategy, 21 (1), pp. 271–300.

Sirois, B. (2010): Discrimination in the NHL: Quebec Hockey Players Sidelined. Quebec: Baraka Books.

Sutter, M. and Kocher, M.G. (2004): Favoritism of Agents: The Case of Referees' Home Bias. Journal of Economic Psychology, 25 (4), pp. 461–469.

Szymanski, S., and Longley, N. (2001): A Market Test for Discrimination in the National Hockey League. Mimeo.

Witt, R. (2005): Do Players React to Sanction Changes? Evidence from the English Premier League. Scottish Journal of Political Economy, 52 (4), pp. 623–640.

Part IV
Ticket Demand and Ticket Pricing

The Effect of 'Superstars' on Attendance: NHL-Players in the German and Czech Hockey League

Christian Deutscher and Sandra Schneemann

Abstract During the 2012–2013 lock-out in the National Hockey League a number of especially European NHL-players signed temporary contracts with European hockey clubs. While the sporting abilities of these players are unquestioned, the attendance effects for the teams signing these players have remained unclear. This chapter analyzes game-level data from the German and the Czech premier hockey leagues to capture attendance effects of these "stars" usually playing in the NHL. We find positive attendance effects for NHL players in the Czech Extraliga, especially if they are on the away team's roster. For the German DEL the impact is considerably smaller and a positive impact can only be found for NHL players on the home team's roster. These results can be explained by differences in the importance of the sport in the two countries and the ensuing differences in the awareness of potential attendees.

Introduction

Labor disputes between team owners and the respective players' union are a common phenomenon in North American sports. If the parties fail to agree on a new collective bargaining agreement a reduction of the number of regular season matches or even the cancellation of an entire season – as in the National Hockey League (NHL) in 2004–2005 – are likely outcomes. Following the third lockout over a period of 20 years, many players left the NHL prior to the postposed start of the 2012–2013 campaign to play professional hockey in Europe. The most recent labor dispute started in the middle of September 2012 when the owners of the NHL teams were unable to agree with representatives of the players' union on the conditions to replace the 2005 collective bargaining agreement.[1] This uncertainty about

---

[1] Major disputes circled around the scope and the distribution of hockey-related revenues. Moreover, team owners advocated for the extension of maximum contract length and the organization of player pensions to reduce costs for the teams. Mediation initiated by the Federal Mediation

C. Deutscher (✉) • S. Schneemann
Department of Sports Science, Bielefeld University, Bielefeld, Germany
e-mail: christian.deutscher@uni-bielefeld.de

© Springer International Publishing AG 2017
B. Frick (ed.), *Breaking the Ice*, Sports Economics, Management and Policy 16,
https://doi.org/10.1007/978-3-319-67922-8_8

the start of the NHL season led 170 players to affiliate with teams overseas by November 2012. Due to restrictions on the number of foreign players allowed by many leagues most of the foreign NHL-players joined teams in their home country. This shift of players caused high media attention in America with ESPN even broadcasting games from Europe during the NHL lockout. Following successful negotiations between the National Hockey League and its players' union on January 6, 2013 the players returned to North America in preparation for a shortened season that started on January 19, 2013, more than 3 month behind its original schedule.

While the impact of the NHL lockout has been carefully investigated in terms of its effects in North America, little is known about the consequences for hockey in Europe. This is surprising as this situation offers a rare opportunity to analyze the impact of superstars who appear and leave in the middle of a season on attendance. Incoming players from the NHL can be considered as "superstars" as the NHL is unanimously considered to be the strongest league worldwide. Hence the question arises how attendance in Europe was affected by the arrival of NHL players. Using game level attendance data for two consecutive seasons from the German DEL (Deutsche Eishockey Liga) and the Czech Extraliga this chapter analyzes the impact of NHL players on hockey attendance in Germany and the Czech Republic. In our analysis we distinguish between NHL players on the home and the away team and find the impact on attendance to dramatically differ between the Czech Extraliga and the German DEL: For the Extraliga our findings document that superstars matter, especially if their appearance is a rare event, i.e. they are playing for the away team. The impact of stars on the home team on attendance is not as strong. For the DEL we find the impact of superstars on attendance to be considerably smaller than in Extraliga. While superstars on the away team do not matter at all they draw additional attendance if they play for the home team. This questions the decision of club managers to sign superstars for DEL-teams, as the clubs had to pay unusually high salaries and insurance premiums.[2]

This chapter starts with a review of the literature on the demand for team sports, the determinants of attendance in hockey and the impact of stars on attendance. In section "Professional Hockey in Germany and the Czech Republic" we describe the organizational structure of the two European leagues under consideration. Section "Data Description and Empirical Approach" describes the data and our empirical approach. In section "Data Description and Empirical Approach" we present the results of our estimations on the impact of NHL players on attendance in the two European leagues. We summarize our findings in section "Conclusion" where we also offer recommendations for team owners.

---

and Conciliation Service was discontinued after few days in November due to the lack of progress in the talks between the two parties. The league repeatedly canceled games as negotiations continued to fail throughout the month of December.

[2] Depending on a player's age, contract value and injury history the teams had to pay insurance fees between $20,000 and $70,000 per player for the 2 month period (www.espn.com/nhl/story//id/8403261/playing-europe-russia-easy-accomplish-locked-players).

Literature Review

Surveys on Determinants of Attendance in Sports

Borland and Macdonald (2003) in their widely quoted review of the literature distinguish five groups of variables as potential determinants of attendance demand for sporting competitions: consumer preferences, economic factors, the quality of viewing, characteristics of the contest and the supply capacity. Consumer preferences are rather complex compared to preferences for other goods, since factors like team loyalty, bandwagon effects and prestige have been found to be important determinants of the demand for sports contests. With respect to economic factors, such as ticket prices, opportunity and travel costs, income of potential fans, market size, unemployment and substitutes seem to affect attendance. The quality of viewing is influenced by the conditions of viewing, the time and the day of the contest, weather conditions and the availability of adequate food and sanitary facilities. Characteristics of a contest refer to the quality of the respective teams, including the presence of star players, the relevance of a particular match, the winning probability of the home team and the uncertainty of outcome. The supply capacity restricts attendance of a match as demand might exceed capacity. With respect to the impact of star players Borland and Macdonald (2003) report mixed evidence: while some studies find a significantly positive effect, others fail to find an effect of the presence of superstars on attendance.[3]

In their survey of the literature, Villar and Guerrero (2009) first distinguish different ways to measure attendance (average attendance, logarithm of attendance, proportion of tickets sold etc.) and criticize that a number of recent studies do not adequately deal with the problem of capacity restrictions by estimating simple OLS regression instead of using e.g. the Tobit estimator. With respect to ticket demand, economic factors, such as e.g. ticket prices, the price of complementary and substitute goods, income, unemployment, market size, stadium capacity and strikes are most important. The quality of a contest (the win probability of the home team, the expected quality of both teams, the presence of superstars, the degree of rivalry and the recent performance of the home team) also have a statistically significant impact on attendance. Moreover, the uncertainty of outcome (match, seasonal and long-term uncertainty) is found to be of minor importance as only long-term uncertainty seems to affect attendance. Finally, opportunity costs and other factors (weather, TV broadcasting, day and time of the contest, parallel events in other sports, the travel distance between the home and the away team, advertising and the racial composition of the teams) seem to matter far less than the variables discussed above.

---

[3] See e.g. Schofield (1983); Kahn and Sherer (1988); Hausman and Leonard (1997).

Analyzing the Determinants of Attendance in Hockey

Studies analyzing attendance in hockey predominantly use data from the NHL. Most of these studies focus on the impact of violence on attendance. Others analyze the effect of uncertainty of outcome, the impact of (re-)location, new arenas and/or of the NHL Lockout 2004–2005 on ticket demand.

Studies focusing on violence mostly find a positive effect of fighting on ticket demand in the NHL, e.g. Jones et al. (1993), Stewart et al. (1992), and Paul (2003). Jones et al. (1993) find violence and match attendance to be positively related and therefore confirm the "blood sport" hypothesis. Aggregate measures of violence are positively related to attendance both in the US and Canada. However, a negative relationship between attendance and extreme forms of violence is found for matches played in Canada while attendance is positively correlated with major penalties in matches played in the US. Assuming that team owners profit maximizers Stewart et al. (1992) argue that violence can be considered an important characteristic of the product "sports entertainment" to influence ticket demand directly and indirectly: On the one hand violence is a major determinant of attendance and therefore affects demand directly. On the other hand violence might have a positive impact on winning and as winning is positively related to attendance, violence can increase demand indirectly. However, the empirical results showing that violence affects attendance directly and indirectly are refuted by Coates et al. (2012).

Paul (2003) investigates the impact of policy changes concerning fighting and scoring on the demand for NHL games. Policy changes were introduced to attract more fans as reducing the extent of violence should improve the league's image while increasing the number of goals should increase the attractiveness of the game. However, the empirical analysis reveals that fighting is positively and scoring negatively related to attendance. Teams displaying a larger amount of violence attract more fans, especially in the USA, while the average number of goals scored in previous matches is negatively related to attendance.

In contrast to these studies Paul and Weinbach (2011) and Coates et al. (2012) find no significant relationship between fighting and attendance. Paul and Weinbach (2011) use data from the Quebec Major Junior Hockey League (QMJHL) while Coates et al. (2012) use information from the German Hockey League (DEL), the Finnish SM-liiga and the NHL. Results of the QMJHL show a strong effect of the win percentage of the home team on attendance, while scoring and fighting do not attract more fans. Coates et al. (2012) find that neither success nor attendance is positively related to violence.

Coates and Humphreys (2012) focus on another potential determinant of attendance: outcome uncertainty. Using data from the NHL, their findings seem to suggest that fans are more attracted by matches the home team is expected to win compared to even matches. Coates and Humphreys attribute this result to loss aversion. Furthermore, they find attendance to be positively related to scoring and negatively related to allowing goals and penalties. The authors conclude that the negative relationship between penalties and attendance confirms policies implemented by the NHL to curb violence.

Leadley and Zygmont (2006) investigate the impact of the quality of viewing on ticket demand by emphasizing the role of the modernity of an arena. Using data from the NHL it appears that an arena attracts approximately 15–20% more fans in the first year after opening, confirming that the age/modernity of an arena is an important factor in determining attendance. The so-called "honeymoon effect" (which also drives franchise values) lasts between 5 and 8 years and largely depends on the observation period chosen (Miller 2009; Büschemann and Deutscher 2011).

Jones and Ferguson (1988) and Cocco and Jones (1997) focus on the impact of the location of a Canadian NHL team on ticket demand. The former find a statistically significant relationship between location attributes (match is played in Canada, size of population and per-capita-income) and attendance. Furthermore, their results show a significantly positive impact of fighting, the number of stars playing for the respective teams, qualification for the playoffs, weekend matches and the teams' ranking on attendance while no effect is found for the uncertainty of outcome of a particular match. The authors conclude that location factors, league rules and team performance are the most important determinants of attendance. Cocco and Jones (1997) investigate the viability of Canadian small market franchises to analyze the relationship between location factors, team quality and ticket demand for Canadian NHL teams. Location factors are captured by the size of the population and per capita income in the city. In their estimations the authors also control for the ranking of the respective teams, outcome uncertainty, the relevance of a match for reaching the playoffs, the day of a match (weekend) and the playing style of the teams (fighting, skating or both) and find that population is negatively correlated with attendance while income and team quality of both the home and away team positively affect attendance.

Winfree and Fort (2008) as well as Rascher et al. (2009) focus on the impact of the NHL lockout 2004–2005 on attendance at minor and junior hockey leagues and the National Basketball Association (NBA). Both studies suggest a positive effect of the NHL lockout on attendance at the games in the leagues considered. Winfree and Fort (2008) find attendance of junior and minor league hockey teams to increase by about 5% during the lockout. However, the lockout variable is statistically significant only for minor league teams. Rascher et al. (2009) confirm the positive impact of the lockout on attendance in leagues competing with the NHL for fan interest: minor hockey leagues and the NBA. All five leagues exhibit a significant increase in demand by about 2% during the lockout.

Determining the Impact of Stars on Attendance

While some of the previously presented studies use variables to control for the presence of superstars in their models explaining attendance, others (Hausman and Leonard 1997; Berri et al. 2004; Berri and Schmidt 2006 as well as Brandes et al. 2008) explicitly focus on the presence of superstars as a (potential) determinant of attendance.

Hausman and Leonard (1997) test the effect of NBA superstars, namely Michael Jordan, Larry Bird, "Magic" Johnson, Isiah Thomas and Shaquille O'Neal, on television ratings and stadium attendance. Their results suggest a statistically significant and positive effect of the presence of a superstar playing for the visiting or the home team on local cable ratings. Among the superstars, Magic Johnson had by far the largest effect on TV viewership. His presence raises TNT's ratings by approximately 38%. Results for NBC data confirm the positive effect of superstars. With respect to gate attendance, Hausman and Leonard (1997) examine whether teams with a superstar on their roster attract more fans in away games than teams without a superstar. Their results suggest a large impact of superstars on road attendance that can be interpreted as a positive externality.

Berri et al. (2004) estimate different models analyzing the effect of superstars on fan interest in the NBA, measured by gate revenues. Depending on the model specification superstars have either a significantly positive or no effect on gate revenues. The two superstar measures are, first, the aggregated number of All-Star Game votes received by the players of a particular team (a measure of star attraction) and., second, dummies for four different players considered superstars: Michael Jordan, Shaquille O'Neal, Grant Hill and Charles Barkley. In addition, Berri et al. (2004) include control variables capturing team performance and quality, franchise characteristics (stadium capacity and age, expansion team, roster stability) and market characteristics (competitive balance, population, income). The authors estimate a double-logged model as well as linear models to examine the relationship between the different determinants of attendance. The effects of the star variables depend on the model specification. The coefficient of the All-Star votes turns out to be positive and statistically significant only in the double-logged model which is from an econometric point of view the more appropriate one, but fails to reach statistical significance at conventional levels in the linear model. Contrary to the results of Hausman and Leonard (1997) none of the four superstar players has a significant impact on gate revenue. Summarizing, Berri et al. (2004) compare the effect of a superstar on gate revenues with the effect of wins. As gate revenue is shown to be a function of wins and stadium capacity, the authors conclude that "it is performance on the court, not star power that attracts the fans in the NBA" (Berri et al, 2004: 44).

Based on Hausman and Leonard (1997), Berri and Schmidt (2006) examine the externality of superstars on road attendance in the NBA. The authors extend the work of Hausman and Leonard using a larger data set (1992–1993 through 1995–1996) and identifying a larger number of superstars. Similar to the Berri et al. (2004) study, Berri and Schmidt (2006) not only focus on individual star players, but on an aggregate measure of star power, again captured by the sum of votes for the All-Star game received by the players of a team. Further explanatory variables are the size of a team's market, the expansion status of a team, roster stability, competitive balance and the racial composition of a team. It appears that road attendance is affected significantly by team wins, star power and racial composition. Following the estimation of star power on road attendance, Berri and Schmidt (2006) examine the effect of individual star players on road attendance and to what extent this effect is due to the star appeal of a player or his on-court productivity. The results seem to suggest that productivity is more important for a team's opponent than star appeal, confirming the results of the previous study by Berri et al. (2004). Nevertheless stars attract fans and generate revenue, especially for a team's opponent.

The most recent empirical study on the impact of superstars on stadium attendance is Brandes et al. (2008). Contrary to previous studies the authors do not use data from the NBA, but the first division of the German soccer league ("Bundesliga"). Brandes et al. (2008) distinguish between "local heroes" and superstars and estimate their effect separately for home and away attendance. Brandes et al. (2008) define a superstar as a player whose market value is in the top 2% of the league's distribution of market values. A local hero is defined as "the most valued player of a particular team that has no superstars" (Brandes et al. 2008: 267). The authors include in their estimations several control variables to isolate the star and the local hero effect from other potential determinants of ticket demand: team characteristics such as reputation (average ranking in the last 20 years), stadium capacity and market characteristics (male population, unemployment rate and competitive balance). Fixed effects regressions reveal that superstars increase attendance both at home and in away matches while local heroes only attract fans in home matches.

Contrary to the available research that identifies superstars by either popularity or salary, we take a different approach. We identify NHL players playing in Europe during the lockout as superstars as none of them would have played here if it was not for the lockout. To control for factors affecting ticket demand we rely on variables used in previous research.

Professional Hockey in Germany and the Czech Republic

Germany and the Czech Republic are both members of ice hockey's umbrella organization IIHF (International Ice Hockey Federation). Since the Champions Hockey League had the inaugural season in 2014–2015, there was no international competition of any importance in the recent history of the sport in Europe. Therefore, the performance in the domestic league is of prime importance for the teams in both countries with respect to revenues and financial success. In the Czech Republic hockey and soccer are the most popular and successful sports in terms of drawing attention from both the media and supporters. When it comes to hockey in Germany, the situation is different: the DEL is certainly one of the more popular leagues but is ranked far behind the first soccer division (Bundesliga) and competes with basketball and handball for second place in terms of attendance and media interest. Total revenues in the 2011/12 season in the DEL was about 86 million Euro[4] (slightly more than 4% of the Bundesliga's revenue in 2011/12 (2.08 Billion Euro[5])).

---

[4] http://www.handelsblatt.com/sport/sonstige-sportarten/handball-basketball-eishockey-profiligen-kaempfen-um-den-silberrang/7369336.html

[5] http://www.bundesliga.de/de/liga/news/2012/dfl-stellt-bundesliga-report-2013-vor-bundesliga-bestaetigt-nachhaltiges-wachstum_0000238084.php

The Czech major hockey league "Extraliga" was founded following the political breakup of Czechoslovakia in 1993. Its antecessor, the "Czechoslovak First Ice Hockey League" started in 1931. The Extraliga organized its inaugural championship season in 1993/1994 with HC Kladno becoming the first champion. A total of 22 different teams has played in the Extraliga ever since with only 6 clubs being permanent members of the league.[6] In the first two seasons only 12 teams competed for the national championship, in 1995–1996 the Extraliga expanded to 14 teams. VHK Vsetín won the most titles, namely 6, but later withdrew from competition due to financial problems. Participation in the open league is regulated by a promotion and relegation system. Until the 2012–2013 season, the four lowest ranked teams had to play a relegation round with the worst performing team playing a best of seven series against the champion of the First League (the second division). Since the 2012–2013 season, the two worst teams of the play-outs play against the two winners of the play-offs in the First League.

In contrast to the Extraliga, the DEL is a closed shop without a relegation system since 2011. The DEL was established in 1994 following a period of financial distress for many hockey clubs. At the time the aim of the league organizers was therefore to offer an attractive competition combined with financial stability for the participating clubs that had not to fear relegation with the ensuing devaluation of their (player) assets. In the inaugural season 1994–1995, 18 teams participated with the Kölner Haie becoming the first champion. In the following seasons, the number of teams varied between 18 and 14. Since 2010–2011 the same 14 teams have been members of the DEL. Overall 31 different teams have participated in the DEL with only six being permanent members. The most successful club is Eisbären Berlin, winning a total of seven titles.

Both the DEL and Extraliga seasons are divided into a regular and a post-season. During the regular season, each of the 14 teams plays against each other four times (twice at each team's arena), resulting in 52 matches per team and 364 total matches per league. In both leagues, eight teams qualify for the playoffs, playing in three rounds for the championship.[7] The top six teams of the regular season directly qualify for the playoffs, and the next four teams play a preliminary round with the two winners advancing to the playoffs.[8] Both leagues have implemented roster restriction rules and limit the number of foreign players on a team. Currently, each DEL team is allowed to contract nine foreign players,[9] while only six foreign players are permitted in the Extraliga.

---

[6] Litvínov, Pardubice, Plzeň, Sparta Prag, Vítkovice and Zlín.

[7] Extraliga: best of seven series in each round. DEL: best of seven series in quarterfinals, best of five in semifinals and finals.

[8] In the Extraliga the preliminary round is played in a best of five series, in the DEL in a best of three series.

[9] Prior to the 2012/2013 season 10 foreign players were allowed to play for each team in the DEL. http://www.welt.de/sport/article12541845/DEL-senkt-Auslaenderquote-in-der-kommenden-Saison.html

Data Description and Empirical Approach

Our data includes information for all matches played during the regular seasons 2011–2012 and 2012–2013 in the DEL and the Czech Extraliga.[10] Overall 728 matches took place in both leagues during the two consecutive seasons. Our subsequent analysis, however, uses only 710 DEL and Extraliga matches: We excluded two games played in the DEL due to their unusual setting. The DEL winter game of the 2011–2012 season took place in a soccer stadium in Nuremberg in front of 50.000 spectators while the game of EHC München against Augsburger Panther was relocated to a different arena. Both games and venues exhibit idiosyncratic features that justify excluding them from the analysis. In the case of the Extraliga we were unable to obtain the betting odds for one particular match that we had, therefore, to exclude.[11] Moreover, during the 2012–2013 season three home games by Rytíři Kladno were played at an arena in Prague.[12] Again, for the sake of rigor we excluded these matches from the empirical analysis. As we control for the rank of the two teams prior to a match, we also had to exclude all matches played on the first day of the two seasons as no rank prior to the first match of a season is available, resulting in a data set including 710 matches for both leagues.

We collected our data from a variety of sources. Game related data was retrieved from the two leagues' official websites (www.del.org and www.hokej.cz) as well as from the widely used hockey website www.hockeydb.com. It includes information on the teams, the day and time of the match, the number of spectators and the respective region and arena. Control variables, such as the number of inhabitants of the cities and their respective unemployment rates were collected from the websites of the Federal Employment Agency of Germany (www.statistic.arbeitsagentur.de), the German Federal Statistical Office (www.destatis.de), the Czech Statistical Office (www.czso.cz) and the Ministry of the Interior of the Czech Republic (www.mvcr.cz/mvcren). To measure the geographical distance between the clubs we rely on information from Google Maps.

Descriptive Attendance Statistics

We follow Villar and Guerrero (2009) and use the capacity utilization (attendance/capacity) as our dependent variable. Welki and Zlatoper (1999) also favor using a proportion instead of the absolute number of spectators because the former controls for varying stadium capacities. "The larger the stadium capacity, the greater the

---

[10] As no NHL-player was in the league at the time of the playoffs, play-off matches are not considered in our analysis.

[11] Vitkovice HC - Mlada Boleslav on October 9, 2011.

[12] Against Pardubice, Brno and Slavia Prag.

Table 1 Descriptive statistics of attendance, capacity and capacity utilization

Variable	League	Obs	Mean	Std. Dev.	Min	Max
Attendance	DEL	726	6,048.3	3,683.0	1,503	18,500
	Extraliga	724	4,950.5	1,890.8	1,801	17,000
Capacity utlization	DEL	726	0.64	0.22	0.19	1
	Extraliga	724	0.63	0.22	0.13	1

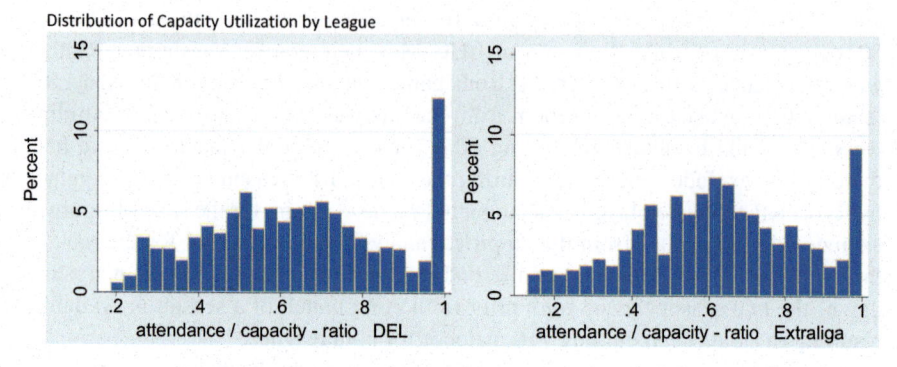

Fig. 1 Distribution of capacity utilization by League

number attending if the inclination to attend is equal across ticketholders in the various cities" (Welki and Zlatoper 1999: 287).

Table 1 shows that the average attendance was about 6,000 (DEL) and 5,000 (Extraliga) during the observation period. The majority of matches in the DEL and Extraliga did not sell out; in only 15% of the matches capacity utilization is above 90%. This eases the interpretation of the results as a large percentage of sellouts would raise the question of how many tickets could have been sold given larger arena capacities. The variance in attendance is much larger for German than for Czech clubs as the standard deviation of *attendance* in the DEL is twice as large as in the Extraliga. This is not surprising as the DEL cities differ very much in size. While the league features teams from Germany's largest cities (Berlin, Hamburg, Munich) on the one hand, there are also teams from rather small places (e.g. Villingen-Schwenningen, Straubing, Iserlohn).

Figure 1 displays the distribution of capacity utilization for both leagues and also shows a certain number of right censored observations, i.e. matches that were sold out. As this ratio is our dependent variable in the subsequent analysis, we estimate the impact of stars on attendance using a Tobit regression model.

Further statistics at the team-level show that the average number of spectators varies considerably between the clubs. This helps explaining the higher standard deviation of *attendance* for matches played in the DEL (Fig. 2).[13] Eisbären Berlin is the most popular club in the DEL with an average attendance of 14,000 spectators. On the other hand, nine clubs have on average less than 5,000 spectators. In the

---

[13] (In 2011/12 Chomutov was relegated to the first league and Mlada Boleslav promoted to the Extraliga, so that in sum there is one team more in the Extraliga compared to the DEL).

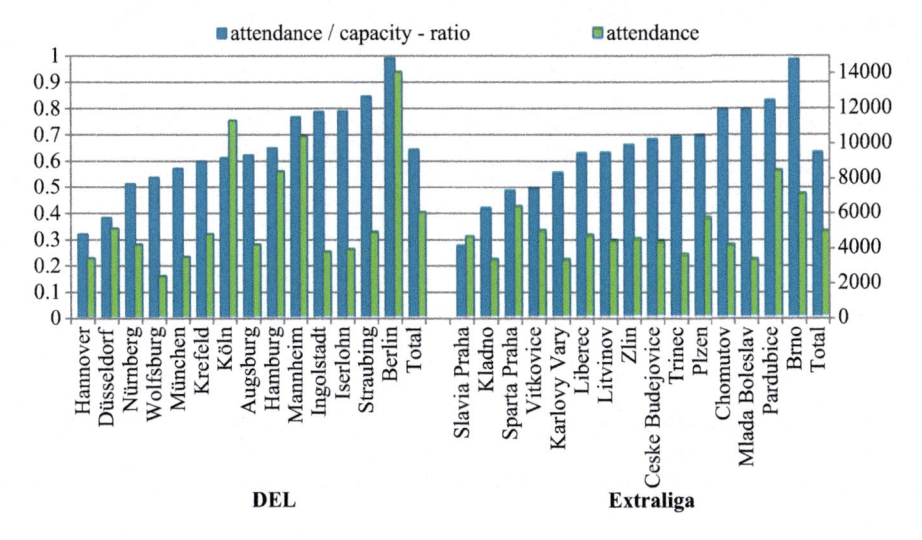

Fig. 2 Average attendance and capacity utilization by club

Extraliga, the most popular club is Pardubice with an average of about 8,500 spectators. Overall, the Czech clubs seem to be more homogenous with respect to attendance, although capacity utilization in Extraliga matches varies almost as much as in the DEL.

Descriptive NHL-Player and Attendance Statistics

Concerning the NHL-players who played in one of the two European leagues during the lockout we have information on the number of NHL-players under contract with the home and away team, their respective date of arrival and departure, their nationality and the number of All-Star Games these players appeared in plus information on the clubs they have previously played for. We define NHL-players playing in the DEL or the Extraliga during the lockout as superstars. As there are teams with up to 5 NHL-players at the same time, we construct different variables to test the impact of these superstars on attendance: dummy variables indicating if there is at least one NHL-player on the home team's or the away team's roster *(NHL home/away)* and variables that represent the number of NHL-Players on the home respectively the away team *(Number NHL home/away)*. For each league we estimate Tobit regressions with both alternatives.

A total of 40 different NHL-players appeared in the German and Czech league during the lockout, 12 in the DEL and 28 in the Extraliga.[14] These NHL-players

---

[14] See Table 8 in the Appendix.

Table 2a Number of matches with NHL-player(s)

		DEL		Extraliga	
		Frequency	Percent	Freqeuncy	Percent
NHL home	0	649	89.39	574	79.28
	1	77	10.61	150	20.72
	Total	726	100	724	100
NHL away	0	645	88.84	568	78.45
	1	81	11.16	156	21.55
	Total	726	100	724	100
NHL home or away	0	595	91.96	520	71.82
	1	131	18.04	204	28.18
	Total	726	100	724	100
NHL home and away	0	699	96.28	622	85.91
	1	27	3.72	102	14.09
	Total	726	100	724	100

were active for 7 different teams[15] in Germany and 11 in the Czech Republic.[16] While the DEL team Adler Mannheim contracted 4 NHL players, the Extraliga clubs Kladno and Ceske Budejovice[17] signed 5 NHL-players each.[18] Altogether we observe 131 (204) matches in the DEL (Extraliga) with at least one NHL-player representing either the squad of the home or the away team (Table 2a).

Only few matches involved teams with more than two NHL-players, especially in the DEL. Here only 18 matches were played with teams that had signed a total of three or more NHL-players (Table 2b). In the Extraliga there is one match with two teams that had contracted 8 NHL-players.

While most of the players from the NHL returned to their home country during the lockout this is not true for everybody. Table 3 provides information on the nationalities of the NHL-players, while Table 4 reports descriptive statistics of different attributes of the NHL-players. Because of the restriction on the number of foreign players in both leagues and the insecurity about the length of the lockout, most clubs only contracted native NHL-players. Half of the NHL-players playing in the DEL were German, in the Extraliga even 75% of the NHL-players were Czech. In Germany every third NHL-player had already played for the respective team in the DEL, in the Extraliga almost half of the NHL-players went back to a club they had played for in the past already *(teamexperience)*. This previous stint with the team was usually at the beginning of the players' careers and prior to their first NHL

---

[15] Adler Mannheim (4 NHL players), EHC Red Bull München (2 NHL players), ERC Ingolstadt (1), Eisbären Berlin (2), Hamburg Freezers (1), Hannover Scorpions (1), Krefeld Pinguine (1).

[16] Ceske Budejovice (5), Chomutov (3), Karlovy Vary (1), Kladno (5), Liberec (4), Pardubice (3), Plzen (1), Slavia (1) and Sparta Prague (1), Trinec (2), Vitkovice (2).

[17] Ceske Budejovice signed 5 different NHL-players, but only 4 were with the team at the same time. One player (Martinek Radek) had already left the team again after 1 week.

[18] The names of the players contracted by the different teams are displayed in Table A in the appendix.

Table 2b Number of NHL-players per match

		DEL			Extraliga		
		Frequency	Percent	Cum.	Frequency	Percent	Cum.
No. of NHL players	0	649	89.39	89.39	574	79.28	79.28
Home	1	52	7.16	96.56	85	11.74	91.02
	2	21	2.89	99.45	24	3.31	94.34
	3	1	0.14	99.59	18	2.49	96.82
	4	3	0.41	100	21	2.90	99.72
	5	0	0	100	2	0.28	100
	Total	726	100		724	100	
No. of NHL players	0	645	88.84	88.84	568	78.45	78.45
Away	1	55	7.58	96.42	91	12.57	91.02
	2	23	3.17	99.59	25	3.45	94.48
	3	2	0.28	99.86	20	2.76	97.24
	4	1	0.14	100	14	1.93	99.17
	5	0	0	100	6	0.83	100
	Total	726	100		724	100	
No. of NHL players	0	595	81.96	81.96	520	71.82	71.82
Home and away	1	71	9.78	91.74	63	8.70	80.52
	2	42	5.79	97.52	48	6.63	87.15
	3	12	1.65	99.17	29	4.01	91.16
	4	1	0.14	99.31	24	3.31	94.48
	5	5	0.69	100	23	3.18	97.65
	6	0	0	100	9	1.24	98.90
	7	0	0	100	7	0.97	99.86
	8	0	0	100	1	0.14	100
	Total	726	100		724	100	

Table 3 Nationality of NHL-players

DEL				Extraliga			
Nation	Freq.	Percent	Cum.	Nation	Freq.	Percent	Cum.
CAN	3	25.00	25.00	CAN	5	17.86	17.86
GER	6	50.00	75.00	CZE	21	75.00	92.86
US	1	8.33	83.33	FIN	1	3.57	96.43
US CAN	2	16.67	100	SK	1	3.57	100
Total	12	100		Total	28	100	

experience. As the start of the NHL season was unsure players turned to their previous club rather than signing with another team in an unfamiliar city.

Figure 3 compares the *capacity utilization* at matches with and without NHL-players for the teams that signed at least one NHL-player. Perhaps surprisingly, the attendance at matches with NHL-players is lower in the DEL than at matches without NHL-players. Considering the individual clubs of the DEL, there are only marginal differences between matches with and without NHL-players, except for the

Table 4 Descriptive statistics of NHL-player characteristics

Variable	League	Obs.	Mean	Std. Dev.	Min.	Max.
Team experience	DEL	12	0.33	0.49	0	1
(Dummy)	Extraliga	28	0.46	0.51	0	1
Matches played in	DEL	12	16.33	8.02	6	32
League in 2012/2013	Extraliga	28	19.14	8.80	4	34
Age	DEL	12	28.84	3.73	23.18	35.25
	Extraliga	28	29.08	4.81	24.07	40.60
All Star game (Dummy)	DEL	12	0.33	0.49	0	1
	Extraliga	28	0.14	0.36	0	1
Years played in NHL	DEL	12	7.67	3.87	3	15
	Extraliga	28	8.29	4.35	3	19
Matches played in NHL	DEL	12	422.75	244.96	38	813
	Extraliga	28	470.32	299.27	102	1,346
Draft number	DEL	12	67.67	51.05	5	172
	Extraliga	28	83.93	80.60	4	241

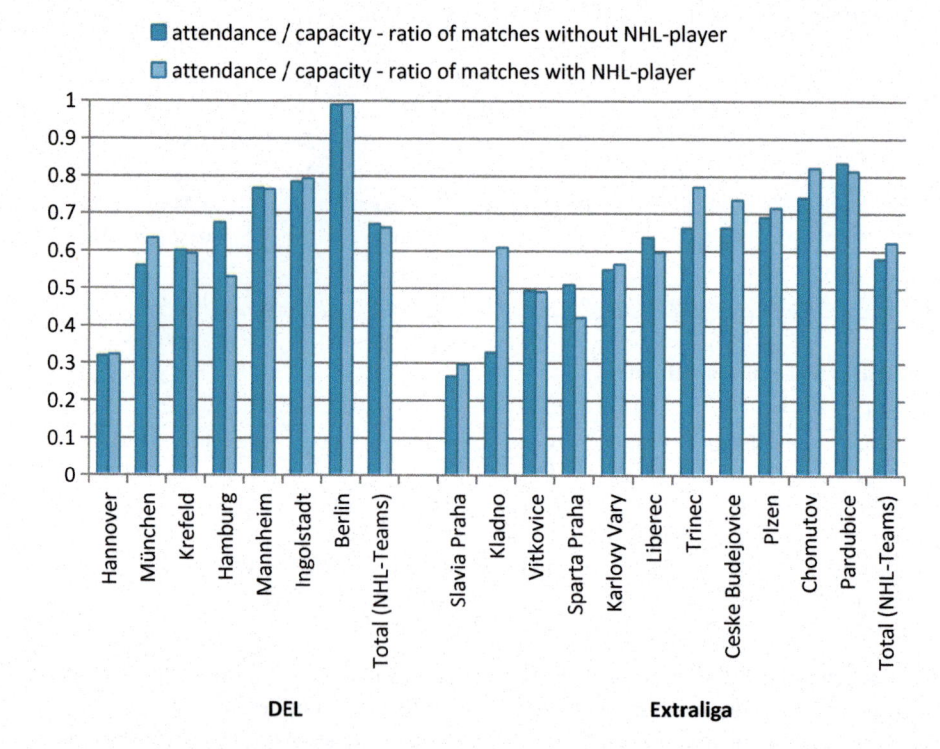

Fig. 3 Attendance – NHL-teams

team from Hamburg. On average 8,700 fans attended a match of the Hamburg Freezers in 2011–2012 and 2012–2013, compared to only about 6,900 spectators per match after contracting Canadian NHL-player Jamie Benn. In general, the average attendance at Hamburg decreased from 9,200 in 2011–2012 to 7700 in 2012–2013. This development has to be attributed to the fact that the club had stopped giving away free tickets in an attempt to increase attendance in 2011–2012.[19] If we exclude Hamburg from the comparison, there are slightly more spectators at matches with NHL-players than without. Contrary to the development in Germany, most of the Czech clubs that signed a NHL-player saw attendance increasing, especially Kladno. The team almost doubled its capacity utilization.[20] Overall, matches with NHL-players attracted slightly more spectators than matches without NHL-players in the Extraliga, even after excluding Kladno from the analysis.

Control Variables

Apart from the presence of star players, other factors are likely to have an impact on ticket demand and, therefore, need to be controlled. Following Borland and Macdonald (2003) who point out that consumer preferences, economic aspects, the quality of viewing, characteristics of the sporting contest and the supply capacity are important determinants of attendance, we control for most of these determinants. As consumer preferences like loyalty and habit should depend on the respective team and be constant over the two considered seasons we control for these factors including team-fixed effects in one of the models. With respect to the economic aspects, we collected data on the size and the economic conditions of the local market as proxied by the number of inhabitants each year *(inhabitants)*, the unemployment rate of the respective cities *(unemployment)* and the availability of substitutes, measured as the distance between a given team and the nearest other first division hockey team *(distancehockey)*.[21] Table 5 reports the descriptive statistics for these variables as well as for additional control variables. In Germany the clubs are located in larger cities compared to the Czech Republic. The unemployment rates in the cities range between 3.3 % (Ingolstadt) and 16 % (Litvinov) and are on average higher in Czech than in German cities. Due to the smaller state territory of the Czech Republic compared to Germany the average distance to the nearest first division hockey club is smaller in the Czech Republic than in Germany.

---

[19] www.taz.de/!107131/

[20] This could be due to the fact that Kladno signed a total of 5 different NHL-players of whom one was Jaromir Jagr, one of the most famous Czech hockey players of all times.

[21] Unfortunately, ticket prices are not available for the two leagues. This should not be much of a problem as studies analyzing the impact of prices on attendance often face the problem of a wide range of ticket prices for different seating categories. As a result empirical analyses of the impact of ticket prices on attendance often fail to produce meaningful results (Villar and Guerrero 2009).

Table 5 Descriptive statistics of control variables

Variable	League	Level	Obs.	Mean	Std. Dev.	Min	Max
Inhabitants (Mio.)	DEL	Team	14	0.74	0.93	0.05	3.44
	Extraliga	Team	15	0.26	0.41	0.03	1.24
Unemployment	DEL	Team	14	7.05	2.35	3.3	11.95
	Extraliga	Team	15	8.60	3.57	4.24	15.80
Distance hockey	DEL	Team	14	94.00	55.27	27	240
	Extraliga	Team	15	62.57	39.38	1	135
Arena age	DEL	Team	14	20.35	9.87	12.58	44.84
	Extraliga	Team	15	39.32	11.39	21.15	51.71
Arena renovation	DEL	Team	14	6.69	2.56	3.22	12.45
	Extraliga	Team	15	11.06	5.64	6.73	26.17
Multifunctional arena	DEL	Team	14	0.64	0.50	0	1
	Extraliga	Team	15	0.67	0.49	0	1
6 pm (Dummy)	DEL	Match	726	0.64	0.48	0	1
	Extraliga	Match	724	0.58	0.49	0	1
Distance	DEL	Match	726	407.95	200.25	27	791
	Extraliga	Match	724	237.49	138.35	1	530
Heterogeneity	DEL	Match	726	0.12	0.15	−0.30	0.55
	Extraliga	Match	724	0.14	0.15	−0.30	0.52
Capacity	DEL	Match	726	9,485.61	4,248.31	4,500	18,500
	Extraliga	Match	724	8,394.85	3,208.78	4,200	17,000

An important factor for the quality of viewing is the age and the modernity of an arena. To capture these factors, we collected data on the years that have elapsed since the respective arena was opened *(arenaage)* and the years since the latest large renovation of an arena *(arenarenovation)*. Czech arenas are almost twice as old as the arenas in Germany and the latest relevant renovation of the Czech arenas also dates back longer (Table 5). In addition, some teams play their home games in multifunctional arenas while others have arenas which are exclusively designed to serve as hockey arenas. In the Extraliga 10 out of 15 arenas are multifunctional while in the DEL 9 out for 15 arenas are multifunctional. An arena exclusively build for hockey has seating fitted to the game and is expected to produce a better atmosphere. We therefore also include a dummy variable, indicating if an arena is a multifunctional place or not *(multifunctional arena)*.

Furthermore, we have information on the time and the day of a match, which has also been found to impact the quality of viewing and attendance (Table 6).

In the Extraliga and the DEL most of the games take place on either Friday or Sunday. Because of the large percentage of matches that are played on one of these days we decided not to include a series of dummies capturing the day of the week but instead use a dummy indicating if the match took place on one of these two more important days *(mainday)*. Most of the games start after 5 pm except for Sunday games in the DEL. Here more than 30% start at 2.30 pm and more than 50% at 4.30 pm. As we assume evening games to draw a larger crowd we use a dummy variable indicating if a game is played at or after 6 pm *(6 pm)*. To control for the time

Table 6 Weekdays of matches

	DEL			Extraliga		
	Frequency	Percent	Cum.	Frequency	Percent	Cum.
Monday	13	1.79	1.79	11	1.52	1.52
Tuesday	79	10.88	12.67	128	17.68	19.2
Wednesday	23	3.17	15.84	64	8.84	28.04
Thursday	6	0.83	16.67	38	5.25	33.29
Friday	311	42.84	59.5	228	31.49	64.78
Saturday	6	0.83	60.33	2	0.28	65.06
Sunday	288	39.67	100	253	34.94	100
Total	726	100		724	100	

of a match during the regular season, we also include the matchday and its square in the subsequent analysis *(matchday)*. Furthermore attendance might be affected by holidays. As studies find that attendance is higher when matches are played on holidays (Borland and Macdonald 2003: 488; Villar and Guerrero 2009: 146) we include a dummy variable *Christmas*, indicating whether a match has been played between December 23 and January 2. During this time, people usually are on vacation and are, therefore, more likely to attend a match. About 2–3% of the matches played in the DEL and Extraliga are played during that particular period.

Characteristics of the sporting contest refer, among other factors, to the quality and significance of a match as well as to the uncertainty of outcome. The quality of a match can be proxied by the playing strength of the respective teams. In the subsequent analysis, the abilities of the teams are represented by the rank of the teams prior to the respective match *(rank)*.

Rivalry has been shown to impact attendance as well. As rivalry is primarily influenced by geographical proximity of the teams facing each other, we collected data on the distance between the home and the away team *(distance)*. The distance between the two cities can also be considered an economic factor: the longer the distance, the higher the travel costs for the fans of the away team. Therefore we expect a negative impact of distance on attendance.

Another characteristic of a sporting contest relates to the uncertainty of outcome of a match. Some fans might be more interested in balanced matches than in matches that seem to be decided in advance. We measure the uncertainty of outcome as the difference in winning probabilities, calculated from betting odds, between the home and away team *(heterogeneity)*. Table 5 shows that matches in the Extraliga seem to be slightly more unbalanced than games in the DEL (0.12 vs. 0.14).

Finally, since Borland and Macdonald (2003) argue that the capacity of a stadium is an important determinant of ticket demand for sporting contest, we include in our estimations the capacity of an arena. The German arenas tend to be larger than the ones in the Czech Republic. On average, the German arenas hold more than 9,500 spectators, whereas the Czech arenas have an average capacity of about 8,500.

As explained above, *capacity utilization* during a particular match played by home team i against away team j at matchday t is our dependent variable. As this ratio is right censored we estimate various Tobit models, which are of the following general form:

$$capacityutilization_{ijt} = \beta_0 + \beta_1 NHL_i + \beta_2 NHL_j + \beta_3 inhabitants_i + \beta_4 unemployment_i$$
$$+ \beta_5 distancehockey_i + \beta_6 arenarenovation_i + \beta_7 arenarenovation_i^2$$
$$+ multifunctional\ arena + \beta_8 mainday_{ijt} + \beta_9 6p$$
$$+ \beta_{10} Christmas_{ijt} + \beta_{11} rank_i + \beta_{12} rank_j + \beta_{13} distance_{ij}$$
$$+ \beta_{14} heterogeneity_{ijt} + \beta_{15} matchday + \beta_{16} matchday^2$$
$$+ \beta_{17} capacity_i + \varepsilon_{ijt}$$

Moreover, we estimate models without team- and time-constant variables as well as with home and away team fixed effects to document the robustness of our findings.

Results

Table 7 shows the impact of the presence and the number of NHL-players on attendance in matches in the DEL (Models 1 and 2, 5 and 6) and the Extraliga (Models 3 and 4, 7 and 8).

It appears that the impact of signing one or more NHL-player(s) on attendance varies between leagues and across model specifications. While Models 1 and 2 indicate that signing an NHL-player does not have a statistically significant effect on attendance in the DEL – neither if that player is appearing on the home or the away team. On the other hand, the appearance of an NHL player increased fan interest considerably in the Extraliga (Models 3 and 4). However, without controls for team fixed effects, the results suggest an increase in attendance only if the visiting team has an NHL player on its roster. Once team fixed effects are included NHL players on both teams increase attendance. Overall, the effect of NHL-players on attendance is much stronger for matches in the Extraliga compared to games in the DEL. The magnitude of the coefficient varies between 1–3 % (DEL) and 1–7 % (Extraliga).

These results remain virtually unchanged when we replace the dummy indicating the appearance of at least one NHL player by a count variable for the exact number of NHL players (Models 5–8). Signing one additional NHL-player increases *capacity utilization* significantly only for matches in the Extraliga. While in the DEL only NHL-players playing for the home team affect attendance (Model 5), there is a stronger effect of NHL-players playing for the away team in the Extraliga. In both models (7 and 8), the coefficient of the number of NHL-players on the away team's roster is positive and statistically significant and exceeds the coefficient of the number of NHL-players on the home team, which is only significant when including team fixed effects. Overall, the appearance of NHL-players seems to have a positive effect on attendance, especially in the Extraliga.

Table 7 Tobit results (Dependent variable: capacity utilization)

	DEL		Extraliga		DEL		Extraliga	
	Model 1	Model 2	Model 3	Model 4	Model 5	Model 6	Model 7	Model 8
NHL home	0.0311	0.0065	0.0096	0.0520***				
	(0.0231)	(0.0158)	(0.0219)	(0.0157)				
NHL away	0.0031	0.0076	0.0717***	0.0330**				
	(0.0215)	(0.0152)	(0.0216)	(0.0162)				
Number NHL (Home)					0.0309**	0.0142	0.0109	0.0276***
					(0.0142)	(0.0097)	(0.0085)	(0.0063)
Number NHL (Away)					0.0063	0.0092	0.0540***	0.0465***
					(0.0140)	(0.0099)	(0.0085)	(0.0067)
Inhabitants	0.1199***		0.2368***		0.1211***		0.2394***	
	(0.0110)		(0.0443)		(0.0110)		(0.0438)	
Unemployment	0.0018		0.0061**		0.0015		0.0066**	
	(0.0050)		(0.0029)		(0.0050)		(0.0029)	
Distance hockey	0.0006***		0.0023***		0.0005***		0.0023***	
	(0.0001)		(0.0003)		(0.0001)		(0.0003)	
Arena renovation	−0.0081*	−0.0104	−0.0093***	0.0103	−0.0079*	−0.0069	−0.0105***	0.0044
	(0.0043)	(0.0191)	(0.0029)	(0.0160)	(0.0043)	(0.0190)	(0.0028)	(0.0152)
Arena renovation2	−0.0002	0.0000	0.0002***	−0.0003	−0.0002	−0.0001	0.0002***	−0.0002
	(0.0002)	(0.0007)	(0.0001)	(0.0004)	(0.0002)	(0.0007)	(0.0001)	(0.0003)
Multifunctional arena	−0.0672***		0.0388**		−0.0675***		0.0345*	
	(0.0210)		(0.0183)		(0.0208)		(0.0177)	

(continued)

Table 7 (continued)

	DEL		Extraliga		DEL		Extraliga	
	Model 1	Model 2	Model 3	Model 4	Model 5	Model 6	Model 7	Model 8
Rank home	−0.0117***	−0.0037***	−0.0048***	−0.0052***	−0.0117***	−0.0037***	−0.0046***	−0.0050***
	(0.0012)	(0.0009)	(0.0009)	(0.0007)	(0.0012)	(0.0009)	(0.0009)	(0.0007)
Rank away	−0.0037***	−0.0011	−0.0035***	−0.0022***	−0.0034***	−0.0010	−0.0043***	−0.0031***
	(0.0012)	(0.0009)	(0.0009)	(0.0007)	(0.0012)	(0.0009)	(0.0009)	(0.0007)
Distance	−0.0002***	−0.0002***	−0.0004***	−0.0003***	−0.0002***	−0.0002***	−0.0003***	−0.0003***
	(0.0000)	(0.0000)	(0.0000)	(0.0000)	(0.0000)	(0.0000)	(0.0000)	(0.0000)
Heterogeneity	0.0653	0.0293	0.1220**	0.0110	0.0535	0.0273	0.1818***	0.0878
	(0.0814)	(0.0664)	(0.0612)	(0.0542)	(0.0822)	(0.0664)	(0.0631)	(0.0602)
Christmas holidays	0.1394***	0.1368***	0.0730*	0.0838***	0.1408***	0.1361***	0.0912**	0.1034***
	(0.0398)	(0.0263)	(0.0413)	(0.0281)	(0.0396)	(0.0262)	(0.0404)	(0.0267)
Mainday	0.0775***	0.0649***	0.0682***	0.0650***	0.0773***	0.0649***	0.0676***	0.0624***
	(0.0162)	(0.0107)	(0.0132)	(0.0091)	(0.0161)	(0.0107)	(0.0129)	(0.0086)
6 pm	0.0136	−0.0130	0.0107	−0.0265***	0.0136	−0.0131	0.0114	−0.0269***
	(0.0130)	(0.0087)	(0.0139)	(0.0099)	(0.0130)	(0.0087)	(0.0136)	(0.0094)
Matchday	−0.0008	0.0001	−0.0015	−0.0015	−0.0012	−0.0003	−0.0026	−0.0029**
	(0.0018)	(0.0012)	(0.0018)	(0.0012)	(0.0018)	(0.0012)	(0.0018)	(0.0012)
Matchday2	0.0001**	0.0001**	0.0000	0.0000*	0.0001**	0.0001***	0.0001**	0.0001***
	(0.0000)	(0.0000)	(0.0000)	(0.0000)	(0.0000)	(0.0000)	(0.0000)	(0.0000)
Capacity	−0.0139***		−0.0474***		−0.0140***		−0.0469***	
	(0.0025)		(0.0044)		(0.0024)		(0.0043)	

Season 2012	−0.0105	−0.0130	−0.0115	−0.0231	−0.0142	−0.0188	−0.0284*	−0.0425***
	(0.0138)	(0.0134)	(0.0175)	(0.0143)	(0.0134)	(0.0131)	(0.0160)	(0.0127)
Constant	0.9187***	0.8714***	0.9208***	0.8573***	0.9284***	0.8474***	0.9233***	0.8744***
	(0.0533)	(0.0962)	(0.0579)	(0.0427)	(0.0534)	(0.0961)	(0.0567)	(0.0406)
Home team dummies	No	Yes	No	Yes	No	Yes	No	Yes
Away Team Dummies	No	Yes	No	Yes	No	Yes	No	Yes
N of observations	710	710	710	710	710	710	710	710
McKelvey & Zavoina's R2	0.806	0.806	0.502	0.779	0.553	0.806	0.526	0.802

Standard errors in parentheses, * $p < 0.1$, ** $p < 0.05$, *** $p < 0.01$

Some of the control variables also have a statistically significant effect on capacity utilization, but often this effect depends on the model specification. In the Extraliga, for example, the coefficient of *arenarenovation* is significantly negative and its square significantly positive only when team dummies are not included in the estimation. Including team dummies often reduces the statistical significance of the explanatory variables while the explained variance increases, suggesting that there the results are to a large extent driven by team specific effects. In almost all models the coefficients of *mainday, distance* and *Christmas* have the expected sign and are highly significant. The demand for hockey is higher, when a match takes place on a Friday or Sunday and especially during (*Christmas*) holidays. The larger the distance between the teams, the fewer spectators watch a match because the degree of rivalry decreases and the travel costs for the fans of the away team increase.

In Germany fans prefer ice hockey arenas compared to multifunctional arenas: the coefficient of the dummy variable *multifunctional arena* is negative and statistically (Models 1 and 5) while it is significant and positive in the Extraliga. Estimations that exclude team dummies yield differences in fan behavior between the DEL and Extraliga: The coefficient of the unemployment rate is insignificant in Germany but positive and statistically significant in the Czech Republic. This is in line with the existing literature that does not agree on the potential effect of unemployment on attendance either. While some authors assume that unemployment is negatively related to attendance, others argue that unemployment can have a positive effect on attendance as sports can help people to "manage personal frustrations" (Villar and Guerrero 2009: 135).

Similar effects for DEL and Extraliga matches occur with respect to city size on attendance: the more inhabitants the city of a hockey's club has the more spectators attend a match. The rank of the home and away team prior to a match has a statistically significant and negative impact on attendance in almost every model. Thus, the further down a team is ranked, the fewer spectators are interested in watching a match of that particular team. The same is true for the away team. This confirms the importance of team quality on attendance.

Conclusion

In contrast to previous studies on the impact of superstars on attendance, we do not focus on players who stay in the league for the entire season but on players who come and go during a particular season due to a labor dispute in another league. The NHL lockout can be used as an ideal test case, because many of its players (whom we term "superstars") moved to European leagues on a short term basis. We analyze the impact of superstar appearances on attendance in Czech and German hockey. Controlling for a large number of other determinants of ticket demand we find attendance to increase significantly with the arrival of superstars in the Czech Extraliga, but fail to find a comparable effect for the German DEL.

The differences in the findings are quite easy to explain: First, the importance of hockey is much higher in the Czech Republic. While average attendance at league games is comparable in both countries, the size of the German population is more than seven times larger than the Czech population. Thus, hockey interest is much higher in the Czech Republic. Second, Czech hockey fans are on average more familiar with the NHL as more prominent Czech players are playing in that league. Moreover, the Czech national hockey team is quite successful in international tournaments such as the World Cup and the Olympic Games. As international success of a national team is an important determinant for increasing the public's interest in a particular sport, hockey attracts relatively more fans in the Czech Republic than in Germany.

Concluding, our results suggest that signing popular players only leads to an increase in attendance if the sport is already very popular in the respective country. Otherwise this strategy is associated with higher costs only.

Future research should investigate the behavior of teams and fans in other leagues, such as the Russian and the Swedish hockey league. Since hockey is very popular in these countries one would expect a positive impact of NHL-players on attendance. However, since the setting is very unique and lockouts in the NBA or NFL rarely cause players to move temporarily to other leagues, analyses across sports will be difficult.

Appendix

Table 8 Name and team of NHL-players playing in Extraliga and DEL

Extraliga		DEL	
Player	Team	Player	Team
Polak, Roman	Vitkovice HC	Seidenberg, Dennis	Adler Mannheim
Kuba, Filip	Vitkovice HC	Goc, Marcel	Adler Mannheim
Klesla, Rostislav	Trinec Ocelari HC	Pominville, Jason	Adler Mannheim
Hudler, Jiri	Trinec Ocelari HC	Hecht, Jochen	Adler Mannheim
Neuvirth, Michal	Sparta Praha	Wheeler, Blake	EHC Red Bull München
Sobotka, Vladimir	Slavia Praha HC	Stastny, Paul	EHC Red Bull München
Rask, Tuukka	Plzen HC	Giroux, Claude	Eisbären Berlin
Kindl, Jakub	Pardubice HC	Briere, Daniel	Eisbären Berlin
Hemsky, Ales	Pardubice HC	Sulzer, Alexander	ERC Ingolstadt
Krejci, David	Pardubice HC	Benn, Jamie	Hamburg Freezers
Pavelec, Ondrej	Liberec Bili Tygri HC	Greiss, Thomas	Hannover Scorpions
Smid, Ladislav	Liberec Bili Tygri HC	Ehrhoff, Christian	Krefeld Pinguine
Simmonds, Wayne	Liberec Bili Tygri HC		
Stewart, Chris	Liberec Bili Tygri HC		
Jagr, Jaromir	Kladno		
Plekanec, Tomas	Kladno		
Zidlicky, Marek	Kladno		

(continued)

Table 8 (continued)

Extraliga		DEL	
Player	Team	Player	Team
Tlusty, Jiri	Kladno		
Kaberle, Tomas	Kladno		
MacDonald, Andrew	Karlovy Vary HC		
Frolik, Michael	Chomutov Pirati		
Jurcina, Milan	Chomutov Pirati		
Chimera, Jason	Chomutov Pirati		
Radek, Martinek	Ceske Budejovice HC		
Ference, Andrew	Ceske Budejovice HC		
Hanzal, Martin	Ceske Budejovice HC		
Michalek, Milan	Ceske Budejovice HC		
Prospal, Vaclav	Ceske Budejovice HC		

References

Berri, D.J. and M.B. Schmidt (2006): On the Road with the National Basketball Association's Superstar Externality. Journal of Sports Economics, 7, pp. 347–358.

Berri, D.J., M.B. Schmidt and S.L. Brook (2004): Stars at the Gate: The Impact of Star Power on NBA Gate Revenues. Journal of Sports Economics, 5, pp. 33–50.

Borland, J. and R. Macdonald (2003): Demand for Sport. Oxford Review of Economic Policy, 19, pp. 478–502.

Brandes, L., E. Franck and S. Nüesch (2008): Local Heroes and Superstars: An Empirical Analysis of Star Attraction in German Soccer. Journal of Sports Economics, 9, pp. 266–286.

Büschemann, A. and C. Deutscher (2011): Did the 2005 Collective Bargaining Agreement Really Improve Team Efficiency in the NHL? International Journal of Sport Finance, 6, pp. 298–306.

Coates, D. and B.R. Humphreys (2012): Game Attendance and Outcome Uncertainty in the National Hockey League. Journal of Sports Economics, 13, pp. 364–377.

Coates, D., M. Battré and C. Deutscher (2012): Does Violence in Professional Ice Hockey Pay? Cross Country Evidence from three Leagues, in: Violence and Aggression in Sporting Contests (R.T. Jewell ed.), New York: Springer.

Cocco, A. and J.C.H. Jones (1997): On Going South: The Economics of Survival and Relocation of Small Market NHL Franchises in Canada. Applied Economics, 29, pp. 1537–1552.

Hausman, J.A. and G.K. Leonard (1997): Superstars in the National Basketball Association: Economic Value and Policy. Journal of Labor Economics, 15, pp. 586–624.

Jones, J.C.H. and D.G. Ferguson (1988): Location and Survival in the National Hockey League. Journal of Industrial Economics, 36 (4), pp. 443–457.

Jones, J.C.H., D.G. Ferguson and K.G. Stewart (1993): Blood Sports and Cherry Pie. American Journal of Economics and Sociology, 52, pp. 63–78.

Kahn, L.M. and P.D. Sherer (1988): Racial Differences in Professional Basketball Players' Compensation. Journal of Labor Economics, 6, pp. 40–61.

Leadley, J.C. and Z.X. Zygmont (2006): When is the Honeymoon Over? National Hockey League Attendance, 1970–2003. Canadian Public Policy/Analyse de Politiques, 32 (2), pp. 213–232.

Miller, P.A. (2009): Facility Age and Ownership in Major American Team Sports Leagues: The Effect on Team Franchise Values. International Journal of Sport Finance, 4, pp. 176–191.

Paul, R.J. (2003): Variations in NHL Attendance: The Impact of Violence, Scoring, and Regional Rivalries. American Journal of Economics and Sociology, 62, pp. 345–364.

Paul, R.J. and A.P. Weinbach (2011): Determinants of Attendance in the Quebec Major Junior Hockey League: Role of Winning, Scoring, and Fighting. Atlantic Economic Journal, 39, pp. 303–311.

Rascher, D.A., M.T. Brown, M.S. Nagel and C.D. McEvoy (2009): Where Did National Hockey League Fans Go During the 2004–2005 Lockout? An Analysis of Economic Competition between Leagues. International Journal of Sport Management and Marketing, 5, pp. 183–195.

Schofield, J.A. (1983): The Demand for Cricket: the Case of the John Player League. Applied Economics, 15, pp. 283–296.

Stewart, K.G., D.G. Ferguson and J.C.H. Jones (1992): On Violence in Professional Team Sport as the Endogenous Result of Profit Maximization. Atlantic Economic Journal, 20, pp. 55–64.

Villar, J.G. and P.R. Guerrero (2009): Sports Attendance: A Survey of the Literature 1973–2007. Rivista di Diritto e di Economia dello Sport, 5, pp. 112–151.

Welki, A.M. and T.J Zlatoper (1999): US Professional Football Game-Day Attendance. Atlantic Economic Journal, 27, pp. 285–298.

Winfree, J.A. and R. Fort (2008): Fan Substitution and the 2004–05 NHL Lockout. Journal of Sports Economics, 9, pp. 425–434.

An Exploration of Dynamic Pricing in the National Hockey League

Rodney J. Paul and Andrew P. Weinbach

Abstract Dynamic pricing of tickets to NHL games are studied through data from three teams that adopted that practice in 2013–2014. Dynamic ticket pricing differs from variable ticket pricing in that prices are allowed to fluctuate throughout the season based upon supply and demand. Through a regression model, it is discovered that the greatest impact on dynamic ticket prices is due to popular opponents. Uncertainty of outcome is only found to be significant in a "non-traditional" hockey market with many entertainment substitutes. Other factors such as weekends and monthly effects due to playoff races are also shown to be important.

Introduction

Dynamic pricing of tickets is the latest innovation in the selling of admission to sporting events. The dynamic revolution began in Major League Baseball and quickly spread across teams in that league. With its apparent success and growing popularity, it was only a matter of time until dynamic pricing made its way into the National Hockey League. For the 2013–2014 NHL season, three teams introduced dynamic pricing of their hockey tickets across different sections within their respective arenas. These three teams were the Anaheim Ducks, Minnesota Wild (St. Paul), and Ottawa Senators.

These teams represent a nice cross section of NHL teams in terms of geographic location and team success. Anaheim is in southern California and would be considered a "non-traditional" hockey market as the nice weather makes playing hockey outside on the pond impossible. Therefore, due to the climate and the scarcity of playing ice, many residents do not grow up playing hockey and therefore the game does not likely draw the majority of fans from those who played the game as children. In addition, being in southern California, the substitute entertainment options

---

R.J. Paul (✉)
Falk College of Sport and Human Dynamics, Syracuse University, Syracuse, NY, USA
e-mail: rpaul01@syr.edu

A.P. Weinbach
E. Craig Wall Sr. College of Business Administration, Coastal Carolina University, Conway, SC, USA

for professional hockey are quite vast including many other sports (two NBA teams in Los Angeles, a MLB team in Anaheim and another in Los Angeles, college football and basketball (USC and UCLA), etc.), other entertainment options (concerts, theaters, shows), and many outdoor activities in the year-round nice temperatures.

In St. Paul, Minnesota, hockey is a very popular sport and is played in most high schools. In addition, NCAA hockey is very well-liked in this region of the country. Fans are generally familiar with the sport and have a genuine passion for the game. St. Paul does offer other sports entertainment options (NBA, NFL, and MLB teams in addition to college), but hockey is likely higher on the list of preferred sports than it is in many other cities across the United States. The weather in St. Paul during the NHL season is generally quite cold, which comes with its own outdoor entertainment options (skiing, ice skating, snowmobiling, etc.), but likely does not offer the plethora of outdoor activities that exists in the warm-weather climate of Anaheim.

Ottawa is the capital of Canada, where hockey is the top draw in terms of sports. Hockey is a national passion of Canadians with the game being a big part of the country's culture. The popularity of hockey is immense in Canada with many leagues for youngsters, popular developmental junior hockey leagues (OHL, WHL, QMJHL), adult leagues, and professional hockey. The climate is typically quite cold and most other sports are quite far behind hockey in terms of popularity.

In addition to how different the three team cities that used dynamic pricing are in terms of geography, climate, and alternative sports and entertainment options, there were also substantial differences in the quality of play of these teams during the 2013–2014 season. Anaheim started out with a high level of success and sustained it throughout the regular season. Minnesota was a middle-of-the-pack team for most of the season that made major personnel moves at the trade deadline and was in a tight and ultimately successful playoff race at the conclusion of the season. Ottawa had high hopes entering the 2013–2014 campaign off of the playoff success of the previous season, but the team played poorly and was eliminated from playoff contention quite early.

Given the introduction of dynamic pricing by the teams in these three cities, coupled with the differences in geography, history with the sport, and team success, the goal of this research is to investigate how different factors influence dynamically-formed ticket prices for NHL teams. We will investigate the role of opponents (regional rivals and the top teams in the league), days of the week, months of the season, on-ice performance variables, and the role of uncertainty of outcome and expected scoring as it relates to ticket prices to NHL games.

The following section describes the process and practice of dynamic pricing and compares it to variable ticket pricing strategies. The third section is the literature review of dynamic pricing, including recent research performed specifically on sports. The fourth section describes the data, explains the regression model, and presents the empirical results. The fifth section compares the results of the highest-priced section to the lowest-priced section to ascertain if there are differences in the factors that influence fans based upon their level of income or wealth. The final section summarizes and discusses the findings and concludes the paper.

Dynamic Pricing in Sports and Comparisons to Variable Pricing Models

Dynamic pricing is the newest advancement in ticket pricing strategy, offering another level of sophistication beyond variable pricing. Variable pricing has been quite common in the NHL for the past decade or more. Just as teams price individual sections of the arena differently, variable pricing strategies set the cost of tickets at different price points based upon factors such as opponents and weekends versus weekdays. This third-degree price discrimination scheme allows for the team to capture higher revenues by recognizing that fans have a major difference in their willingness to pay for different games. Prime opponents and weekends are generally more popular with fans and the increased demand for these games lead to higher prices. Teams recognize differences between games and price accordingly before the season begins. Variable ticket prices are announced in advance and do not change once released.

Dynamic ticket pricing offers a different model for consumers purchasing tickets. Instead of announcing fixed ticket prices of distinct price points for different games and having those prices persist throughout the selling period; dynamic ticket pricing allows for supply and demand to alter prices in real time. These market generated prices for tickets fluctuate throughout the season, up until game time, based upon the level of demand and the number of tickets remaining. Prices will rise and fall based upon a variety of factors in the marketplace.

The advantage of a dynamic pricing strategy over a variable pricing strategy is that dynamic pricing allows for a considerable upside in terms of revenue generation. If a team is playing particularly well, a playoff race is intensifying, or if opponents become more interesting due to their success or a rivalry grows, prices can move to reflect actual demand at the time of the game, rather than the perceived level of interest based upon preseason expectations. Dynamic pricing can capture upside movements in prices, much like a secondary market seller on Stubhub, when the game generates a high level of fan interest. Likewise, if things turn sour for a particular team, dynamic pricing allows for decreases in ticket prices to a level where fans will still purchase admission to the game. The use of dynamic pricing allows for a maximization of revenues throughout the season based upon factors which may not be obvious when ticket prices are first released to the public (as in variable pricing strategies).

The dynamic marketplace for tickets is not a pure open market, however, as it is likely that price floors are put in place to prevent ticket prices from falling to a level that would irritate season ticket holders. Most season ticket purchasers are earning a discount compared to individual game ticket purchases, which is one of the advantages of being a season ticket holder (many teams offer other benefits as well such as season ticket holder events, special merchandise, discounts at the team store, etc.). If the true level of demand for a game is quite low, however, it may not make sense to drop the price below a certain floor so as to not irritate the season ticket base, which creates immediate transactions costs in terms of customer service and may impact future season ticket sales in a negative fashion.

Under situations of reduced ticket demand (i.e. poor team performance), ticket prices in a variable pricing model cannot directly fall, but the teams could offer other deals to stimulate sales such as two-for-one coupons, meal or merchandise coupons, reduced-price or free parking at the arena, etc. Dynamic pricing offers the advantage of being able to impact consumers directly through price as the cost of tickets is lowered to the customer. In addition, secondary market prices (i.e. Stubhub) would already have fallen below the set price under the variable pricing model, leading to fewer sales. Dynamic pricing offers a level of defense against this as tickets offered directly from the team will reflect the overall level of supply and demand. In terms of situations of increased demand for tickets, variable pricing strategies are impotent as prices have already been set, the game will sell out, and secondary market prices will be much higher than the posted ticket prices. In dynamic pricing, however, the team captures the additional revenues of increased prices due to the high level of demand.

Literature Review on Dynamic Pricing

Dynamic pricing is a relatively new phenomenon in the sports ticket marketplace. Although the practice is recent, some literature has already explored the subject matter. Using data from EBAY and Stubhub, Sweeting (2012) captured both prices and quantities in a dynamic ticket pricing setting for Major League Baseball. Through monitoring prices over a window of time, Sweeting (2012) found that sellers cut price by 40% as the game approaches. Overall, however, Sweeting (2012) found that the use of dynamic pricing allowed for an increase in the expected payoff of the seller by 16%. In this study, however, the gains went to individuals reselling tickets in the secondary market, not to the teams directly.

Drayer et al. (2012) also examined ticket prices and quantity sold with data provided from a secondary market firm for the National Football League. Using the number of tickets sold and the average ticket price, they showed that prices respond to consumer demand in the secondary market. Their findings revealed that resellers of tickets are able to capture $260,000 worth of consumer surplus when tickets are priced in a dynamic setting.

In relation to primary ticket market sales, through the teams themselves, Paul and Weinbach (2014) studied dynamic pricing through data gathered on four Major League Baseball teams during the 2011 season. In investigating the key determinants of demand for dynamically priced tickets, their research revealed that prices differ due to weekend games, key opponents, promotions, and starting pitchers. Many similarities did exist in terms of significant determinants of prices across teams, but there were some individual marketplace differences across cities that suggest some heterogeneity among fans purchasing baseball tickets.

The sports ticket marketplace research on dynamic pricing is based on other industries that have used dynamic pricing for some time. A review of the literature on dynamic pricing that distinguishes between posted-price and price-discovery markets is noted in Elmaghraby and Keskinocak (2003). Bremaud (1980) and Gallego and van Ryzin (1994) derived optimality conditions using models of the continuous-pricing problem based on intensity control theory. Both studies showed that at any given point in time, the optimal price is lower as inventory increases and is higher the longer the time remaining in which to sell the product.

Empirical research on dynamic pricing by airlines has been studied by Burger and Fuchs (2004). They described a model where airline seats are initially sold at a preset price and are then automatically adjusted over time based on the number of remaining seats and the level of observed demand. Escobari (2009) also analyzed airline pricing and found statistically significant higher fares when there was a higher percentage of seats sold, significantly lower rates for flights on Tuesday (relative to Thursday) and for flights further into the future. Their study focused on the market for non-stop flights from Miami to Boston.

Data and Regression Model

The data for dynamic pricing used by Anaheim, Minnesota, and Ottawa was gathered directly from the team websites. Each day prices for all games remaining in the season were captured. Given that the data was obtained by observing changes in prices on the team website, we did not have access to quantity sold data. Our only piece of information available directly from the website were ticket prices for each game. Data for the other variables mentioned below come from www.nhl.com except for the gambling market odds which was gathered from www.covers.com.

Our dependent variable is the average price across all ticket sections for each of the three teams that used dynamic pricing during the 2013–2014 season. In each case, we use the closing price (day of the game) to attempt to incorporate all information about each game on the schedule. We run each team as a separate regression equation focusing on the key factors that are likely to influence prices in this market.

The independent variables include on-ice team attributes, a measure of uncertainty of outcome in the game, the market-based expected scoring in the game, key opponents, the day of the week, and the month of the season. On-ice attributes related to the performance of the home team include fights-per-game and points-per-game (a measure of team success).

The fights-per-game variable was calculated by taking the number of fights in each game and creating a moving average throughout the season. Fighting has been shown to increase attendance in professional leagues in North America where they are allowed (Jones 1984; Jones et al. 1993, 1996; Paul 2003; Paul et al. 2011, 2013). Fighting was shown to have a positive and significant effect on attendance in these studies. Although fighting is not allowed in the DEL league in Germany, evidence was found that physical play (penalty minutes) increased attendance (Coates et al. 2011). The same result related to physical play was not found to affect attendance in the SM-Liiga in Finland (Coates et al. 2011). Fighting was not shown to have an impact on attendance in junior hockey in the Quebec Major Junior Hockey League (Paul and Weinbach 2011).

In all of the studies of fighting and attendance, however, fighting was included across the pool of teams in the league. In that setting, the fighting variable may capture the impact of different levels of fighting across teams. In this research, we run the regression model for each of the three teams individually and therefore the variable captures only the changes in ticket price based upon changes in the frequency in fighting over the course of the season.

Points-per-game was calculated on a moving average basis in a similar fashion to the fighting variable. In an NHL game, a team earns two points for a win, one point for an overtime loss or a shootout loss (ties no longer exist in the NHL), and zero points for a regular loss. The points-per-game variable was calculated by dividing the number of points earned divided by the total possible number of points (two times the number of games). For both the fights-per-game and points-per-game variables, the value of the variable going into the game was used as the independent variable. If fans prefer more fights and better team success, these variables will be positively related to ticket price in the dynamic pricing setting.

The uncertainty of outcome hypothesis is an important and well-studied topic in sports economics (e.g. Coates and Humphreys (2012) on the NHL). Our measure of uncertainty of outcome for individual NHL games comes from the betting market. The use of the betting market prices as a measure of uncertainty of outcome first appeared in studies of soccer in England by Peel and Thomas (1988, 1992). The link between uncertainty of outcome, as measured by game odds, and attendance has been shown for soccer (Forrest and Simmons 2002). In addition, the case for betting market odds being the best measure of match uncertainty for soccer matches has been made by Buraimo et al. (2006). Betting market odds were used as a measure of uncertainty of outcome in Major League Baseball by Knowles et al. (1992) and Rascher (1999). Lemke et al. (2010) established the link between betting market odds and ticket sales in baseball.

The betting market odds on the game are converted into home team win probabilities. The probability of a home team win is then included as an independent variable in the regression model. If fans prefer more uncertainty of outcome, this variable will positively influence demand and will have a positive relationship to ticket price.

Given that betting market prices were available to use for our measure of uncertainty of outcome, the betting market also provides a measure of expected scoring in terms of the total. Totals in hockey are generally five-and-a-half goals or five goals, with an odds adjustment. We tried the model using the probability of an over coupled with the goal line, but the odds adjustment did not appear to provide meaningful results. Therefore, to simply distinguish between games that are expected to be higher-scoring from those expected to be lower-scoring, we use a dummy variable for games with a total of 5. If these games that are expected to be relatively low scoring are of less interest to fans because they prefer more scoring to less, then the sign on this variable should be negative.

A major factor that differs from game-to-game is the opponent. Some opponents are more popular than others due to star players, team success, and local/regional rivalries. Given the limited number of degrees of freedom within the data set due to a single year of observations of teams using dynamic pricing, we selected two of the most popular opponents in the league and then added regional rivals for each of the teams. We tried other specifications, but factors such as division rivals did not contribute significantly to the results.

The two premier opponents we included as individual dummy variables were the Chicago Black Hawks and Pittsburgh Penguins. Chicago was the defending champion for the year studied and had star players Jonathan Toews and Patrick Kane. Pittsburgh had the premier player in the league in Sidney Crosby and another superstar in Evgeny Malkin. For other possible key opponents, we used the Los Angeles Kings for the Anaheim Ducks (cross-city rival), the Winnipeg Jets for the Minnesota Wild (popular Canadian team across the border) and Canadian teams (other than Calgary and Edmonton who did not reveal significant results and were dropped from the regression specification) for the Ottawa Senators. Canadian opponents are very popular in Canada due to regional rivalries and media coverage of all Canadian teams on Hockey Night in Canada and other television outlets. We would expect these key opponents to have a positive and significant effect on ticket prices due to increased fan interest for these contests.

To round out the independent variables in our regression model, we included dummy variables for the days of the week and the months of the season. Fan interest in NHL games is likely to be different due to opportunity costs of time during the work week as opposed to weekends. We allow for variability for each day of the week by using dummy variables for each day except Monday, which all results are compared to as the omitted dummy variable. The months of the season may see differences in fan interest due to weather concerns, holidays, other sporting seasons, and playoff races. The omitted dummy variable for the months in the regression model is January, with all other monthly dummies compared to this month.

Summary statistics for the non-binary variables are shown in Table 1 above. Included are the averages, median, and standard deviations for each of the variables. Summary statistics of the individual price levels for each team is noted in the Appendix at the end of the chapter. Table 2 presents the frequencies for the dummy variables used as independent variables in the regression model.

Regression results are presented in the table below. Due to initial heteroskedasticity and autocorrelation issues with the data, Newey-West HAC standard errors and covariances are used and are presented in the results below. For each independent variable, its coefficient is presented along with its t-statistic (in parentheses).

The regression results reveal that there are both similarities and considerable differences in the factors that influence prices for the three NHL teams that adopted dynamic pricing for the 2013–2014 season. To discuss the results, we will note the important findings by variable (and variable groupings) for each of the three teams.

Table 1 Summary statistics for non-binary variables

	Total	Fights per game	Points per game	Win probability	Closing ticket price
Anaheim- average	5.44	0.49	1.50	0.63	84.22
Anaheim- median	5.50	0.43	1.46	0.63	80.00
Anaheim-Std. dev.	0.17	0.18	0.10	0.06	10.49
Minnesota-average	5.06	0.51	1.19	0.56	99.54
Minnesota-median	5.00	0.41	1.19	0.57	92.82
Minnesota-Std. dev.	0.17	0.32	0.10	0.07	15.31
Ottawa-average	5.43	0.43	0.99	0.55	65.00
Ottawa-median	5.50	0.47	1.00	0.55	49.84
Ottawa-Std. dev	0.18	0.15	0.07	0.06	29.78

Table 2 Summary statistics – frequency table for days of week and months of season

	Sun	Mon	Tue	Wed	Thu	Fri	Sat
Anaheim	9	4	6	9	2	8	2
Minnesota	6	3	8	3	10	3	8
Ottawa	6	6	2	2	12	5	8
	Oct	Nov	Dec	Jan	Feb	Mar	Apr
Anaheim	4	6	6	9	4	7	4
Minnesota	7	8	6	7	2	7	4
Ottawa	4	9	11	4	2	7	4

First, fights per game, which measures the level of physical play and violence throughout the season, were not found to have significant impacts on ticket prices in any of the three cities studied. This is different from what was found in other studies of hockey, where fighting was found to have a large and statistically significant impact on attendance at hockey games. From the three teams that use dynamic pricing in the NHL, however, there is little discernable impact of increasing (or decreasing) fighting over the course of the season impacts ticket prices.

Although fighting has been shown to be an important determinant of attendance in studies of the NHL and minor North American leagues that allow fighting, those studies pooled data across each of the teams in the league. At an individual team level, as in the data set studied here, this impact may not be as pronounced, as the importance of fighting may differ in terms of the relative number of fights seen by fans across different NHL cities. In any case, the moving average of fights per game throughout the 2013–2014 season did not play a significant role in prices of hockey tickets (Table 3).

The points per game variable, measuring home team success as a moving average throughout the season, was also shown not to have a significant impact on ticket prices. It needs to be remembered that the probability of a home team win is included in the regression model, as our measure of uncertainty of outcome, and the home

Table 3 Regression results of the determinants of dynamic pricing in the NHL (Dependent variable: average closing price for each home game)

Variable	Anaheim	Minnesota	Ottawa
Fights per game	−3.6764	−25.6648	−56.4819
	(−0.7923)	(−1.3912)	(−1.1962)
Points per game	0.7739	−29.7524	102.2448
	(0.0486)	(−0.7190)	(1.5698)
Win probability	−43.0950***	−14.5742	−20.1218
	(−4.0159)	(−0.5537)	(−0.6349)
Total of 5	−0.5393	6.1758	14.9846
	(−0.3110)	(1.1031)	(1.6405)
Chicago	34.1618***	18.5161**	53.6415***
	(9.6411)	(2.2592)	(7.9015)
Pittsburgh	39.7892***	5.9974	39.6791***
	(13.4182)	(1.1278)	(12.2422)
Los Angeles	15.8321***	–	–
	(3.1099)		
Winnipeg	–	21.3667**	14.3909**
		(2.7169)	(2.1496)
Detroit	–	–	50.7122**
			(2.5310)
Montreal	–	–	53.2343***
			(7.3122)
Toronto	–	–	92.4102***
			(6.1054)
Vancouver	–	–	34.4868**
			(2.1386)
Sunday	6.3478***	9.9254**	11.0068
	(2.8593)	(2.1224)	(1.4687)
Tuesday	−1.7887	9.1246*	2.2895
	(−0.7051)	(1.7275)	(0.4006)
Wednesday	−1.4362	16.5151**	−12.4287
	(−0.4763)	(2.7692)	(−1.3947)
Thursday	1.9215	8.2685*	−10.3712
	(0.4713)	(1.7935)	(−1.3844)
Friday	2.7140	21.0228**	7.9435
	(0.9442)	(2.3527)	(1.0842)
Saturday	4.4558**	33.1864***	5.9051
	(2.6642)	(6.2840)	(0.7491)
October	−5.7452	−3.6367	−34.5736
	(−1.3984)	(−0.3329)	(−1.7074)
November	−4.4766**	−4.3247	−19.3810*
	(−2.2735)	(−0.4763)	(−1.7793)

(continued)

Table 3 (continued)

Variable	Anaheim	Minnesota	Ottawa
December	−5.4726**	8.9750	2.9115
	(−2.7740)	(0.9555)	(0.2780)
February	−4.0005	−4.5823	−7.1804
	(−1.3678)	(−0.6488)	(−0.5017)
March	−2.8251	7.9057	−8.9882
	(−1.3519)	(1.5993)	(−1.3251)
April	−1.8583	13.3730**	8.7569
	(−0.8853)	(2.3730)	(1.4381)
Intercept	111.32***	130.7312**	−10.6446
	(10.5957)	(2.3925)	(−0.2265)
R2	0.9343	0.8391	0.9445
Adjusted R2	0.8718	0.6783	0.8647

*Denotes statistical significance at the 10% level
**At the 5% level
***At the 1% level

team points per game is related to the uncertainty of outcome measure in relation to the quality of opponent played. That said, however, changes in the points per game earned by the three NHL teams studied was not found to play an important role in the determination of prices.

The probability of a home team win, based upon the betting market odds on the game, was shown to have a negative and statistically significant effect on attendance, but only for the Anaheim Ducks. The negative relationship between the probability of a home team win and ticket prices illustrates the importance of the uncertainty of outcome hypothesis in this market. The greater the favorite in the marketplace, the less interest there is in the game, which led to decreased prices for these games. The square of the probability of a home team win was also tried in the regression model, but it did not reveal statistically significant results.

What is interesting about this result, in this sample of three teams using dynamic pricing, is that Anaheim is the one "non-traditional" market for hockey. Many people grow up playing hockey in Minnesota and in Ottawa and hockey would be at (or near) the top of the list of favorite sports for many in these cities and surroundings. In addition, Anaheim offers many more sport and entertainment substitutes than Minnesota and Ottawa. Combining both of these factors is the likely rationale of why uncertainty of outcome plays a much more important role in Anaheim than it does in the other cities.

The independent variable which represented expected scoring, a dummy for a betting market total (over/under) of five (compared to five-and-a-half), was not found to have a statistically significant effect on dynamic ticket prices. Although scoring was shown to play an important role in NHL television ratings on NBC Sports Network (Paul and Weinbach 2013), it does not appear to play an important role in the determination of individual ticket prices for teams that adopted dynamic ticket pricing.

A set of variables that did play an important role in the determination of dynamically priced NHL tickets was the opponent. Key opponents, whether the best teams in the league, those having marquee players, or traditional rivals, were found to have a major effect on prices on a game-to-game basis. In Anaheim, previous season Stanley Cup Champion Chicago, the Pittsburgh Penguins (featuring NHL stars Sidney Crosby and Evgeny Malkin), and the cross-city rival LA Kings all were shown to increase prices substantially when they were the opponent. Similarly in Minnesota, large and statistically significant ticket price increases were seen when Chicago and the cross-border rival Winnipeg Jets (who recently were re-formed after moving from Atlanta) came to town. Ottawa fans showed a high level of demand, driving ticket prices higher, when the opponent was Chicago, Pittsburgh, or the Detroit Red Wings (marking the return of former team captain Daniel Alfredsson to Ottawa), in addition to the Canadian rivals of Toronto (increased price by over $90 a ticket on average), Montreal, Winnipeg, and Vancouver. Canadian fans often enjoy seeing other Canadian franchises, likely due to national pride in the game, but also due to coverage of Canadian teams in the media and on television (Hockey Night in Canada, TSN national games, etc.) that likely breeds familiarity and perhaps contempt for these opponents.

The days of the week were also important determinants of ticket prices in Anaheim and Minnesota. In Anaheim, weekend games commanded a premium, as expected due to the opportunity cost of time for fans. In Minnesota, each day was statistically different from the omitted dummy variable day of Monday. Weekends in Minnesota commanded the highest premiums, as expected, but Wednesday games were also popular, with prices exceeding those seen on Sundays, Tuesdays, and Thursdays. Perhaps surprisingly, the days of the week were not statistically significant in Ottawa. Given the considerable interest in hockey in Canada, perhaps the day of the game matters less to fans than seeing a quality opponent or rival on any day of the week.

The months of the season, which were thought to capture weather effects and seasonal interest due to the long length of the NHL season and the late season playoff push, where applicable, were found to play an important role in the determination of ticket prices in some instances. Prices in April in Minnesota were shown to increase considerably and by a statistically significant margin, likely due to the playoff push of the Minnesota Wild during the 2013–2014 season, which ultimately was successful and led to a first round playoff upset of the division champion Colorado Avalanche. In addition, November was found to have a negative impact on ticket prices in Anaheim and Ottawa and December was also found to be negative in Anaheim. These effects could be due to a brief pullback in demand in these cities after the initial euphoria of the start of the season. It could also be attributable to the holiday season and less of an interest in attending games during that often hectic time.

The summary of this section is that the key variable that has the most impact on ticket prices is the opponent. In addition, some day of the week effects exist (across all days in Minnesota and weekend games in Ottawa) in addition to monthly effects (playoff race impacting late season prices in Minnesota and some early-season discounts in Anaheim and Ottawa). Uncertainty of outcome was found only to play a statistically significant role in Anaheim and on-ice variables such as team points-per-game and fights-per-game were not found to have statistically significant results.

Regression Results for High and Low Ticket Price Sections for the Teams Using Dynamic Pricing

Another consideration the data set allows is to study any differences that might exist between the factors that impact ticket prices at the high- and low-ends of the ticket pricing scale. Each of the three teams offered multiple sections where dynamic ticket pricing was available for purchase by fans. To determine if fans that purchase the most expensive tickets (likely wealthy fans) and fans that purchase the least expensive tickets (likely less-wealthy fans) are influenced by the same factors to the same degree.

To undertake this study, we use the highest-priced section and lowest-priced section of available tickets for each team and use the closing price on the day of the game for each available game for the Ducks, Wild, and Senators. The one exception that we made was that there was almost no variation at all for the highest-priced section next to the glass in Anaheim. The Ducks appeared to keep these prices almost identical across games. Therefore we used the Plaza Center section, the second-highest priced section as there was considerable variation in prices across games in that seating section. Summary statistics for each section of the team arenas using dynamic pricing is shown in the Appendix.

The independent variables remain the same as in the regression model in the previous section. Our main interest in this section is to investigate if purchasers of the highest-priced tickets and lowest-priced tickets have similar responses toward on-ice performance, uncertainty of outcome, expected scoring, opponents, and weekends vs. weekdays.

The results are shown in the tables below. The results for the highest-priced sections are presented first and the results for the lowest-priced sections follow. As in the average price regressions in the previous section, heteroskedasticity- and autocorrelation-consistent standard errors and covariances are used and are presented in the results below (Table 4).

In relation to the highest-priced tickets under dynamic pricing for these three NHL teams, the main commonality is that key opponents led to higher prices for the top-end seats in all three cities. In Anaheim and Minnesota, the days of the week also played an important role for the highest priced tickets, as each day was statistically different from the other in Minnesota, with Monday being the lowest-priced day and Saturday seeing the highest premiums. Anaheim had the curious result at the top-end of ticket prices where Thursdays and Fridays were offered at a very slight (but statistically significant) discount and Sundays sold at a slight premium. The days of the week were not statistically significant in Ottawa, as the lure of hockey in Canada may not be overly dependent upon the day of the week in this Canadian city.

Table 4 Regression results for the highest-priced dynamic tickets for NHL teams (Dependent variable: Closing price for the highest-priced section in the Arena)

Variable	Anaheim – Plaza center	Minnesota – On the glass	Ottawa – Club
Fights per Game	−7.3674*	−58.5121	−181.89**
	(−1.8214)	(−1.0910)	(−2.1855)
Points per game	−5.8242	−99.561	338.5750**
	(−0.4903)	(1.9654)	(2.1120)
Win probability	−26.3425***	−13.8099	−39.4089
	(−3.5930)	(−0.2004)	(−0.6081)
Total of 5	−1.4666	14.8746	21.7668*
	(−0.9771)	(0.9936)	(1.8795)
Chicago	8.2698***	43.9681*	80.7420***
	(4.6069)	(1.9791)	(4.8489)
Pittsburgh	16.3423***	26.3215	53.5574***
	(14.3628)	(1.4863)	(6.4703)
Los Angeles	11.2220***	–	–
	(5.8355)		
Winnipeg	–	54.0726**	23.3366*
		(2.4283)	(2.0752)
Detroit	–	–	72.6226***
			(3.3934)
Montreal	–	–	98.1284***
			(11.6666)
Toronto	–	–	163.0360***
			(4.9277)
Vancouver	–	–	102.6726***
			(4.1257)
Sunday	3.0267**	27.8375*	28.8809
	(2.3852)	(1.9654)	(1.3026)
Tuesday	−2.4027	22.0195*	11.8359
	(−1.4823)	(1.7643)	(1.1977)
Wednesday	−0.9625	33.4585**	−4.8264
	(−0.6512)	(2.2685)	(−0.2018)
Thursday	−4.6318***	25.4620*	−15.5440
	(−2.9003)	(2.0639)	(−1.0923)
Friday	−2.2616**	41.1617**	16.8170
	(−2.3914)	(2.7117)	(0.9022)
Saturday	0.7757	73.5389***	4.9936
	(1.0833)	(3.9531)	(0.3282)
October	−0.5957	−2.5611	−119.3384***
	(−0.2026)	(−0.0785)	(−3.2452)
November	−0.3491	6.8030	−70.1821***
	(−0.2452)	(0.2756)	(−3.9188)

(continued)

Table 4 (continued)

Variable	Anaheim – Plaza center	Minnesota – On the glass	Ottawa – Club
December	−4.4093***	34.8868	9.4979
	(−3.2778)	(1.1478)	(0.4063)
February	−4.1733***	−2.0923	−34.1056*
	(−3.4417)	(−0.0956)	(−1.7877)
March	−3.5176**	29.1731*	−20.6649
	(−2.7215)	(1.8243)	(−1.6553)
April	0.8976	32.1080*	−0.0374
	(0.5451)	(1.9224)	(−0.0030)
Intercept	318.1575***	363.9280**	−31.7005
	(24.1918)	(2.7497)	(−0.2573)
R2	0.8705	0.7808	0.9477
Adjusted R2	0.7475	0.5616	0.8724

*Denotes statistical significance at the 10% level
**At the 5% level
***At the 1% level

The months of the season also showed some commonality with some months showing statistically lower prices compared to January in Anaheim and Ottawa and the late-season months (March and April) selling at a premium in Minnesota. The late-season premium in Minnesota is most likely due to their team's successful playoff push at the end of the season. Anaheim and Ottawa, on the other hand, were not in the thick of playoff races late in the season as Anaheim had locked into a playoff spot quite early and Ottawa was eliminated from contention relatively early compared to other teams.

Team performance and game expectations did matter in two of the three cities for the highest-priced tickets. The win probability variable (based on betting market odds) was shown to be negative and significant in Anaheim, but not in the other two cities. As mentioned in the previous section, the importance of uncertainty of outcome in Anaheim is likely due to substantial competition for sports and entertainment dollars and time, in addition to Anaheim being a "non-traditional" hockey market. The points-per-game variable was shown to have a positive and significant effect on the most expensive tickets in Ottawa, which may be due to their disappointing season compared to the previous year.

Fights per game appeared to have a negative and statistically significant effect in Anaheim and Ottawa as the purchasers of the highest-priced tickets seemed to have an aversion to fighting in the game. This could represent different preferences based upon income level of fans, which may be interesting to pursue as an avenue of future research, especially given that more fighting has been shown to increase attendance at various levels of professional hockey in North America.

In relation to the lowest-priced tickets for the three teams that used dynamic pricing, the common factor which had a significant influence on price was the opponent. Day of the week effects were also quite common, with Minnesota seeing statistically significant differences across each day of the week and Anaheim (Saturday) and Ottawa (Friday) showing price increases on individual weekend nights. The only monthly effect seen at the low-end of the price scale was for games in April in Minnesota, which was during their playoff push at the end of the season (Table 5).

Uncertainty of outcome and expected scoring played a significant role in pricing in Anaheim. Win probability (based on market odds) was found to have a negative impact, suggesting the fans that purchase seats in the upper levels do care about uncertainty of outcome and prefer a more competitive hockey game. In addition, games with a betting market total of 5, representing an expected low-scoring game, also had a negative impact on ticket prices, suggesting that fans purchasing the less expensive tickets (likely highly correlated with having lower incomes) prefer more scoring to less in NHL games.

Minnesota also saw some effects of on-ice performance at the lowest-end of their ticket scale, with dynamically priced tickets in their upper levels being impacted by points-per-game and fights-per-game. The points-per-game variable was surprising,

Table 5 Regression results for the lowest-priced dynamic tickets for NHL teams (Dependent variable: Closing price for the lowest-priced section in the Arena)

Variable	Anaheim – Terrace value east	Minnesota – Upper level red	Ottawa – WCR300
Fights per game	−5.4478	−38.5487**	−16.3257
	(−1.6659)	(−2.4551)	(−0.6294)
Points per game	15.4820	−62.0687*	32.8210
	(0.7267)	(−2.0049)	(1.1814)
Win probability	−29.3926**	12.3053	−0.3348
	(−2.7103)	(0.6476)	(−0.0217)
Total of 5	−6.2692*	5.0718	5.0274
	(−1.7727)	(1.1125)	(0.6730)
Chicago	27.1106***	14.1774***	41.4694***
	(6.1991)	(3.2347)	(11.9251)
Pittsburgh	26.4605***	−6.9889	22.2150***
	(6.4949)	(−1.7033)	(14.7255)
Los Angeles	19.2845**	–	–
	(2.6967)		
Winnipeg	–	19.2434***	5.9437
		(4.5776)	(1.3108)
Detroit	–	–	45.8936***
			(5.5271)
Montreal	–	–	43.0329***
			(12.9659)
Toronto	–	–	50.8332***
			(11.5325)
Vancouver	–	–	11.3954
			(1.3108)

(continued)

Table 5 (continued)

Variable	Anaheim – Terrace value east	Minnesota – Upper level red	Ottawa – WCR300
Sunday	3.6496	12.1769***	4.4661
	(1.4000)	(3.5557)	(1.5453)
Tuesday	−0.6627	9.8986**	2.8074
	(−0.2110)	(2.1896)	(0.9013)
Wednesday	0.0825	15.3877***	−0.9062
	(0.0264)	(3.2935)	(−0.2198)
Thursday	2.9041	11.0661**	−1.8094
	(0.5138)	(2.0959)	(−0.8718)
Friday	2.9590	24.5282***	5.8810*
	(0.7585)	(4.1552)	(1.9733)
Saturday	6.3491**	24.7765***	3.5785
	(2.1082)	(6.0205)	(1.0830)
October	−3.3762	3.9524	−7.3356
	(−1.2177)	(0.4412)	(−0.7394)
November	−3.1413	−2.5933	−4.0279
	(−1.6753)	(−0.4321)	(−0.6667)
December	−3.9053	10.1369	7.1315
	(−1.6213)	(1.6871)	(1.5975)
February	−0.5842	−1.2614	−3.7623
	(−0.1538)	(−0.3171)	(−0.7154)
March	−1.1887	0.8317	0.1351
	(−0.5555)	(0.2634)	(0.0503)
April	−0.6585	9.0052***	4.2705
	(−0.2992)	(3.2286)	(1.4349)
Intercept	38.8940***	102.2473***	−1.2137
	(3.0285)	(2.9047)	(−0.0696)
R2	0.8790	0.8467	0.9662
Adjusted R2	0.7641	0.6933	0.9177

*Denotes statistical significance at the 10% level
**At the 5% level
***At the 1% level

as it was found to have a negative effect on price for the lowest-priced tickets. Fights-per-game was also shown to have a negative and significant effect on price for the lowest-priced tickets. The negative reaction of the fans that purchase upper-level seats in Minnesota may have something to do with their familiarity with hockey that does not allow fighting, such as their popular high school and college programs. When compared to Canada, which allows fighting at the junior level, this societal difference across the border may help to explain the significant negative effect seen in Minnesota.

Overall, the common factor that influences the prices of both the high-priced and low-priced tickets was the opponent. Prime opponents led to substantial price increases across all three cities. Days of the week also had an important impact, but was much more evident in Minnesota, where each day revealed its own significant price level, and in the higher-priced seats rather than the lower-priced seats. Months of the year also appeared to be a bigger factor for the higher-priced seats, but the main impact of the month was the playoff push at the end of the season, which increased prices in Minnesota (whereas there was not a significant increase in Anaheim or Ottawa due to more certainty about making or not-making the playoffs in these cities, respectively).

On-ice performance did matter to consumers of dynamically-priced tickets, but in different ways in different cities. For both the highest- and lowest-priced tickets (in addition to average ticket prices overall), Anaheim was the only city where uncertainty of outcome played an important role. Fights per game was shown to have a negative and significant effect for the highest-priced tickets in Anaheim and Ottawa and for the lowest-priced tickets in Minnesota. These findings are different than what was discovered in researching the effects of fighting on attendance, which have been positive. These differences may suggest that fighting has more of an impact across cities rather than within the same city over the course of a year (as this sample represents). There could also be considerable differences in attitudes toward fighting as it relates to the income level of fans and regional preferences.

Conclusions

Dynamic pricing is a recent innovation in the sports industry. Using a pricing model from the airline and hotel industries, dynamic pricing was introduced in baseball and quickly spread to many teams across that sport. In 2013–2014, three National Hockey League teams introduced dynamic pricing as the means to sell tickets. These three teams were the Anaheim Ducks, Minnesota Wild, and Ottawa Senators. These three cities are quite different in terms of hockey history, geographic location, availability of substitutes, and demographic factors.

Dynamic pricing is the next step in the evolution of ticket pricing beyond variable pricing. Variable pricing allowed for differences in ticket prices based upon opponent, weekday, and other factors. Once variable prices for the season were set, however, prices remained constant throughout the season of ticket sales. Dynamic pricing alters the relationship by allowing ticket prices to change throughout the course of the season. Ticket prices fluctuate throughout the season based upon various factors that impact demand as it relates to the number of tickets remaining to sell.

This chapter explored the variables that played a pivotal role in the determination of ticket prices for the three NHL teams that used dynamic pricing. Through the capturing of data from team websites, we used the closing price of tickets for each section for each team as the dependent variable in a regression model. The independent variables consisted of a variety of factors that were likely to impact demand for individual game tickets, such as opponent, weekday, on-ice performance factors, and uncertainty of outcome.

When estimating the regression model with the average closing ticket price as the dependent variable, a few key determinants revealed themselves. The factor with the biggest impact in explaining differences in ticket prices across games was the opponent. Popular and successful teams such as the Chicago Black Hawks and Pittsburgh Penguins were found to have substantial premiums associated with games where they were the visiting team. In addition, regional rivals and Canadian rivals for Ottawa also saw big premiums associated with games where they were the opponent.

Days of the week also had an effect, but it was found to be different across cities. In Anaheim, most of the significant impact of days of the week came from weekend games. In Minnesota, each day was significantly different from the others, with larger premiums occurring on weekend games. In Ottawa, the days of the week were not a significant determinant of dynamic ticket prices.

Months of the season did not have much of an impact on prices, but November was found to have lower prices in Anaheim and Ottawa (compared to the omitted month of January in the model) and December prices were significantly lower in Anaheim. Minnesota saw late-season increase in prices, but they were the only team involved in a meaningful playoff race at the time, as Anaheim clinched a playoff spot early and Ottawa had a disappointing season with an early exit from playoff contention.

In terms of on-ice performance and game expectations based upon uncertainty of outcome and expected scoring, the only impact of any of these variables was found in Anaheim as it related to uncertainty of outcome. The home team win probability on the game, based upon betting market odds, was found to have a negative and significant effect on dynamic ticket prices, implying that Anaheim fans prefer more uncertainty of outcome. This variable did not have a statistically significant impact in Minnesota and Ottawa. The importance of uncertainty of outcome in Anaheim may have to do with Anaheim being a "non-traditional" hockey market and due to the many entertainment opportunities, both indoors and outdoors, in southern California.

In addition to average closing prices for dynamic-priced tickets in the three cities, we also analyzed the high- and low-ticket sections in each arena. The results revealed most of the same information as was seen in the average price regression model in terms of the impact of days and months, but it was discovered that uncertainty of outcome in Anaheim appeared to matter more at the high-end of the ticket pricing scale and the increase in ticket prices at the end of the season in Minnesota appeared to be more of a factor at the low-end of the ticket pricing scale.

One interesting finding concerning the high- and low-ticket price sections was in relation to the fights-per-game variable. Although this variable was not statistically significant in the regression model with average price as the dependent variable it was found to be negative and statistically significant at the high-end of prices in Anaheim and Ottawa and at the low-end of prices in Minnesota. In Anaheim and Ottawa, perhaps the wealthiest fans are not as big a fan of fighting in the game of hockey as fans of other income levels. In Minnesota, where high school and college hockey is quite popular and does not allow fighting in their games, perhaps people buying the upper deck tickets prefer the game to be more like high school and college and do not enjoy fighting in the games as much as some others do. In other words, there may very well be income and cultural differences in attitudes toward fighting in the sport of hockey that deserve further research and attention.

Overall, this chapter has illustrated some of the key factors that impact dynamic pricing in hockey. As more teams and sports adopt dynamic pricing, it will be interesting to observe the similarities and differences across both cities and sports. Dynamic pricing offers upside on ticket prices when particular games become in high demand. This is beneficial to the teams in the sense that market prices are offered directly by them, rather than solely in the secondary market on websites such as Stubhub. This allows the team to capture additional revenues that were the sole propriety of secondary market sellers in the past. As technology evolves and more teams and sports adopt this practice, we believe that research in this area will be very important in understanding consumer demand, on the average and in specific subsets of the population, and the pricing practices of firms in this industry.

Appendix

Individual Section Prices for NHL Teams Using Dynamic Pricing

Anaheim Ducks

	Glass	Plaza center	Plaza main west	Plaza main east	Plaza goal lower west	Plaza goal lower east	Plaza goal upper west	Plaza goal upper east
Average	292.40	140.68	127.08	111.33	114.55	107.78	86.28	79.85
Median	290.00	134.50	120.00	106.00	105.00	100.00	85.00	75.00
Std. Dev.	4.60	15.41	13.65	14.72	18.15	18.73	14.68	13.03
	Premium gold	Premium silver	Premium bronze	Premium wheel chair	Terrace lower center	Terrace lower west	Terrace lower east	Terrace center
Average	110.95	81.95	98.50	98.20	82.35	62.25	53.30	43.45
Median	105.00	80.00	95.00	95.00	76.00	60.00	50.00	39.00
Std. dev.	11.25	11.80	10.53	9.31	13.54	10.81	11.64	10.72
	Terrace main west	Terrace main east	Terrace center upper	Terrace goal west	Terrace goal east	Terrace value west	Terrace value east	Average price
Average	41.55	39.83	32.20	35.90	34.85	30.88	30.95	84.22
Median	38.00	37.00	30.00	33.00	33.00	27.00	27.00	80.00
Std. dev.	9.40	9.37	8.46	7.11	7.85	7.64	8.62	10.49

Minnesota Wild

	On the glass	Club level purple	Club level blue	Lower level green	Lower level beige	Lower level orange
Average	277.64	109.85	98.23	108.92	94.59	87.10
Median	260.00	105.00	92.00	102.00	90.00	80.00
Std. dev.	34.44	18.21	16.10	17.52	16.11	14.92
	Lower level brown	Lower level white	Upper level yellow	Upper level red	Standing room only	Average price
Average	86.85	81.62	55.38	39.59	55.13	99.54
Median	81.00	74.00	54.00	38.00	50.00	92.82
Std. dev.	14.37	15.78	8.80	10.41	7.91	15.31

Ottawa Senators

	Club	100 Ends	200 Centre	200 Ends	300 Centre lower	300 End lower
Average	208.17	166.05	183.73	139.10	100.07	73.98
Median	187.61	144.61	167.61	125.61	78.61	54.61
Std. dev.	51.50	57.05	52.21	43.68	50.55	44.18
	300 Centre upper	300 End upper	Sport chek zone	Subway zone	Coke lower	Coke upper
Average	65.88	57.80	50.44	44.12	58.32	36.71
Median	47.61	39.61	38.61	31.61	42.61	21.61
Std. dev.	38.90	35.44	21.75	25.07	32.04	28.05
	WCR 200	WCR 300	The ledge	Standing room only	Average	
Average	64.39	37.10	88.53	28.61	65.00	
Median	56.61	26.61	73.61	18.61	49.84	
Std dev.	15.09	19.12	31.19	17.72	29.78	

References

Bremaud, P. (1980): Point Processes and Queues, Martingale Dynamics. New York: Springer.

Buraimo, B., Forrest, D., and Simmons, R. (2006): Outcome Uncertainty Measures: How Closely Do They Predict a Close Game? In Statistical Thinking in Sports (J. Albert and R. Koning eds.), Boca Raton, FL: Chapman and Hall.

Burger, B. and Fuchs, M. (2004): Dynamic Pricing – A Future Airline Business Model. Journal of Revenue and Pricing Management, 4, pp. 39–53.

Coates, D. and Humphreys, B. (2012): Game Attendance and Outcome Uncertainty in the National Hockey League. Journal of Sports Economics, 13, pp. 364–377.

Coates, D., Battre, M., and Deutscher, C. (2011): Does Violence in Professional Ice Hockey Pay? Cross Country Evidence from Three Leagues, in: Violence and Aggression in Sporting Contests (R. Todd Jewel ed.), New York: Springer.

Drayer, J. Rascher, D. and McEvoy, C. (2012): An Examination of Underlying Consumer Demand and Sport Pricing Using Secondary Market Data. Sport Management Review, 15, pp. 448–460.

Elmaghraby, W. and Keskinocak, P. (2003): Dynamic Pricing in the Presence of Inventory Considerations: Research Overview, Current Practices, and Future Directions. Management Science, 49, pp. 1287–1309.

Escobari, D. (2009): Systematic Peak-Load Pricing, Congestion Premia and Demand Diverting: Empirical Evidence. Economics Letters, 103, pp. 59–61.

Forrest, D. and Simmons, R. (2002): Outcome Uncertainty and Attendance Demand in Sport: The Case of English Soccer. The Statistician, 51, pp. 229–241.

Gallego, G. and Ryzin, G. van (1994): Optimal Dynamic Pricing of Inventories with Stochastic Demand over Finite Horizon. Management Science, 40, pp. 999–1020.

Jones, J.C.H. (1984): Winners, Losers, and Hosers: Demand and Survival in the National Hockey League. Atlantic Economic Journal, 12, pp. 54–63.

Jones, J.C.H., D.G. Ferguson, and K.G. Stewart (1993): Blood Sports and Cherry Pie: Some Economics of Violence in the National Hockey League. American Journal of Economics and Sociology, 52, pp. 87–101.

Jones, J.C.H., K.G. Stewart, and R. Sunderman (1996): From the Arena into the Streets: Hockey Violence, Economic Incentives, and Public Policy. American Journal of Economics and Sociology, 55, pp. 231–249.

Knowles, G., Sherony, K. and Haupert, M. (1992): The Demand for Major League Baseball: A Test of the Uncertainty of Outcome Hypothesis, American Economist, 36, pp. 72–80.

Lemke, R.J., Leonard, M. and Tlhokwane, K. (2010): Estimating Attendance at Major League Baseball Games for the 2007 Season. Journal of Sports Economics, 11, pp. 316–348.

Paul, R.J. (2003): Variations in NHL Attendance: The Impact of Violence, Scoring, and Regional Rivalries. American Journal of Economics and Sociology, 62, pp. 345–364.

Paul, R.J. and Weinbach, A.P. (2011): Determinants of Attendance in the Quebec Major Junior Hockey League. Atlantic Economic Journal, 39, pp. 303–311.

Paul, R.J. and Weinbach, A.P. (2013): Uncertainty of Outcome and Television Ratings for the NHL and MLS. Journal of Prediction Markets, 7(1), 53–65.

Paul, R.J. and Weinbach, A.P. (2014): Determinants of Dynamic Pricing Premiums in Major League Baseball. Sport Marketing Quarterly, 22, pp. 152–165.

Paul, R.J., Weinbach, A.P. and Chatt, R. (2011): Regional Differences in Fan Preferences for Minor League Hockey. New York Economic Review, 42, pp. 63–73.

Paul, R.J., Weinbach, A.P. and Robbins, D. (2013): American Hockey League Attendance: A Study of Fan Preferences for Fighting, Team Performance, and Promotions. International Journal of Sport Finance, 7, pp. 21–38.

Peel, D.A. and Thomas, D.A. (1988): Outcome Uncertainty and the Demand for Football. Scottish Journal of Political Economy, 35, pp. 242–249.

Peel, D.A. and Thomas, D.A. (1992): The Demand for Football: Some Evidence on Outcome Uncertainty. Empirical Economics, 17, pp. 323–331.

Rascher, D. (1999): A Test of the Optimal Positive Production Network Externality in Major League Baseball, in: Sports Economics: Current Research (J. Fizel, E. Gustafson and L. Hadley eds.), Westport: Praeger.

Sweeting, A. (2012): Dynamic Pricing Behavior in Perishable Goods Market: The Case of Secondary Markets for Major League Baseball Tickets. Journal of Political Economy, 120, pp. 1133–1172.

Index

A
Aggressor, 22
American Hockey League (AHL)
  arenas and attendance, 21
  clubs, location of, 21
  fighting
    aggressor, 22
    American and Canadian fan preferences, 29
    attendance and ticket demand, effects on, 28–29
    data, 32–33
    deterrent and monitoring effect, 28
    econometric model, 29–32
    estimation results of profit-maximization, 33–36
    franchise relocations, 24–27
    "goon" players, 28
    instigator, 22–23
    motivations for players, 27
    and NHL, 23–24, 28
    number of fights *vs.* total points, 29, 30
    penalty, 22–23, 27–28
    Rule 46, 22–23
    Slap Shot strategy, 24, 27
  number of teams, 21
  parent NHL club, affiliation with, 21–22
  salaries, 22
  schedule, 21
  ticket prices, 21
  top-tier minor hockey league, 21
American Labor Law, 4
Arena Football League, 8

B
Balanced penalty, 135
Barkley, Charles, 156
Bernoulli process, 141
Bird, Larry, 156
Birth cohort size
  baby-boom and subsequent baby-bust, 57–58
  birth rate cycles, 58, 60
  data set, 59–60
  NHL player outcomes, 86–87
    average player salaries, 82, 86
    career earnings paths, 62–64
    data sources and sample, 68–70, 88–89
    demand for player talent, 63
    Easterlin's hypothesis, 60–61
    free-agency, 63–64, 71, 72
    larger-than-average cohort (1990–2008), 77–78
    player performance (1990–2008), 74–76
    player salaries (1990–2008), 71–74
    player types/phases/stages, 61
    pre-post lockout and league expansion, player salaries, 82, 84–86, 88
    regression specifications, 70
    relative age effect (*see* (Relative age effect (RAE)))
    Rosen's optimal life-cycle model, 61
    substitution elasticity, 63
  positive demand-side effect, 58
  pro-athletes, 59
"Blood sport" hypothesis, 154

C

Canadian Hockey League (CHL), 21
CBAs, see Collective Bargaining Agreements (CBAs)
Close-game penalty, 135
Coefficient of variation (COV), 9, 10
Cohort size, see Birth cohort size
Collective Bargaining Agreements (CBAs), 4, 5, 8, 14
Contaminated hypothesis tests, 136
Co-worker discrimination, 98, 99, 109
Cultural and language diversity
    German manufacturing plants, production levels in, 114
    NHL players, productivity levels
        estimation results, 121, 124–126
        ethnic specific players, team specific proportion of, 117–121
        European players, 114–115, 127
        game level analysis, 117
        game of hockey, 116
        game summary and play-by-play reports, 116–117
        home and visiting team specific summary statistics, 121–123
        inferences, 127
        new skills, learning of, 115
        on-ice and off-ice player interactions, 115, 117
        reduced communication costs, 128
        season-game and season-game-goal level information, 117
        semi-parametric linear model, 121
        U.S.-born residents, average real wage and rents, 114
Customer-based discrimination, 98, 106, 107, 109
Czech Extraliga, see Superstars, German and Czech hockey league

D

Deutsche Eishockey Liga (DEL), see Superstars, German and Czech hockey league
Discretionary penalties, 133
Discrimination, in NHL
    co-worker discrimination, 98, 99, 109
    cultural, political/linguistic factors, 96
    customer-based discrimination, 98, 109
    definition, 98
    employer discrimination, 98, 109
    entry/hiring discrimination, 96
    national origin/ethnicity, 96
    salary discrimination (see (Salary discrimination, in NHL))
    statistical discrimination, 98
    taste-based discrimination, 98–99
    team-level referee discrimination (see (Team-level referee discrimination))
    team owners and managers, 99
Dynamic ticket pricing
    airlines, 181
    Anaheim Ducks, 177–178, 187, 195
    data and regression model
        betting market prices, 182, 186
        dependent variables, 181
        dummy variables, 183, 184
        fights-per-game variable, 181–182
        independent variables, 181, 183, 186
        Newey-West HAC standard errors and covariances, 183
        NHL, determinants, 185, 186
        non-binary variables, 183, 184
        points-per-game variable, 182, 184
        uncertainty of outcome hypothesis, 182, 186, 188
    high and low ticket price sections, 188–193
        average price regressions, 188–190
        betting market, 191
        fights-per-game variable, 190–192
        on-ice performance, 193, 194
        points-per-game variable, 190, 191
        regression results, NHL teams, 189–192
        seating section, 188
        team performance and game expectations, 190
        win probability variable, 190, 191
    intensity control theory, 181
    Minnesota Wild (St. Paul), 178, 187, 196
    Ottawa Senators, 178, 187, 196
    posted-price and price-discovery markets, 181
    primary ticket market sales, 180
    secondary market firm, 180
    variable pricing models, sports and comparisons, 179–180

E

East Coast Hockey League (ECHL), 21
Easterlin's hypothesis, 60–61
Employer discrimination, 98, 106
Entry discrimination, 96, 134

Index

F
Fan-based discrimination, 107, 109
Fighting
  in AHL
    aggressor, 22
    American and Canadian fan preferences, 29
    attendance and ticket demand, effects on, 28–29
    data, 32–33
    deterrent and monitoring effect, 28
    econometric model, 29–32
    estimation results of profit-maximization, 33–36
    franchise relocations, 24–27
    "goon" players, 28
    instigator, 22–23
    motivations for players, 27
    and NHL, 23–24, 28
    number of fights *vs.* total points, 29, 30
    penalty, 22–23, 27–28
    Rule 46, 22–23
    Slap Shot strategy, 24, 27
  in ice hockey, 19–21
  NHL's Philadelphia Flyers players, 18
  professional boxing matches, 18
  Slap Shot (movie), 17–19
  television coverage, 18

G
Gini Coefficients, 8
Goal differential (GD), 11
"Goon" players, 28

H
Handedness, 55
  hockey, right and left-handed shooters in
    assists per game, 49
    average goals and average goals per game, 48–49
    forward positions, 44
    goals per game, p-values, 48
    ice hockey, 43
    mean salary, difference in, 46–47
    "off-wing" position, 45–46
    salary determination and returns, 49–54
  right *vs.* left-handed individuals
    autism and learning disabilities, 41
    baseball players, 43
    cognitive to environmental, 42
    compensation, 42
    intelligence and creativity, 41
    left-handed females, penalty for, 41, 42
    left-handed males, premium for, 41, 42
    wage loss, 42
Hershey Bears club, 24
Hill, Grant, 156
Hiring discrimination, 96
"Honeymoon effect," 155

I
Ice hockey
  fighting, 19–21
  IIHF, 157
  right and left-handed players, 43
Instigator, 22–23
International Ice Hockey Federation (IIHF), 157
Invariance principle, 7

J
Johnson, Magic, 156
Jordan, Michael, 156

L
Labor market discrimination, 95–96
Language diversity, *see* Cultural and language diversity
League revenues, 132
Lockouts, *see* Strikes and lockouts

M
Major League Baseball (MLB), 4, 7, 14, 132, 180, 182
Major League Soccer (MLS), 8
Multicollinearity, 139

N
National Basketball Association (NBA), 4, 6, 8, 14–15, 131, 155, 173
National Football League (NFL), 4, 6, 8, 173, 178
National Hockey League (NHL), 132–134
  Canadian players, majority of, 101
  cohort size effect (*see* (Birth cohort size))
  cultural and language diversity (*see* (Cultural and language diversity))
  discrimination (*see* (Discrimination, in NHL))

National Hockey League (NHL) (*cont.*)
  Eastern and Western Conference, 100
  fighting, 23–24, 28
  players' union and owners (*see* (Players' union and owners, NHL))
  superstars, attendance effects (*see* (Superstars, German and Czech hockey league))
  teams of, 100–101
  ticket prices (*see* (Dynamic ticket pricing))
  US players, percentage of, 101
National Hockey League Players' Association (NHLPA), 4, 5
Non-discretionary penalties, 133

O
O'Neal, Shaquille, 156

P
Penalty, 22–23, 27–28, 134, 135, 140–145
Players' union and owners, NHL
  CBAs, 4, 8, 14
  2003–2004 championship season, 5
  cracks in union's solidarity, 5
  federal labor law, 4
  labor policy, changes in, 8
    competitive balance, 7
    invariance principle, 7
    property rights to players' labor service, 6–7
  modified CBA, 4–5
  NHLPA, 4, 5
  salary caps
    bounds on payroll, 8
    competitive balance, improvement in, 8
    effects on sports leagues, 6, 8
    hard payroll cap, 4–6
    individual player's compensation, limits on, 8
    payroll limits, demand for, 5
    pre and post salary cap, 9–13
    salary distribution within and across teams, improvement in, 8
    soft payroll cap, 4, 6, 8
  strikes and lockouts, 4, 14–15
    income-eliminating work stoppages, 14
    1994–1995 lockout, 5
    2012 lockout, 6
    1994 MLB championship tournament, cancellation of, 4
    NBA lockout, 14–15
    public relations damage, 14
    2004–2005 schedule of games, cancellation of, 4
    1998–1999 season's games, cancellation of, 14

Q
Quebec Major Junior Hockey League (QMJHL), 154, 182

R
Racial discrimination, 96
Relative age effect (RAE), 58, 60
  amateur athletics, 59
  NHL player outcomes, 67–68, 87
    accumulative advantage, 65
    cutoff date hypothesis, 65–66
    data sources and sample, 68–70, 88–89
    drafted, team captaincy, 78–79, 82
    initial better performers, 65
    large birth cohort size effects, 80–81, 83
    path dependence, 65
    physical/psychological maturity advantage, 67
    player performance (1990–2008), 78, 80, 81
    player salaries (1990–2008), 78, 79
    regression specifications, 70–71
    relative age disadvantage, 66
    skewed birthdate distributions, 65–66
  positive "peer effects," 59

S
Salary caps
  bounds on payroll, 8
  competitive balance, improvement in, 8
  effects on sports leagues, 6, 8
  hard payroll cap, 4–6
  individual player's compensation, limits on, 8
  payroll limits, demand for, 5
  pre and post salary cap
    average payroll, standard deviation, and COV, 9–10
    SDGD/games, 11, 12
    SDWP and RSD results, 10, 11
    SRCC, 12–13

salary distribution within and across teams, improvement in, 8
soft payroll cap, 4, 6, 8
Salary discrimination, in NHL, 96–97, 103–104, 133, 134
   customer-based discrimination, 106, 107, 109
   employer-based discrimination, 106, 109
   fan-based discrimination, 107, 109
   franchise information, 102
   free agency, 108
   game-team player time, 108–109
   individual characteristics, 102
   individuals' "plus-minus-statistics," 105
   language/cultural barriers, 100, 106–107
   less favorable compensation packages, 100
   market-based approach, 97, 107, 108
   player ethnicity and team locations, 105–107
   productivity measures, 102
   reservation wage hypothesis, 100
   salary and performance data, 97, 105
   style of play, 99
   team performance, 107
   team-specific, 106
   wage expenditures, 107
   young players, 106, 108
SDGD, *see* Standard deviation of goal differential (SDGD)
Season-game-penalty level, 134
Slap Shot (movie), 17–19
Spearman's rank correlation coefficient (SRCC), 12–13
Standard deviation of goal differential (SDGD), 11, 12
Statistical discrimination, 98
Strikes and lockouts, 4, 14–15
   income-eliminating work stoppages, 14
   1994–1995 lockout, 5
   2012 lockout, 6
   1994 MLB championship tournament, cancellation of, 4
   NBA lockout, 14–15
   public relations damage, 14
   2004–2005 schedule of games, cancellation of, 4
   1998–1999 season's games, cancellation of, 14
Stubhub, 179, 180, 195
Superstars, German and Czech hockey League attendance, determinants of
   double-logged model, 156
   gate revenues, 156
   in hockey analysis, 154–155
   linear model, 156
   lockout, 157
   road attendance, 156
   sports, 153
   ticket demand, 155, 157
capacity utilization
   average attendance and, 161
   dependent variable, 169–171
   distribution of, 160
collective bargaining agreement, 151
control variables, 159
   arenaage, 166
   arenarenovation, 166
   clubs, 165
   consumer preferences, 165
   descriptive statistics of, 166
   economic aspects, 165
   matchday, 167
   multifunctional arena, 166
   rivalry, 167
   Tobit models, 167–171
descriptive NHL-player and attendance statistics
   characteristics, 164
   Kladno, 165
   lockout, 161, 162
   matches, number of, 162
   nationality, 163
   team experience, 162
   Tobit regression, 161
game level attendance data, 152
model specification, 172
multifunctional arenas, 172
professional hockey, 157–158

T
Taste-based discrimination, 98–99
Team-level referee discrimination
   anti-discrimination, 145
   data
      chi-square tests, p-values, 137, 139
      coincidental discretionary penalty, 136, 137
      ethnic specific players, 138
      identity and ethnicity, refereeing crews, 137
   decision-making, 131
   empirical model
      motivation, 134–136
      specifications, 139–140

Team-level referee discrimination (*cont.*)
   English Canadian players, 142–145
   English Canadian referees, 142–145
   estimation procedure, 141
   French Canadian players, 142–145
   French Canadian referees, 142–145
   homogeneous referee pairings, 142
   intermediate specification, 142
   NBA referees, 131
   NHL and game of hockey, 132–134
   null hypothesis, 142
   parsimonious specification, 142
   penalty rates, 132
   referee ethnic mixes, 143–145
   saturated specification, 142
Thomas, Isiah, 156
Ticket prices, *see* Dynamic ticket pricing

W
Wald test, 34
Women's National Basketball Association (WNBA), 8
Work stoppages, *see* Strikes and lockouts
World Hockey Association (WHA), 7, 21, 28

Printed by Printforce, the Netherlands